Border Junkies

ADDICTION AND SURVIVAL ON THE STREETS OF JUÁREZ AND EL PASO

By Scott Comar

UNIVERSITY OF TEXAS PRESS
Austin

In the new "Inter-American" epoch to come, our borderland zones may expand well past the confines of geopolitical lines. Social knowledge of these dynamic interfaces offers rich insights into the pressing and complex issues that affect both the borderlands and beyond. The Inter-America Series comprises a wide interdisciplinary range of cutting-edge books that explicitly or implicitly enlist border issues to discuss larger concepts, perspectives, and theories from the "borderland" vantage and will be appropriate for the classroom, the library, and the wider reading public.

Copyright © 2011 by the University of Texas Press
All rights reserved
Printed in the United States of America
First edition, 2011

Requests for permission to reproduce material from this work should be sent to:
    Permissions
    University of Texas Press
    P.O. Box 7819
    Austin, TX 78713-7819
    www.utexas.edu/utpress/about/bpermission.html

♾ The paper used in this book meets the minimum requirements of ANSI/NISO Z39.48-1992 (R1997) (Permanence of Paper).

LIBRARY OF CONGRESS CATALOGING-IN-PUBLICATION DATA
Comar, Scott.
    Border junkies : addiction and survival on the streets of Juárez and El Paso / by Scott Comar. — 1st ed.
    p.   cm. — (Inter-America series)
    ISBN 978-0-292-72658-1 (cloth : alk. paper) —
    ISBN 978-0-292-72683-3 (pbk. : alk. paper)
    1. Comar, Scott.   2. Drug addicts—Texas—El Paso—Biography.   3. Drug addicts—Mexico—Ciudad Juárez—Biography.   4. Heroin abuse—Case studies.   I. Title.
    HV5805.C63A3 2011
    363.29′3092—dc22   [B]
                                                            2011005075
ISBN 978-0-292-73537-8 (E-book)

This book is dedicated to the memory of Jesus "Jesse" Martinez and Víctor Manuel Vásquez Reyes.

CONTENTS

Foreword   ix

Preface   xiii

Acknowledgments   xv

ONE   Viajes   I

TWO   *Arrivals*   15

THREE   *Down and Out*   31

FOUR   *Assimilations*   45

FIVE   *La Navidad*   66

SIX   *New Millennium*   77

SEVEN   *Insanity Repeats Itself*   94

EIGHT   *Migrations*   113

NINE   *Vigilance*   135

TEN   *Endings and Beginnings*   160

Conclusion   200

Epilogue   211

Photo section follows page 112

Howard Campbell

FOREWORD

*Opium expands what has no bound, lengthens the illimitable,
deepens time, furrows pleasure, and fills the soul with dark
wearisome felicities more than the soul can hold.*
CHARLES BAUDELAIRE, *THE FLOWERS OF EVIL*
(TRANSLATED BY KEITH WALDROP)

The lineage of opiate narratives in Western societies
stretches from the nineteenth century to the modern era: Samuel Taylor
Coleridge, Thomas de Quincey, Charles Baudelaire, Arthur Rimbaud,
Jean Cocteau, William S. Burroughs, Alexander Trocchi, Piri Thomas,
Richard Hell. Across decades and centuries, the experience of opium,
morphine, and heroin addiction has generated its own logic. Existence
is reduced to the cellular need for dope, punctuated by bouts of euphoric delirium. Excess baggage is discarded or pawned as the junkie
desperately acquires the money needed to buy the next fix, get high,
and repeat the cycle. In the literary re-creation of this quest, florid details are disdained in the lean, narrowly focused prose of the panicked,
hustling search to cop, but lush colors describe the pandemonium of
opiate dreams, and a dark palette sketches in the excruciating pain of
withdrawal and the inevitable physical and mental deterioration.

Often, the ethnographic portrait of a heroin user mirrors its literary
counterpart in its depiction of the single-mindedness of the addict. An-
thropological accounts of addicts, however, pay much more attention
to the economics and practical details of junkie life and less attention
to the lyrical or morbid inner landscape of the addict—with some exceptions, especially the verbal poetry of the "righteous dopefiends" in
Bourgois and Schonberg's brilliant study.

Comar's narrative echoes the stark realities, the depths of despair, and the sensations of instant glory that permeate the classic opiate literature, and its emphasis on survival strategies and oppositional cultures contributes to the social science literature on addiction. While avoiding the narcissistic excesses of popular heroin-chic memoirs, Comar chronicles the specific dilemmas of the junkie life amid the transnational, bilingual context of the U.S.-Mexico border.

In the process of absorbing this fine account, the reader gains insight into the underworld cultures of border dealers and addicts, and obtains a street-level sociological vision of drug trafficking and addiction in Ciudad Juárez, currently the world's most dangerous city for murder and kidnapping and home to one of the largest drug cartels in the world. *Border Junkies* will be of considerable interest to students of the mental dimensions of drug addiction, the cultural bases of junkie adaptations, and the dynamic and evolving societies of the U.S.-Mexico border.

Ciudad Juárez, the quintessential Mexican border city, has been an important center of contraband smuggling since at least Prohibition. In the aftermath of Prohibition, Ignacia Jasso de González (alias "La Nacha") built a powerful heroin-smuggling organization from her home near the Paso del Norte international bridge that links Juárez and El Paso. Despite the visibility of her operation—physically observable from the U.S. side of the Rio Grande (Río Bravo)—La Nacha sold one-hit doses of Mexican black tar heroin to American GIs and Mexican addicts for immediate consumption, and larger quantities to smugglers who took La Nacha's product far into the heartland of the United States. Although both the Mexican and U.S. governments pursued her aggressively, La Nacha resisted attempts to extradite her, and though she served several stints in Mexican prisons (including in the infamous Islas Marías), La Nacha did not let go of the heroin business until she died, a multimillionaire, of natural causes in 1977.

Although La Nacha's business was robust and multinational—linking the opium fields of Sinaloa and Durango through various clandestine processing laboratories in Jalisco and elsewhere to smuggling routes all the way to Chicago—domestic consumption of narcotics was relatively low in Mexico until the rise of the cocaine cartels of the 1980s. La Nacha had maintained street dope-selling corners in Juárez since the onset of her business, but it was not until the 1990s that the evil bloom of the *tiendita* ("little store") or *picadero* (shooting gallery) system spread beyond the central city to encompass much of the surrounding areas.

The Juárez cartel, founded by a federal police commander and a butcher in the 1980s, became a major international drug-trafficking organization, far exceeding the scope of La Nacha's drug business. In the 1990s, the cartel's supplies of illegal drugs so far surpassed even the gargantuan demand of the American market that the cartel, then controlled by Amado Carrillo Fuentes, the "Lord of the Skies," began dumping product on the local market by selling through the *tienditas* located on the barrio streets of Juárez, from the windows of run-down buildings, inside small retail businesses, etc.

La Nacha's old whitewashed adobe house still stands in the Bellavista neighborhood, the historic and contemporary center of the barrio heroin trade in Juárez. Comar's odyssey took him through the maze of unpaved alleys, trails, and dusty concrete streets of Bellavista as well as nearby Altavista, Felipe Angeles, Colonia Postal, and Arroyo Colorado. These frontline border neighborhoods have provided soldiers for the Mexican Revolution, workers for the ASARCO copper smelter of El Paso, undocumented immigrants fleeing north, and combatants and victims in the drug wars of the current era, including the massacre of eighteen gang-related addicts at a drug rehabilitation center in 2009. These areas, including one of the most notorious drug selling points in all Juárez, La Cima ("the Zenith"), present a startling panorama of poverty and degradation as well as resilience and hope to motorists speeding down Interstate 10. The freeway parallels the international boundary embodied in the Río Grande (Río Bravo), which both separates and brings together the United States and Mexico.

From border neighborhoods, Juárez residents can clearly observe the comparatively stunning wealth of El Paso and its large state university, the University of Texas at El Paso, where Comar is now a graduate student. Perhaps nowhere else in North America are the contradictions and binational causes—supply and demand, inequality and dependence—of the international drug trade more evident. Comar's searing account of junkie life on the streets of El Paso and Juárez puts a human face on the border drug debacle that has claimed more than 8,000 lives since 2008.

FURTHER READING

Important ethnographic studies of drug abuse (and related trafficking issues) include Philippe Bourgois, *In Search of Respect:*

Selling Crack in El Barrio, 2nd ed. (Cambridge: Cambridge University Press, 2003); Philippe Bourgois and Jeff Schonberg, *Righteous Dopefiend* (Berkeley and Los Angeles: University of California Press, 2009); Michael Agar, *Ripping and Running: A Formal Ethnographic Study of Urban Heroin Addicts* (New York: Academic Press, 1973); and Lee Hoffer, *Junkie Business: The Evolution and Operation of a Heroin Dealing Network* (Belmont, Calif.: Wadsworth, 2005).

PREFACE

This book concerns cycles of addiction, surrender, and early recovery. It may seem repetitive because the spiraling descent one experiences while actively addicted to narcotics tends to occur in repeated patterns. Its emphasis is on my own lived experience in Ciudad Juárez, Mexico, and El Paso, Texas, from 1998 to 2003. This story is not just my story; it is also the story of those whose experiences paralleled my own. It is the story of my progressive and downward spiral within the whirlwind of active addiction, my ultimate surrender, and my emergence into the "new." Because both change and reflection are essential elements in the process of recovery from active addiction, this book focuses on them through my analysis of past and present. (Note: "Active addiction" refers to the condition in which an addict is pursuing the substance he craves; in recovery, a former user is still considered an addict, just not an active one.)

Faded and forgotten, my lived experiences are too numerous and elusive to recall in their entirety. In this narrative, I have attempted to share some of the basic trends and patterns of active narcotics addiction along with my life experiences on the U.S.-Mexico border. In no way do I wish to glamorize or minimize the pains, fears, and uncertainties associated with the lifestyle of a drug addict. Many of these feelings are indescribable—and practically impossible to reproduce within a written account.

ACKNOWLEDGMENTS

First, I thank Dr. Howard Campbell for encouraging me to follow through with this memoir. Second, I want to thank Richard A. Dugan of the University of Texas at El Paso for the myriad hours that he spent proofreading my original manuscript and suggesting corrections during the summer of 2009.

Finally, I want to share my respect and gratitude with everyone mentioned in this story, including the nameless and faceless people whom I encountered daily on the streets of Juárez and El Paso. It was their unconditional grace that kept me alive during some of my darkest moments. Also, I am indebted to the various treatment centers in El Paso that patiently tried to help me during our various encounters between 1999 and 2002. Ultimately, I am grateful to Aliviane in El Paso and especially to Jesse Martinez, who worked there as a counselor during the 2002 Christmas season.

BORDER JUNKIES

One   *VIAJES*

Sometimes it's better to stick to what you know.

When things go wrong, they always seem to go wrong at the worst possible time. One morning, in the late summer of 1998, I was driving through the streets of Colonia Felipe Angeles in Ciudad Juárez, Mexico, with my girlfriend's brother Jorge. Jorge and I were about a minute away from his family's place. We had just copped five *globos* (small balloons) of Mexican black tar heroin and made an extra stop at the pharmacy to buy insulin syringes, *jeringas*. As we headed back to Jorge's, two Juárez municipal police cars approached us from the opposite direction, passed us, did an immediate U-turn, and pulled us over. The cops searched the car and found our jeringas, but didn't find the dope, because Jorge had swallowed it before I stopped the car. That didn't matter to them—they arrested us anyway. The car had New York plates, and they must have thought that they could get an easy *mordida*, or bribe. My girlfriend was at work and had left Jorge and me to babysit her daughter. Because the eight-year-old child was in the back seat of the car, the cops brought us to Jorge's family's place so we could drop her off before they took us in. They could have let us leave the car, but they towed it in instead. It was a decent car, a Nissan sedan, but since we didn't have the mordida money then and there, the cops took us downtown.

For a junkie, it is a nightmare to get busted two minutes before you are about to shoot up your morning fix. The Delicias Municipal Jail in downtown Juárez was an impregnable fortress built of stone. It was nicknamed Las Piedras, "The Rocks." The cops put us in a room full of younger guys who were delirious after being locked up all night, drunks with hangovers, and junkies going through the various stages of heroin withdrawal. Cement benches extended around the perimeter of the bare, rock-walled holding cell. Las Piedras was dingy and hard, and I just wanted to get out of there as fast as possible. Jorge and I sat there for three hours until my girlfriend finally showed up and got us out. My car was parked outside the jail. Laura, my girlfriend, seemed angrier at the police than she was with Jorge and me. Her mother was there, cursing the cops out in Spanish for not letting us go in the first place. I think the real reason the cops ran us in was because we were short fifty pesos—that was about five U.S. dollars—for the mordida. Laura's mom was pretty upset about the whole bust, but she too directed her anger at the municipal police rather than at us.

I was just grateful that I had given Laura a thousand dollars just in case something went wrong while I was living with her and her family. As we drove back to the house, the conversation quickly turned to Jorge and me and how we had screwed up. Together, we concluded that we should have taken the main road back to the house from the pharmacy instead of the back road that paralleled the Rio Grande. Silence followed. Back in Felipe Angeles, I parked the car, and Jorge and I decided that this time we would just walk over to the heroin connection's house.

Moving to Juárez to live there with Laura and her family was an attempt to remake my life. I grew up in New York State and in Hartford, Connecticut. When I was thirteen, my family moved from New York to Connecticut. Sometime before the move, I began experimenting with marijuana with some of the neighborhood kids. My parents were from upstate New York and had met each other at community college. They were both from large, low-income, rural families and had moved up the American social hierarchy from lower- to middle-class status. I see my own childhood as having been a transition from country boy to city kid. The move to Connecticut put my family in the partially integrated community of Bloomfield. It was not long after our arrival there that I began to hang around with other kids who were using drugs and alcohol. This was around 1979, when the influence of rap music was spreading from New York City into the tristate area. Although I had grown up on rock music, I became heavily involved in the local drug culture that associated itself with rap and hip-hop. After I was expelled from two high schools in the Hartford area and another in upstate New York, I ended up in a long-term rehab program in Hartford. I spent six months there.

As a teenager, my life was full of chaos. I stopped living at home when I was sixteen. For a while, I lived with another family in Hartford and then tried to live with my grandmother in upstate New York. Both experiences were marked and marred by drugs, alcohol, and chaos. By seventeen, I was in the long-term rehab program. Rehab was great: it steered me away from the ignorant path of adolescent self-destruction and put me on track with life. I got a GED (general equivalency diploma) while I was there, and I began to work full-time, changing tires at a local auto shop. One day, about a week before my eighteenth birthday, a friend from the tire shop told me that I should leave rehab and move in with him and his family. My goal was to keep working, get a place of my own, live independently, and pay my own way.

I went AWOL from rehab and began my adult life in the working world. A month later, I got laid off from the tire shop. Business was slow, so the main office, which was located out of town, was cutting back. But the guys at the shop introduced me to one of the regular customers—a guy named Mario, who bought tires from us for a fleet of furniture-delivery vans. The very next day, I had a job delivering furniture for a furniture distribution center. The guys at that job were either into drugs or alcohol, which were all one and the same to me. I worked as a driver's helper, delivering furniture, and most of the guys I worked with drank and smoked reefer all day, every day. I ended up working with a guy named Richard, who did not smoke weed and drank only on special occasions. I developed a stable work routine as his helper, but one day, while delivering to a very upscale home on Cape Cod, we broke a very large crystal chandelier while moving a sleeper sofa up a set of stairs. When we picked the sofa up after breaking the chandelier, a piece of the crystal got wedged between the sofa and my finger and sliced my finger pretty deep. That night I was at the hospital getting stitches.

I was too young to know about workman's comp and decided to quit after a week of light duty. I worked odd jobs around Hartford for a while until I found a job at a moving and storage company. Working for the moving company changed my life. I applied myself, worked hard, and became friends with two drivers named Gary and Woody. Gary's wife, Betty, was the union steward, and it wasn't long before they taught me how to drive a truck and I became a member of the Teamsters. I worked obsessively during my late teens and early twenties. By the time I turned twenty-one, I had left the union and begun driving for different van lines and trucking companies. I was lucky: the way I learned to drive a truck, on the job, was probably one of the last vestiges of the tradesmen-apprentice relationships formerly found in the Northeast.

Life in Hartford gave me a multidimensional perspective on class, gender, and race. The room I rented was in a boardinghouse populated by lower-income working-class men. My neighbors were black, white, and Puerto Rican. Everyone there drank and used drugs. I watched the drug use in the neighborhood switch from marijuana and heroin to cocaine and crack cocaine. Sometimes the guys in the boardinghouse stayed up drinking and smoking crack all night. In those days, I smoked reefer and drank, and although I tried crack cocaine, I really did not like it. When I was not at work, I mostly hung around with the guys from the rooming house in the Parkville neighborhood on Hartford's west side.

In my early twenties, I began driving a truck cross-country and worked my way up in the business from being a company driver to an owner-operator, still mostly moving furniture. Eventually, I owned my own truck. If I could have accepted this move up the social scale—going from living in the boardinghouse to owning my own truck—as my destiny, I think I would have had a very solid and stable life as a truck driver. But at this point, I saw Hartford as my home, and I just couldn't conceive of leaving the streets and the people I knew. My job driving back and forth across the country conflicted with my microscopic vision of success, which demanded that I settle down in Hartford and have a social life outside of work. One day when I was off the road and relaxing in town, a friend of mine from the boardinghouse turned me on to some heroin. It was "China white" powder, so we could sniff it rather than use a needle. I soon started sniffing China white during my breaks from work.

The little cellophane bags that the stuff came in had nicknames stamped on them, names like "Rush Hour" or "DOA" (for "dead on arrival"). Most of the stamps had connotations of death, trauma, or paradise. Once, I bought some dope in New York City that was stamped "Tropicana," just like the Tropicana orange-juice label. I rationalized sniffing dope by telling myself that it was okay because I wasn't shooting it up. But whether you sniff it or shoot it, heroin is highly addictive. In my early experiences with heroin, I did not use enough to become hooked. I used only occasionally and recreationally.

Around this time in my life, I became involved with a woman

named Marilinda. Marilinda was older than me and had two daughters. I was introduced to her by the guys from the boardinghouse. One of my friend's brothers was living with Marilinda's sister. Marilinda was pretty, and I obsessed over her. I was inexperienced with serious relationships and saw only what I wanted to see. We had some good times together. Marilinda had grown up in Puerto Rico, and we traveled there a couple of times. Despite the good times, our relationship was a dysfunctional roller-coaster ride.

It was during one of the lows of that ride that I got hooked on heroin. During one of our many breakups, I began to use every day. One day I woke up feeling really crappy and just couldn't shake it. One of my running partners told me it was the dope and that I caught "a chippie," or a small habit. I sniffed some more dope and felt better. Before I knew it, I was really and truly hooked and progressing further into addiction. I continued to move furniture, but I used dope before, during, and after work. If I went out of town, I tried to bring enough dope with me to make it through the trip. This never worked, of course, and I went through my first detox while I was on the road in Georgia and Florida. It's really messed up to try to move furniture while detoxing from heroin, but I was still new to the whole experience, and my body bounced back because I had not yet been debilitated by years of active addiction.

Eventually, my addiction progressed to the point that I got sick and stayed strung out all the time. It wasn't long before I got busted for heroin possession in New York City. After that, I stopped driving and moved back to Hartford. The dope was synthetic, so my lawyer got the charges dropped, but the company I was working for did not want to deal with me or my problems. As a result, I began to lose all of the money I had saved and all the material possessions that I had accumulated over the years that I worked. I went in and out of various treatment centers and programs, but still could not kick the habit. Subsequently, I found myself alone and hooked on methadone.

Methadone is like liquid heroin. You drink it once a day and it holds, or maintains, you and keeps you from experiencing the pain of withdrawal. The problem with methadone is that it gets you just as high as dope and hooks you into another physical dependency. Withdrawing from methadone is worse than withdrawing from heroin. Some methadone facilities try to systematically lower the dosage so that addicts can withdraw gradually, but this takes a lot of discipline on the part of the addict. At the methadone clinic in Hartford, the addicts would line up every morning, take their daily dose, and go about their business. Many of us met up at a large McDonald's near the clinic and sat there half the morning drinking coffee. Coffee enhances the effect of methadone, helping it kick in faster. Many of the people on the methadone program used heroin also, but they did not have to if they did not want to. I was taking fifty milligrams of methadone daily when I decided to detox. The clinic tried to bring my dosage down slowly, but I messed up that plan by continuing to use heroin on the side.

The first time I shot up heroin with a needle was long before I was on methadone. It was after I got good and hooked from sniffing. A couple of guys I knew taught me how to use a spoon and needle, and my first time mainlining felt real good. The stuff hit me fast and gave me an instant rush of satisfaction, followed by a nod: the sleepy sensation that someone under the influence of heroin experiences. It is similar to falling in and out of sleep. Sometimes the sleep is intense and deep, and other times it is light and short, like a catnap. Using a needle and nodding out with a lit cigarette between my fingers drove Marilinda away from me. Most people are terrified of needles and people who use them. At that time, I thought I would be hooked on methadone and heroin forever and that my life was pretty much finished.

By the end of 1997, I had resolved to clean up, detox, and go back to work as a truck driver. The people at the methadone clinic all looked half-dead. I looked half-dead myself. I was in my early thirties and on the fast track to the graveyard. During the winter of early 1998, my father took me to a house he owned in upstate New York, near Vermont and Canada, where I had parked my big rig the year before. Now I wanted to stay there, detox, and then drive the truck to Chicago for a new job that I had lined up. My father left me there alone and told me he would be back in a month. I had walked off the methadone program when my daily dose was down to fifteen milligrams, but I had also started to shoot up again. In upstate New York, so far from anywhere and anyone familiar, there was no way to find any dope. I ended up so sick from withdrawal that I did not sleep for three weeks. There was some food there, but I was so dope-sick that I could not eat for the first week. I did force myself to eat some oranges. Of all the bad withdrawals I went through, and there were a lot, that was one of the worst. It was very cold that winter, but after a while, the long solitary walks in the cold northern woodlands felt refreshing, and I knew that I had finally kicked the habit!

FIRST TRIP TO JUÁREZ

That spring I was back in business, driving my truck again. I had assumed that my addiction was behind me and that my life was changing for the better. I was hauling household goods from Texas to the Northeast, and on one of those runs, the company sent me to El Paso. I had been to El Paso a few times before, during the late 1980s and early '90s. During the summer of 1998, I went on a trip to Juárez with a small tour company called Bandit Lady Mexico Tours, which operated out of a local truck stop. The Bandit Lady called out to all the truck drivers on her CB radio, telling them to come on over for a tour and a "good time." I decided to check it out. The tour lasted only a few hours, but it was the first time I had ever been to Mexico. I got laid that night, and afterward, I drove back to the Northeast with pleasant memories of El Paso and Juárez. When I reloaded, I was happy to discover that my next run included a one-week layover in El Paso.

As soon as I got back to El Paso, I went back to Bandit Lady Mexico Tours and said that I wanted to stay in Juárez for five days. When I got to Juárez, I went to the Pink Lady bar, and one of the local tour guides took me to rent a hotel room in downtown Juárez. I could tell by his frantic manner that the guide was a cokehead (someone who uses cocaine). He tried to get me into one hotel, but it was full. Finally, we ended up at the Plaza Hotel in downtown Juárez on Calle Ugarte.

Calle Ugarte is a great place; it's a busy downtown street, full of buses, street vendors, taco stands, and small stores. I spent my first day wandering around, drinking at the bars and trying out the food at various restaurants. On my second morning there, as I was leaving the hotel lobby, I heard a young woman's voice speaking to me from behind. The voice asked me, in plain English, how was I doing. It was the voice of a woman named Laura, who was at the hotel visiting a friend who worked at the front desk. I did not have any plans, so I talked with the two girls for a few minutes. Laura asked me whether I wanted to go get something to eat, and I was happy to accept her offer. She had a car, and the next thing I knew, she was driving me around Juárez and telling me all about herself. Laura worked for a dairy company, taking orders from supermarkets. I liked tagging along with her to the different markets around town. She was a bright person, and it was nice to meet someone who was from Juárez and knew her way around.

The next day, Laura picked me up at the hotel and took me to meet her family. They lived in a neighborhood called Felipe Angeles on the west side of Juárez. Her mom was quite lively, and we drank a few beers while she cooked a nice dinner for us. That night, Laura spent the night with me at the hotel. We had become good friends real fast. I spent the next night with her at her mother's place, which had a main house with two smaller cottages behind it. Laura lived in one of the small cottages, or *casitas*, and her younger brother, Jorge, lived in the other. In the main house lived Laura's mother and younger sister. Laura's daughter lived with her, but while I was there, the daughter slept in the main house with Laura's younger sister. I ended up spending the rest of my layover in El Paso with Laura in Juárez. When it was time for me to go back to work, I told her I would definitely be back in a few weeks.

The rest of the trip was a blur: Florida, Georgia, Pennsylvania, and then back to Hartford, where I finished my run and parked my truck. It was late August by then, and shutting down for a while, after running the road for the better part of the spring and summer of 1998, seemed like a good idea. I was still clean, and the thought of returning to Juárez kept me from hanging out up north for too long. One of my moving partners, a guy named Roger, said that he wanted to go along with me to El Paso. Roger was an old road hand who had worked the moving and storage business all his life. We had lived as neighbors at the boardinghouse in Hartford and had known each other for years. Roger had also run the road with me as a driver's helper, and his efforts had helped me pay off my first truck. The thing about Roger was that he liked to drink, and he drank every day. He walked with a limp and had a bad wrist, which he wrapped in a heavy bandage when he worked. The younger guys at the local moving companies called Roger "Captain Hook" because of his limp. Roger always shared tales about being on the road, which he told like a pirate telling tales of trips out to sea. Roger was my helper and friend. He had practically killed himself working for me on some of the big moving jobs we did together. I think the thing that kept him alive was his beer. He did love to drink beer and move furniture.

In 1998, I hooked up with Roger after returning to Hartford from the Juárez trip. He helped me deliver the trailer-load of furniture from the return trip from Texas. I told him that I was going back to El Paso and Juárez to hang out with a girl that I just met and asked him whether he wanted to go. I knew he would take the trip because of his predicament.

Over the years that I knew Roger, he had lived in truck stops, abandoned cars, and various rooming houses. He was practically home-less for many years of his life. In fact, he had been staying at one of the homeless shelters in Hartford when I returned that summer from Texas. He told me that he had just been approved for Social Security payments and that he had enough money on him to pay his own way once we got to El Paso. Because he knew that I had been strung out on dope, he was happy to see me clean and back on the road again. Subsequently, the two of us left Connecticut, picked up a car in New York, and drove straight through to El Paso. It took us just two and a half days to make the trip in a little Nissan sedan.

Once we got to El Paso, Roger checked into a motel room near the truck stop, and I went back to Laura's place in Felipe Angeles. Laura was excited to see me, and I brought Roger over to visit them and have a few beers with her mom. I cooked spaghetti for everyone that night. It was still summertime in Juárez. I remember Roger, after he had had a few too many beers, grinning from ear to ear behind his large plastic-framed glasses and saying that "this was the life." Roger was French-Canadian; although life had dealt him a shitty hand, he was no push-over. I once watched him attack four guys in a barroom brawl, running at them while shouting at the top of his lungs. He seemed to enjoy El Paso and Juárez. And when I told him that I planned to stay in Mexico for a while, he decided that he would stay in El Paso.

During those first few days in El Paso, I periodically went back to check on Roger at the motel room. He was spending his money too fast, so I helped him rent a room from a nice family in El Paso's Lower Valley. He got his Social Security case straightened out and settled down there at the room. I think it was the best thing for him. Roger smoked when he drank, and the stench from the cigarettes must have driven that family crazy. I was happy that I was able to introduce him to a place where he had a chance to experience something beyond the homeless shelters of Hartford, Connecticut.

Meanwhile, back at Laura's house, I became familiar with her fam-ily and their friends in Felipe Angeles. I found a part-time job in El Paso and began to work right away. At this time, I still owned my own truck, although it was parked in New York, and still had my commer-cial driver's license. When I was looking for something to do to make money, Laura told me, "Sometimes it's better to stick to what you know." So I found work at a local moving company in El Paso. After my first week of crossing the bridge every morning in the little Nissan and working at the moving company, the weekend became a festive reprieve from the bump and grind of the daily routine. Yet it was good to be out working. Moving furniture in El Paso seemed easy compared to moving the large estates and homes of New England. Most of the work was on Fort Bliss in military housing, and most of the houses there did not have any stairs.

However, the weekend after my first week of working in El Paso was a major turning point for me. I was staying at Laura's, and she had to work that Saturday. I was bored, pacing the floor, planning to go out for a ride just to get out of the house for a while. On my way out I decided to stop by and visit Laura's brother, Jorge. I knocked on his door, and he welcomed me into his casita. He was there with a few guys from the neighborhood, including one named Víctor, who was going out with Laura's sister. I noticed a spoon on the dresser with some brown liquid in it. It was then that my not too distant past caught up with the present. Next to the spoon sat a needle, the type of syringe that a diabetic uses to inject insulin. The needle was small and not as intimidating as the big needles that are used to give flu vaccinations. And it was all there for the taking. It didn't take long to break the ice with Jorge's buddies; I had walked in and caught them in the act. They were even more surprised when I showed them some of the old track marks on my arms. Just the sight of the dope in the cooker gave me an internal rush. They began to pick up where they had left off when I walked in, preparing the heroin in the spoon and putting it in the syringe. They did not have to ask me whether I wanted any because I was already asking them where to get more. A moment later, I was sticking the needle in my arm. It was in that instant that I threw away about six months of clean time and reverted to the allure of the instant euphoria that had almost killed me the previous year.

Over the next few days, life at Laura's became very different. I was hooked on heroin and began to shoot up every day. Jorge and I were arrested by the municipal police. My addiction progressed into a daily habit, and I stopped going back to Laura's casita at night. Her sister's boyfriend—Víctor—became my dope-shooting partner; we spent a lot of time together, and he became like a brother to me. It wasn't long before I was really strung out again and losing weight. One day as we walked back to Felipe Angeles after copping dope in nearby Altavista, Marcos, a friend of Víctor's who spoke some English, told me that once I was accepted by the people—the Mexican people of Juárez—I would be like family and it would be a beautiful thing. Marcos had lived in Denver for a while, and his English was good. We always got along, and he translated for me when we hung out with other guys from the neighborhood.

Marcos, Víctor, and Jorge all belonged to a gang called La Quinta ("The Five"). The gang had peaked a few years before I arrived, but the feeling of oneness and solidarity among its members was still there among the dope addicts in Felipe Angeles. Many of the gang members had become strung out on heroin and lost their warrior stature. Jorge once showed me an old picture of the gang, its members all carrying sawed-off shotguns and pistols. The neighborhood of Felipe Angeles was even nicknamed "La Quinta" because it had been controlled by that gang. Part of the Altavista neighborhood, where heroin was sold, was known as La Quinta Loma because the same gang had controlled that area as well. I bonded with the guys from the neighborhood. Yet out of all the guys there who were strung out on dope, it was Víctor who became my regular running partner.

Laura was patient as I became a junkie again. Maybe it was because she didn't know anything about my life before we met; maybe she felt bad because I had returned to Juárez just to be with her. Anyway, by the time I was good and hooked, I didn't really care what she felt. The dope was good, cheap, and plentiful. As fall arrived, I was spending most of my time hanging out at Víctor's and shooting dope at least three to five times a day. We set up a small camp on his family's property and used it as our own little shooting gallery. After a couple of weeks, I went back to Laura's and tried to kick the habit. As I felt the withdrawal setting in, I knew that getting back to normal would involve a painful detox. I still had about a thousand dollars deposited in a Mexican bank, and because I knew I had to do something fast, I withdrew the money and closed the account. I visited the office of a Mexican doctor, who prescribed some narcotic pills that were supposed to ease the pain of withdrawal, and then I tried to go cold turkey at Laura's casita.

It was no use. I was too sick, and as soon as Laura left for work, I got either Jorge or Víctor to go down the block and cop some dope from the neighborhood dealer. After a week of this, I decided that I needed to leave Laura's. I packed my stuff and left one day while she was at work, leaving her a note that thanked her for her hospitality. It was early November, and the weather was turning colder, and I decided that I had to get back to my truck and make some money. I had about four hundred dollars left when I finally drove away from El Paso that night, leaving Roger there.

To take the edge off the withdrawal, I took some of the narcotic pills that I had got from the doctor in Juárez; by the time I got to Indiana, I dozed off at the wheel and totaled the car. I still had some money, so after spending the night going through withdrawal in a small-town Indiana motel, I rented a car and drove obsessively through the night to New York City, where I went to the Bronx and picked right back up where I had left off in Juárez. The most insane part of it all was that I still had to return the rental car to Indiana. I drove upstate to my mom's and dropped off my luggage; then I drove down to Hartford and picked up what I thought would be enough dope to make the trip back to Indiana. What a mess! There I was, lying to myself about what I was going to do and what was going to happen. The next thing I knew, I was riding back from Indiana on a Greyhound bus and going through heroin withdrawal. The trip took forever, the bus stopped at every small town and crossroads, and by the time the bus arrived in Philadelphia, I could practically smell the dope getting closer and closer. When we finally arrived in New York City, I took the subway up to the Bronx. The next thing I knew, I was being woken up by two paramedics after nodding out in a Dominican restaurant. I had ended up face first in a plate of rice and beans, and the restaurant owner had called an ambulance. I told the paramedics that I was all right, just a little overtired from too much traveling. They looked me over, decided that I really was okay, and left. With nowhere else to go, I went back to my mom's house and spent Thanksgiving withdrawing from heroin. I remember the smell of the food making me feel even sicker.

By December, I had the strength to drive my truck again. I drove to Hartford and found Marilinda, my old girlfriend, and we took a trip, moving furniture to California, for Christmas. I had scored more dope in Hartford after withdrawing, but by the time we got to Tennessee, it was gone. The sickness from the subsequent withdrawal was painful, but in Albuquerque, New Mexico, I managed to score some more dope, which lasted until we got to California. There is lots of heroin in California, and I stayed hooked while Marilinda and I spent Christmas together at a Motel 6 in San Jose. On the return trip east, Marilinda and I even stopped in Juárez to visit Víctor in Felipe Angeles. Víctor and I copped and ended up spending the day together talking about life and enjoying the moment. The dope lasted all the way back to New York, where there was always more. I dropped Marilinda off in Hartford, not knowing that it was the last time that I would ever see her.

Then I hauled another load of furniture out to California and stopped again in Juárez on my way back. As I approached El Paso and Juárez from the west, I began going through heroin withdrawal. By the time I got to Juárez, I was real sick. I showed up at Víctor's place barely able to walk. Víctor invited me in and told me to lie down and relax while he went out and got some dope. A few minutes later, we were cooking the shit up in a spoon and I shot myself up, despite the sweats and the shakes. I stayed at Víctor's for a couple of weeks, then decided to go back east. Once I was there, I tried to reload for California again, but my drug habit was getting the better of me and really interfering with my ability to work.

It was during that last run back east, that last attempt to keep my footing on what had become an insane treadmill of van lining (cross-country furniture moving), mainlining, and outright lying, that fate finally caught up with me. Someone may have called the company and said that they had seen me driving around New York City with a junkie hooker from Hunt's Point (in the Bronx). Or it may have been all the money that I blew over the course of the weekend. But whatever it was, the company cut off my fuel card, which I used to draw cash; and without any fuel money, the trip was over. Deciding to pull the plug myself, I called the company from New Jersey to tell them that my truck had broken down and would not pass inspection.

The next withdrawal was not as bad as it could have been, and it surely wasn't as bad as the methadone withdrawal. I used very small amounts of heroin to bring myself down incrementally. Perhaps this is why it was a little bit less painful than the other withdrawals I had experienced; moreover, it was certainly less painful than some of the subsequent withdrawals that I would experience. It wasn't long before I thought of returning to Juárez. Life up north was a drag, and I just didn't feel as if there was anything there for me anymore. I felt empty and aimless and wanted a change; I wanted to experience something different, something more out of life than what it had offered me so far. I believed that the kind of newness and opportunity that I was looking for was there in Juárez, and I set my mind on returning there.

I sold my truck during the spring of 1999. My rig was the last link to my success as an owner-operator in the moving and storage business—the last link to my struggle to find regular employment and make ends meet while living in a boardinghouse in Hartford. Everyone who knew me from those days would have spoken of me as a success story, the exemplification of the Horatio Alger idea of pulling yourself up by your bootstraps. All those years of visions, hopes, and dreams faded into the past as I relinquished my truck for a quick five thousand dollars. It didn't really matter to me at the time, because I was eager to leave everything behind.

No hay nada.

On the Trailways bus headed south on the New York State Thruway, I spoke to a guy who had just been released from of one of the prisons upstate. He was heading back to New York City and said he had some people down there who would look out for him. I was kind of envious, since I had always liked the city and my journey wasn't even going to bring me close to it. In Albany, I transferred to a bus that was destined for Buffalo. It was already late afternoon, and I knew that I was in for a long ride. Syracuse, Rochester, Buffalo, Cleveland: it was like a trip through the twilight zone, standing outside the bus station, waiting to reboard in the wee hours of the morning. I knew that the ride was going to be tedious. It seemed as if every little town and gas station on the route had to be visited. I had run this route before as a line driver, but that was like the express compared to this monotonous journey, which dragged on through the night.

As the sun came up, we arrived in Louisville, Kentucky. As the bus chugged through the depressed areas of Louisville, I remember thinking to myself, asking myself, and telling myself, "I know that they have got to have some dope somewhere around here—just look at how messed up this whole place is." I got off the bus and had a ham, egg, and cheese sandwich, the kind that a hungry bus passenger can get in most greasy-spoon diners and truck stops anywhere in mainland America. The bus serviced various little towns along the route, and by the time we got down to Tennessee, the sun was going down again.

I was bound for El Paso—more specifically, for Juárez—and had been on the road for twenty-four hours. We stopped in Nashville, then Memphis, and drove on through the night into Texas, down I-30. I felt as if I were on just another run, another line haul across country to some remote destination that I would figure out once I got there.

As the sun rose, the bus pulled into Dallas, and it reminded me of Hartford. How had my life come to this? It was beyond my ability to comprehend. Life had turned into one hell of a roller-coaster ride, and the down slope seemed long and relentless. Thankfully, though, I was in pretty damn good shape, the result of having spent the better part of my early adult life working in the moving and storage business. In Dallas, a drug dog sniffed at a luggage rack. I remember thinking to myself, "Who would be stupid enough to try to transport illegal drugs on the bus lines." I suppose that after driving a tractor-trailer across country for all those years, I just couldn't fathom transporting drugs any other way.

A bus ride through West Texas can be a very enjoyable experience. What had previously been a monotonous peddler's run, skipping from one town to the next, was transformed into a series of longer trips through scenic landscapes that kept me spellbound with an almost natural elation for the duration of the journey. Dallas and El Paso are nearly 600 miles apart, so there was a lot of time to think. As the bus pushed ahead, the ride became more and more euphorically refreshing. I began to sense the good times ahead in Juárez and El Paso.

Near Pecos, the bus stopped at a fast-food restaurant, and a small group of people got on. A young Mexican woman sat down across the aisle from me. Not long after, a couple of U.S. Border Patrol officers got on the bus and asked anyone who looked Mexican for identification. They took the young woman away, into custody. On the rest of the ride through the desert to El Paso, the remaining passengers were silent. It's funny how a piece of paper can make all of the difference in the world.

In El Paso, the sun was shining, and although it was only early spring, the whole place seemed baking hot. I didn't want to waste any time, so I went directly to the Plaza Hotel in Juárez and rented a room. I had about twenty-five hundred dollars on me, and the safest thing to do was to get off the street. Because I had lived in Juárez before, I was somewhat familiar with the area and knew where I could cop some dope. After I got settled in the room, I caught a bus across town to the area of Colonia Altavista called La Quinta Loma, where I managed to cop about ten dollars worth of *chiva*, or Mexican brown tar heroin. On my way back to the hotel, I stopped at a pharmacy next to the bus stop and bought a new jeringa for five pesos, about fifty cents. Then it was back to my hotel room. Everything was going exactly as planned. I had just made a three-day bus ride across country so that I could start shooting up all over again, and I was finally on the brink of my reaching my objective.

Shooting up heroin is a process that involves the successful completion of many small procedures. First, you need to know where to buy the stuff. Second, you need to be continually vigilant, since cops and robbers come in all shapes and sizes. Third, you need a secure place to shoot up and the proper tools for the act. Most importantly, you need to know what the fuck it is you're doing, or else you could end up killing yourself or someone else. Mexican dope comes in small packages called globos, or balloons. They are about the size of a Tic Tac, and when I showed up in Juárez in the spring of 1999, they cost about three dollars each. If the dope was good, one globo would get a beginner off. Since I was no beginner and had already built up a tolerance, I started off with two.

As soon as I got back to the room, I unwrapped two globos and put the little pieces of brown tar onto a spoon. This in itself is a delicate procedure that takes practice, since dropping and losing dope is like watching a good dream turn into a nightmare. The best way to explain the process is to imagine that the heroin is like a piece of chewing gum stuck in some cellophane; you push the "gum" side onto a spoon, then quickly peel back the plastic. This probably best describes how to get that shit from the inside of a plasticized globo and onto the surface of a spoon without losing any of it. Mexican brown tar heroin is gummy, like Play-Doh, and a globo is about the size of a BB. Anyone who knows anything about insulin needles and shooting dope will likely use about a thirty of water—that's 30 cc, or *treinta rayas*—on a 1 cc or 0.5 cc insulin syringe. Once you use the syringe to measure the amount of water, you spray the water onto the spoon, which already has the dope on it, and stir it up. This takes practice, and with brown tar, you can either heat the spoon or scrape the brown tar into liquid form without heating it. Whether or not you heat the spoon, the fastest way to liquefy brown tar heroin is to use the end of the plunger from a syringe, stirring the stuff around on the spoon until it looks like brown water. Once the water turns brown—the darker the better—and there is no doubt that the dope is liquefied, then it's ready. The next step is to put a very small piece of cotton into the liquefied tar and then put the tip of the needle into the cotton, drawing up the liquid into the syringe. Then a couple of taps on the syringe and a careful leveling off of the liquefied magic should reveal the same amount of water with which you initially began, only now the water is brown. Once the works are fully loaded, you still have to be patient.

The ability to locate a blood vessel and inject the dope is also an art; you know you've hit a vein when you stick the needle in and see blood when you pull back on the plunger. When a connection is made with a vein, you slowly push the plunger in until it reaches the plastic and the syringe is empty. Once the stuff is in your bloodstream, you are overcome with a euphoric rush that levels off, leaves you feeling somewhere between numb and dreamy, and lasts between six and twenty-four hours, depending upon the quality of the dope, the quantity used, and the tolerance of the user.

Some junkies, *tecatos*, chew on the small used piece of cotton that filtered the liquefied dope into the tip of the syringe. However, if you miss the shot, which happens occasionally, be ready for one hell of a nasty sensation: it feels like getting stung by a swarm of bees in the area of the injection. The bad thing about missing is that the dope doesn't take effect as fast; worse yet, the pain lasts for a long time. Some people miss on purpose: this is called skin-popping. Most junkies who skin-pop have really messed-up skin after they do it for a while. Shooting into a vein is called mainlining, which is generally the preferred method among junkies.

I had been clean for almost a week before the bus ride, so the dope hit me pretty good. One thing that heroin users like to do when they get high is to smoke lots of cigarettes. Sometimes you can spot a heroin user by the burn marks on their fingers. This is usually the result of nodding out while holding a lit cigarette. If the nod is good, not even a cigarette burning their fingers will wake up a junkie. My tolerance was low, so I decided to go out and see what was happening on the street. One nice thing about Juárez was that food vendors were in abundance. Taco stands, burrito stands, and small restaurants with signs announcing *comidas corridas* (small fixed-price meals) abundantly occupied the urban landscape. Once junkies' addictions to heroin start getting heavier, it's normal for them to fix so that they can eat. It's never the other way around.

After I ate, I decided to visit a local bar and house of prostitution known as the Pink Lady. While I was there, drinking beer, smoking cigarettes, and nodding out, I ran into the Bandit Lady. She was still running her Mexico tour business out of a truck stop in El Paso. I told her that I had moved to Juárez to live and that I was looking for an apartment and a part-time job. She told me that she needed another driver, that there were always plenty of apartments for rent in Juárez, and that she would help me find one. My previous contacts turned out to be crucial for building and maintaining my drug habit. Even though I had lived in Juárez a year earlier, this time was different because I was alone and I was here to stay.

During my first week back in Juárez, I stayed at the Plaza Hotel in El Centro, the central part of town, on Calle Ugarte. I hadn't done much of anything yet except shoot up and hang around the hotel room. I hooked up with my friend Víctor and also visited another tecato named Pepe, who lived near one of our connections. Most of my time, however, was spent alone or just hanging out on the streets of downtown. I was anxious to find something to do, and after a few days of this hanging around, I was bored. I found the Bandit Lady, and she introduced me to a couple who agreed to rent me an apartment. The guy was an American and the girl was a *Juarense*. Her family owned the apartment, and they all seemed pretty friendly about the whole deal. They took me out to look at the place, and I liked the view. I was also pleased at the prospect of getting out of the hotel room.

It was a little bungalow, a casita on Calle Fray García de San Francisco in Colonia Postal, which is on the west side of Juárez, close to the Avenida 16 de Septiembre. The neighborhood is called Barrio Magnesio because Calle Magnesio is the big cross street that runs through it. The casita was a nice little cottage on a hill, with a tree in the front and undergrowth extending down the far side of the small yard. The street, which is really just a set of steps going up a hill to a schoolhouse located on the mesa, is lined with small casitas. And the view was great: a panorama of downtown El Paso, the mountains, and the surrounding area. I agreed to rent the place on the spot and paid for six months' rent up front. At fifty dollars a month, I figured it was a bargain.

Since the Plaza Hotel was located in downtown Juárez, it was surrounded by small corner stores, restaurants, taco stands, bars, and strip clubs. Every night, music rattled the walls and drunks roamed the streets. The sounds of *corridos* (folk songs) and the reek of stale beer and liquor drifted from the barrooms and mixed with the smell of fried food from nearby restaurants. Most doors never closed, although a few were curtained off by a small sheet to keep the cool air from a working swamp cooler from spewing directly onto the street. Restaurants displayed roasted chickens in their windows, and the smell of food cooking was all around, mixed with the exhaust of buses and automobiles, the sounds of motors, and the chanting yells of street vendors. The whole street in front of the hotel was a major bus stop, and many of the buses that ran through downtown parked in designated areas, waiting for passengers until it was time to move along. The traffic was constant well into the night. El Centro was a good place for keeping my identity as a junkie undercover, but the intensity of the noise and the crowds was bothersome. There was an upstairs pool hall two doors down from the hotel; it was one of my favorite hangouts when I was high. The owner was friendly and talkative, and he charged by the hour for the pool tables. It was nice and inexpensive, and it kept me off the street during my early days in Juárez, when I didn't know much Spanish. I knew just enough to get by, but since the city was on the border, many of the people spoke a little bit of English.

I would often shoot up in the afternoon and hang out at the pool hall. The place would start to fill with people, the music would start to play, the beer would flow, and I would play pool with whoever was there. I was never good at pool until I started shooting dope. For the most part, the people were friendly, and I didn't sense any animosity. The pool hall always smelled like beer because there were always accidents involving broken beer bottles and beer spilled on the floor. The best thing about the pool hall was that I stayed active even while I was under the influence, and getting out of the hotel room made me feel good about being in Juárez. It made me feel connected. If I shot up and just sat in the room watching TV, I usually nodded out and felt isolated and depressed. Getting out and interacting with the people was what it was all about. Interaction signified involvement, at whatever level. It represented a sort of progress, since it meant that I was closer to the mainstream of life in Mexico.

Before I moved from El Centro to Colonia Postal, I met a young woman named María de los Angeles. We met one morning in a taco shop on the Mariscal, the red-light district. María seemed as if she were just floating through life the same way that I was. She was from somewhere in Chihuahua, a *morena* (brown-skinned woman) who had come to the border to get ahead. She worked in a bar, but after I visited her at work, I realized that she was working in one of the sorriest establishments in town. I think she worked there for the companionship and the safety of being part of a group rather than to make money. There were always half a dozen young girls there, hanging around and hoping someone would buy them a beer. María and I became partners for a while, and she started to spend nights with me at the hotel. I asked her whether she wanted to move with me to the casita, and she agreed. Moving was a simple process: we threw our bags into the back of a taxi, and off we went.

IN COLONIA POSTAL

We arrived at the casita about five in the afternoon, unpacked, and settled in as best we could. The next day, we went shopping on Avenida 16 de Septiembre, and I bought some new sheets and pillows. The apartment came furnished, but the extras weren't included. The casita had only cold water; there was no water heater, and the cold water was really cold. The first few days at the casita with María were nice. I wasn't strung out real bad, so we spent a good amount of time messing around in bed and going out to eat. María worked at the bar from two in the afternoon until two in the morning. She never really made any money, and I was forever telling her to leave that place and find a better job, but I didn't really care what she did, and neither did she.

Soon, I began crossing the bridge to El Paso to try to find work in the moving business. During this period, the summer and fall of 1999, when I was still new to Juárez and El Paso, my years of experience in the moving business could still help me get jobs. In the morning, I would get up early and cross the bridge into El Paso to work. After knocking off, I would go to La Quinta Loma, which was near the casita, and score a couple of globos. I still had some money left from the cash that I had brought with me, but I wanted to support myself by working. At this point, I still liked to think that I had some kind of control over my addiction.

One day I went to work and started feeling a slight case of the *malilla* (heroin-withdrawal symptoms). I stuck it out, but the trip to the dope dealer after work couldn't come fast enough. This went on for a few days. One day when work was slow and I went home early, I copped on the way home, the way I usually did, and planned on spending a nice afternoon in the euphoria of heroin and nicotine. When I got home, the door was locked and my key wouldn't open it. I thought to myself, "What the fuck is going on?" Finally, María opened the door, and I walked in to discover some guy sitting at our kitchen table. I felt betrayed, although I didn't really care that much about anything except shooting up. María used to come home from work late at night with beer and cocaine on her breath. I knew what that shit smelled like from experience. I also knew from the start that our relationship was short term and that her lifestyle would eventually clash with mine. I shook this motherfucker's hand and pretended that it was all cool, acting as nice as I could. I didn't give a fuck whether they knew what I was about, so I sat down at the table, pulled out the dope and my works, and proceeded to shoot up right in front of them both. Neither of them said a word, and they seemed thankful that I wasn't mad. In a sense, I felt liberated to be able to be what I was; after all, I had been shooting up for some time. After a couple of hours of sitting there and smoking cigarettes, María announced that she was leaving for work. Before she could say another word, I told her to leave her key to the casita with me and take her clothes with her. I guess they probably both expected it. María knew that I was no pushover. She packed her stuff into two plastic shopping bags and left me the keys, and that was that for María de los Angeles.

I felt as if a burden had been lifted from me: I didn't have to carry somebody else's extra weight around along with my own addiction. After I kicked María out, I stopped going to work and started to run through the money I had left in my pocket. At that time, I didn't know about the shortcuts through the neighborhood, so I would walk down the main street, Calle Magnesio, to get to Altavista to score. One morning, I went out and bought ten globos and two new jeringas. In Juárez, the police have pickup trucks with little campers on the back; the cops drive around looking for people to pick up and throw into the back. The street slang for this Mexican version of the paddy wagon is *camper*. When a group of junkies are shooting up someplace and they hear someone shout, *"Camper!"* everyone runs, and I mean they haul ass as if their lives depended on it.

Well, as I was walking back to the casita that morning, with the globos and jeringas, a *camper* passed me and did a U-turn. I was still new in the neighborhood, and these cops saw me as an easy target. They ran the usual routine, frisked me, and found the dope and the needles; it was enough to put me away for at least a few years, even in Mexico. I knew it, and so did they; when I lived in Felipe Angeles, Víctor and the rest of the crew had filled me in on how the Mexican law worked, and I knew they had me. I did the only thing that I knew would work: I took my sneaker off and pulled out ten hundred-dollar bills from under the insole. As I was digging out the cash, I asked the cops how much it would cost to get me out of this mess. My Spanish wasn't great, but it always got better real fast when I was in a predicament, and it was certainly good enough for this conversation. They looked at each other and took the money. As the cops contemplated how much to keep, I explained that I lived only two blocks away and that what I had given them was all the money that I had in the world. The cops smiled, told me not to worry, and gave me back six hundred dollars. Yes! This might not have been the greatest day to be me, but at least I wasn't on my way to jail. The cops confiscated the globos and jeringas, so I turned around and walked back to Altavista and bought some more.

The whole incident shook me up pretty bad, and I wasn't going to again risk being as exposed as I was that morning. I decided that I was going to have to learn a little more about how to survive in Mexico. The last time I had lived in Juárez, I spent a lot of time hanging around with Víctor and getting to know my way around the local *barrios*, or neighborhoods. In Altavista, two brothers, Víctor and Pepe, had a little casita behind their family's house. Pepe's brother Víctor is not to be confused with my friend Víctor from Felipe Angeles, who dated Laura's sister. There was a cinder-block wall around Pepe and Víctor's backyard, which could be entered through a little iron gate. I hoped that they would remember me from my visits to shoot up there with Víctor from Felipe Angeles. Happily, they did remember me and were hospitable. I offered to get them high, and we all shot up in their one-room casita. Their place was the neighborhood shooting gallery, and practically as soon as we shot up, more tecatos showed up with their works and more dope.

Víctor from Felipe Angeles always told me that I could trust Pepe, so I told him about my run-in with the municipal police. Pepe told me that I should avoid the main streets as much as possible. Pepe and his brother Víctor showed me a shortcut to my place via unpaved back streets and footpaths and told me that I could shoot up at their place anytime. Pepe and his brother treated me with a lot of respect because I had been introduced to them by my friend Víctor from Felipe Angeles, a member of the old gang—La Quinta. My association with Víctor had given me a pass into their network, but I knew it would be short-lived if I didn't solidify the bond. There wasn't much of an option if I were going to survive as a junkie in this neighborhood: I needed to establish a network that would help me support my habit. I went back to Felipe Angeles and found Víctor and explained my situation to him; he went with me back to Pepe's shooting gallery. I knew that as long as I was down with the local *onda* ("groove"), nobody would go out of their way to fuck with me. This helped me avoid any unnecessary drama. Being strung out is bad enough, but being strung out and hunted by *la policía* and targeted by other junkies is pure damnation.

For the next few weeks, I tried to slow down and think carefully before I acted. My money was running out, and I alternated my shooting patterns so that I could take the shortcuts either early in the morning or after dark, or else I would hang out at Pepe's and get high with the rest of the *tecatos del barrio*. My tolerance was increasing fast, and I needed more and more dope to feel normal. It was around this time that Víctor from Felipe Angeles disappeared. His family told me that he was in the CERESO (a prison in Juárez), so I stopped going to Felipe Angeles for a while. My lack of income started to bother me, so I went downtown to the Pink Lady bar in order to take the Bandit Lady up on her job offer. I never did learn her real name, but that wasn't important as long as I got paid. The Bandit Lady was no fool and probably sensed that I was a little bit rough around the edges—she just didn't know exactly how rough. She gave me a big lecture about how she would take care of me if I were loyal to her. Fine, whatever, I had the job.

WORKING FOR THE BANDIT LADY

I drove lonely truck drivers from the truck stop in El Paso to the Pink Lady in Juárez. If the Pink Lady wasn't happening, we would use a bar called Chito's. If given a choice between the two, I always recommended the Pink Lady. The job itself was unusual: I would arrive at the truck stop and pick up customers from the Bandit Lady's little office, located nearby. It had a big sign out front that read "Bandit Lady Mexico Tours." The Bandit Lady, or one of her female associates, sat at the desk in the office and talked to truckers on the CB radio, explaining the ins and outs of "touring" Juárez and having a good time. Make no mistake about it: Bandit Lady Mexico Tours proved to me that sex sells just as well as, maybe even better than, drugs do.

I had never been much into prostitution, and by the time I started working for the Bandit Lady, my heroin habit was really starting to kick my ass. I would go into the bars and translate for the truckers; it made them feel safer with an American chauffeur. Of course, if they had known what I was doing after I dropped them off at the clubs, they probably would have been more than a bit uncomfortable. I would usually fix in the morning and then go downtown and meet the Bandit

Lady at the club around noon; she would have another woman working the CB up in El Paso at the truck stop. I would take her van and head up to the truck stop from Juárez, and by the time I got there, there would usually be a few customers already lined up. Sometimes, between runs, I would pick up some chiva and stop off at my casita to fix.

Working for the Bandit Lady was interesting, and driving a bunch of drunken truck drivers over the bridge had its moments. You never knew what might come out of the mouth of an intoxicated truck driver at two in the morning at an international checkpoint. I also got to be pretty good at playing pool while on the job, and for me, the sodas were on the house. I never drank beer, because it didn't mix well with heroin, so I kept to a strict regimen of dope, cigarettes, and nonalcoholic beverages. On the other hand, sex and dope always went well together. One of the biggest problems for a junkie working in a whorehouse is the lack of money. At first, I tried to feel sorry for the girls, but that didn't last very long. My relationship with the girls involved convenience and necessity. I brought them the customers, and they put up with me on the pool table. Because of the economic dilemma that every addict faces, I was never a paying customer. Over time, mutual respect developed between us, and some of them taught me a few words in Spanish.

The girls were unique in their own ways. Most of them were younger than forty and physically active. Some walked to work or took the bus, while others had cars. Most of them were from places like Chihuahua, Zacatecas, Torreón, and Durango, although some were local girls from Juárez. Others were from as far away as Mexico City, Michoacán, and Veracruz. Later, I met girls from Chiapas and Oaxaca. Many of the girls would hang around the Pink Lady and Chito's all day and night. In my opinion, the Pink Lady was the classier of the two places. The girls would curse, drink, and laugh until the customers arrived; then they would get the customers to buy them drinks and eventually persuade them to go upstairs to one of the private rooms to have sex. I never joked with them about their job, and they just seemed to play the cards that life had dealt them. Some of them lived on the premises, while others lived in the city. According to the system in place, if a customer wanted to take one of the girls out of the bar for the day or the evening, he had to pay; if a customer wanted to marry one of the girls, he had to pay. It seemed to me that the girls were virtual slaves. But some of them weren't as helpless as others, and if a patron in the club got too bossy, they wouldn't put up with it.

The girls didn't fight among themselves that much; in fact, they often shared with one another. Even the bare necessities, such as food, clothing, and shelter, seemed to be community property. This informal network within the bar helped these women survive. Although some of the dirtier and more strung-out women walked the streets alone, away from the protection of the *cantina*, those who were healthy and accepted as part of the community operating in the bars had developed a support system that increased their chances for survival. In 1999 there wasn't much talk about the ongoing murders of young women in Juárez. Most of the girls at the Pink Lady and Chito's either were unaware of the danger or didn't have the luxury of considering the possibility that something bad might happen to them. In the clubs, every day was another adventure in the quest for survival.

One day, I caught the Bandit Lady's boyfriend having sex with one of the girls from Chito's. He told me to be cool and keep it quiet, and I really had no reason to do otherwise. It was kind of funny because this girl was also going out with Chito's son, Tommy. Tommy was a junkie who always stayed close to daddy's cantina and hooker bar. This kept enough money in his pocket that he was able to maintain his dope habit. Every once in a while, I would hang out and rap with Tommy, but he was too sheltered to be a street junkie. He was also one hell of a manipulator. We were amigos, but I knew that he was too self-centered in his addiction to be trusted fully. I got along better with Chito himself, and he mentioned to me from time to time that if I ever became tired of working for the Bandit Lady, I should come work for him. As always, when I brought him some business, the sodas were on the house.

Chito's place had two large pool tables, and the atmosphere wasn't as businesslike as at the Pink Lady. Many of Chito's girls were hooked on cocaine, and they would run in and out of the bar all night to score and get high in the private rooms they used next door. Chito knew that I was strung out, and he knew his son was also hooked on heroin. I think that was one of the reasons he liked it when I came around and brought customers. Maybe in his own convoluted way, he envisioned us cleaning up and really running a top-notch operation, one where the girls were cleaner and prices were higher. On the other hand, maybe he had surrendered to the reality around him and was trying to cope in the best way that he could. Some of the women who worked the bar for him would ask me things like, why did I do that shit? They were pretty nice to me at Chito's and would sometimes surprise me with a plate of food in the morning. They may have noticed that I was losing weight and wanted to pump me up for the work that needed doing. After all, American customers meant good times and money, and it took someone like me to go out to the truck stop, pick them up, and bring them over.

In general, I was never really exposed to prostitution before living in Juárez. When I drove a truck, every once in a while I would get propositioned, but the "lot lizards," truck-stop prostitutes, were a nasty-looking bunch that didn't really turn me on. Prostitution in Juárez seems to have a hierarchy of its own. On the bottom is the street-junkie prostitute, working out of flophouses and on street corners. Working at this bottom level is the riskiest type of hooking because the women are accessible to the general public and have practically no protection. Anyone from a policeman to a homicidal maniac can show up and wreak havoc in a street prostitute's life. Then there are the hole-in-the-wall clubs that at least offer some protection, but the conditions are usually dirty, and drug use is heavy at this level. Then there are the clubs that are just a notch above the local dives. These are the types of places that I was driving for; they offer greater protection for the girls as well as housing and a more solid network between owners and workers. This must involve some human trafficking, I assume, since some of the girls seemed to be trapped in their lives at the bar. Some of them never went anywhere, and if someone wanted to leave with one of them, the bar would always want a fee to be paid. I had heard rumors about people paying for long-term excursions, sometimes leading to marriage, but I never witnessed anything like that. I knew one truck driver who supposedly married one of the girls from the bar, and rumor had it that he had paid for her to be able to leave with him. This couple showed up at the bar from time to time as if to romanticize their initial encounter, and always ended up stumbling drunk. The next level up on the prostitution hierarchy involves massage parlors and the more bourgeois bordellos that the wealthier clients frequent. I suppose there must be others, such as call girls who work by phone, but most of my experience was on the street level.

Usually, the police didn't mess with the customers at the bars where I worked, although I was frisked once during a crackdown at Chito's. Chito's wasn't as upscale as the Pink Lady, and the cops may have been tipped off about drug use in the bar. I never shot up in any of the clubs—it was just too risky. After working for the Bandit Lady for a few weeks, I started to have problems at work. The work, if you could call it that, wasn't that difficult, but my heroin addiction was becoming too much to balance with the burdens of shepherding drunken truckers across the bridge, not to mention the presentation of myself to the U.S. and Mexican customs officials, customers, and club workers.

I usually woke up and walked to La Quinta Loma to buy enough dope to keep me maintained for the day. The clubs stayed open very late, and it was too risky and uncertain to try to buy dope late at night. Sometimes I didn't get home until after three in the morning. This created a recurring morning ritual of waking up sick, dragging my ass to the dealer, and then making it back home or over to Pepe's to shoot up. My options were limited. Additional problems occurred when my main dealer didn't have any dope, since I absolutely had to have it in order to function. The dependence was both physical and mental.

Mornings around the casita in Colonia Postal were quiet, and I started to really get to know my way around the unpaved streets and shortcuts. The barrio was also full of other junkies out looking for their morning fix, and some of them showed me other heroin dealers. A few people tried to deal in a fly-by-night way, but I could never depend on a part-time dealer. They were easy to spot, and an experienced junkie could tell they were inexperienced and just in the game to make a few pesos. Soon, I made a new connection just down the hill from the casita, as well as another just a few blocks farther into the barrio.

Now I was starting to feel the urge to use during work, and the nights were becoming too long to wait until morning, when I would wake up sick and desperate to fix. So I began to score in the afternoon and early evening after I dropped the customers off at the club. I would go to the casita and shoot up and save a little stash for later. I did this for some time until one night, on a run back to the truck stop to pick up more customers, the Bandit Lady confronted me. She wanted to know what had taken me so long. Apparently, some of the "tourists" waiting at the office had become impatient and left. When she called the bar, someone told her that I had already left. Her suspicions were high, but I played it off and placated her, telling her that there had been a long line on the bridge.

One morning I woke up sick and had trouble finding a fix. What usually happens when the connections go dry and no one has any dope, *no hay nada*, is that, especially in the mornings, sick junkies start to gather around the dope spot like flies on shit. Then, finally, when the dope arrives, there's a mad rush and the crowd dissipates. By the time I finally got downtown, I was a half hour late. On this particular day, the

Bandit Lady was at the Pink Lady and her van was gone. She told me that she sent her boyfriend to pick up the customers. We were standing outside the bar on the street when I just gave her the keys and told her that I couldn't do it anymore. She looked me over and told me that she had known all along that I was hooked, and then she gave me forty bucks and wished me luck.

It didn't bother me to leave that job behind; I just walked back to the barrio, copped some globos, and went to the casita to shoot up. I was still fairly new in Juárez, and I still had a little bit of my own money put away for what I thought would probably be a very short rainy day. I didn't go back downtown looking for work, because I figured that everyone who knew me knew that I was strung out. On the street, once people know this, they tend to keep their distance. Usually, the gossip goes something like, "Did you hear about so-and-so?" "Yeah, that's too bad. Don't trust him." No, I didn't need any of that, so I decided to hang out around the casita instead. The casita offered some protection and a chance for survival.

I wouldn't miss all the phony bar bullshit. I didn't even drink! The whole scene was just too much. The prostitutes saw everyone as targets instead of as people. I was still soft, and the girls were hard. They didn't give a fuck, because they were already out there. As for me, I knew how to defend myself, but I surely didn't want to hurt anyone in order to support my drug habit. Stealing was too much of a risk because there was too much to lose. Getting caught meant going to jail, and that meant sitting through five weeks of hell while detoxing from heroin. Also, getting a reputation as a thief wasn't the best move for someone who was a foreigner. The girls at the bars knew that their alternatives were limited, so they stayed where they were, made the best of things, and used the handiest means to get what they wanted. Although I was still new to the desperation that the bar girls were already familiar with, it wouldn't be long before I was operating in the same realm of survival. In Juárez, nobody asked me for anything. Perhaps the taxi drivers near the bridge on Juárez Avenue were a bit aggressive, but I never took a taxi unless I had a pocket full of money and was too sick to walk. The buses in Juárez were dependable and consistent, and for thirty cents, or three pesos, you couldn't go wrong.

Víctor taught me how to ride the bus; we sometimes had to take the bus to score dope in the morning when the local connections were dry. The neighborhood around my casita didn't dry up that often, but in Felipe Angeles, where I used to live, the supply wasn't always as abundant.

A bus ride in Juárez was always exciting. Sometimes, recovering addicts from Christian recovery homes would get on and pass out candy to everyone; if you gave the candy back, that meant that you didn't want to buy it. If you kept it, you had to give them something. Ice cream vendors with plastic coolers, singers and guitar players, and crazy people just shouting out their problems all boarded regularly, working to get people to part with their spare change. Sometimes the musicians were pretty good, and even I gave up a few pesos, about thirty cents, to make them feel like there was still some kind of hope in the world.

I enjoyed the bus rides, and when the buses were full and the aisles filled up with people, it felt like being crammed into a can of sardines. But even this didn't stop the destitute from worming their way from the front to the back of the bus while trying to bum some change. Sometimes the buses were so full that one had to get on or off through the rear emergency doors; in fact, this was an everyday occurrence. The Juárez buses were old American school buses, repainted on the outside, with interiors that would be familiar to anyone who grew up in the States. Some of the Juárez lines had newer buses, but this was more the exception than the rule.

I rode the bus practically everyday. The bus to the casita went, usually hastily, up and down some pretty intense little hills, and since it was often full of people, the ride was somewhat dangerous, although most passengers never really considered the danger. At times, bus drivers would race each other to the next pickup for an extra one or two passengers. Even when I was high on heroin, the bus-ride experience was enough to keep me on the edge of my seat. Some bus drivers smoked cigarettes, and smoking on the bus was generally considered acceptable unless all the windows were up because it was cold outside. Just to be sure, I would usually ask the driver if it was all right to smoke. From my perspective as a former truck driver, I thought that many of the bus drivers took too many unnecessary risks, almost in the same way that a junkie who steals takes too many unnecessary risks. The bus drivers varied from impulsive maniacs to older and smoother operators. I think that you can usually judge the level of someone's serenity by the way they drive.

¡Caballos!

Colonia Postal and the surrounding neighborhoods are a maze of paved and dirt roads that intertwine and crisscross through hilly terrain. As the summer of 1999 wore on, I became more familiar with the shortcuts, connections, and networks near my casita. I also started to become part of the barrio in more ways than one. After I gave up driving for the Bandit Lady, I had more time to explore the neighborhood. Since moving into the casita, I had found three primary heroin connections in the surrounding neighborhoods: dealers in the neighborhood of La Quinta Loma, and the local dealers Marcos and Polo. Marcos's place was down the hill from the casita, just within the perimeter of the maze of unpaved streets. Polo's was deeper inside the maze itself. La Quinta Loma was a bit farther away, but still within walking distance. I usually started at the closest connection, since I always wanted to cop a fix and return to the casita as quickly as possible. The Juárez police patrol the backstreets and pathways of the barrios on horseback, and when I walked the streets, I was always on the alert for fresh horse manure or the sound of hooves. Around the connections, if anyone shouted, "¡*Caballos!*" ("Horses!"), it was time to either run or act as though you were doing something besides trying to buy drugs.

Whenever the dope ran out and a group of junkies were waiting for the dealer to re-up, some junkies would be so sick from withdrawal that they wouldn't even try to run. Then it would be up to the mounted patrol officers whether to take them in. Sometimes the cops just rode by as if nothing were wrong. This was because the cops were often paid off to leave the dealers and customers alone. Once the flow of heroin (chiva) began, or when it was consistently available, a lot of junkies shot up close to the dealers' locations. Some of the dealers didn't let this happen, while others let it happen right on their property or even right on the premises. If a horse patrol came around when junkies were outside shooting up, the group would make a mad dash and the chase would be on! Some junkies would get caught and others would escape; the ca-ballos conducted these roundups in conjunction with the *campers*. To avoid these dragnets, I always got tight with the local dealers. Because I bought from them every day, they often tried to protect me, or at least warn me, when things got hot.

Marcos, who lived down the hill from the casita, was the closest connection. He used to live in Los Angeles, California, and spoke good English. An old-school West Coast junkie who identified as a Chicano, Marcos was married, or living with a woman, and together they had about seven kids. Marcos's story was one of the many tragedies that I witnessed in Juárez. Getting tight with Marcos wasn't too difficult, be-cause he spoke good English and was an honest dope dealer. Since I was a steady customer, it didn't take long for me to become an insider in his world.

Relationships between pushers and junkies usually take some time to develop, and dealer–customer trust issues aren't the same in Juárez as they are in the United States. For example, there was no way that Mar-cos was going to worry about me, an American, being an undercover cop. One morning I went to Marcos's place when I was so sick from heroin withdrawal that I could barely walk. He invited me in and sold me some dope in his kitchen. Then, since he was the only one there, he let me shoot up there. As the days passed, Marcos and I developed a reciprocal trust, but it lasted only as long as there was a steady sup-ply of dope. Marcos, his wife, and the kids lived in the rearmost casita of three within a compound that was fenced in by plywood and pal-lets; the shared outhouse was at the very front of the compound. A vis-itor entering the gate had to pass by the other casitas to get to Marcos's, which was half kitchen and half sleeping area; the family all slept in one room. The place was hot in the summer and cold in the winter; liv-ing there was practically like camping. His wife's relatives lived in the neighboring casitas. Between the casitas, his sister-in-law and her boy-friend resided in a little shack built of pallets. They were both junk-ies, and their makeshift shelter often served as a shooting gallery. After I'd been buying dope from Marcos for a while, I felt comfortable with the proximity and safety of his setup. The only problem was that when he didn't have any dope, I would have to drag my dope-sick ass farther into the barrio in order to connect.

The next nearest connection was Polo. Many street junkies hung around Polo's. Like Marcos, Polo was both a dealer and a junkie, but he was a reckless junkie. Polo, who often shot up in front of the customers, was strung out pretty bad. He didn't speak English, but we got along pretty well anyway, despite my broken Spanish. Polo sold quality dope, but he was as crazy as they came. If I was sick when I got to Polo's, I had to either shoot up there or go home and shoot up alone. I often chose to go back to my casita, but if I was real sick, I would shoot up right there at Polo's. The thing about Polo's is that it was public. Some junkies would shoot up in the street, right in front of the place! Polo's place, like Marcos's, was in the middle of a neighborhood that didn't have paved streets; streets of dirt and stone often tapered off into little paths and horse trails. Polo's small house sat off a hilly dirt road that resembled a wide trail. It was hard to reach by car, especially after it rained. The police often patrolled the neighborhood with their *campers*, which fared badly on the rocky roads, or on horseback. Junkies were always hanging around Polo's looking for a fix, and many of them acted as lookouts.

By this time, most of the regular junkies in the barrio knew my face from seeing me around the different connections. I networked with them a little, but most of the time I ran alone. The bad thing about a place like Polo's was that there were always dope-sick junkies hanging around, begging for someone to give them a fix: "*Préstame diez rayas, compa*" ("Front me 10 cc worth of dope, friend"). As money got tighter, I had nothing to give away. But if a dealer who used, like Marcos, was sick and I helped him out of it, it was a good investment, since he would return the favor later on. This was important: withdrawal sickness was always lurking in the life of a tecato, just waiting for him to let his guard down or experience some misfortune. Reciprocity occurred at the most surprising moments and strengthened the ties between the neighborhood pushers and me.

THE WAY OF THE PANHANDLER

Up to this point, I had been a house junkie. I had sustained enough economic security to stay off the street and still maintain my habit. For a junkie, losing a house or apartment and moving onto the street means crossing a threshold, stepping over a line and experiencing a new bottom. Living on the street to maintain your habit means accepting that you have sunk to a new level in heroin addiction. With this shift comes a change in perception: others around you go from being seen as people in their own right to simply becoming possible ways to get more money to feed your addiction.

The vampire metaphor is a good one for considering the lifestyle of a street junkie. Vampires hunt their victims for the life-sustaining blood they require for their deathlike existence. Without blood, vampires perish. For junkies on the street, dope becomes the blood of life, and without it, they get sick and certainly wish they were dead. And just as slain vampires are released from the eternal addiction to blood, dope addicts who go through the deathlike experience of detox and make it through to the other side of physical dependency are released from the perpetual need for heroin as they resurrect themselves from the depths of their addiction. A more in-depth comparison between the folkloric particulars of vampirism and the general patterns of addiction reveals some interesting correlations. I think that for nineteenth-century theorists trying to explain addictive behavior in general, vampire folklore served as a rational symbol of the process.

Getting back to coming out onto the street: my experience went from desperation to hopelessness. By the end of the summer of 1999, I was flat broke and strung out. Having exhausted all of my economic resources, I found myself alone and desperate. One evening, I shot my last globo and just went to sleep. When I awoke up the next day, I began to feel a little sick. It was hot out, and my body felt as if it were on fire. I lay in bed and wondered whether I had the strength to go cold turkey with no money, no food, and no one to help me. By late afternoon, I knew that the answer was no. I went outside and found some of the local kids hanging around on the steps in front of the casita. The neighborhood kids knew what was up with me. By this time, I was very weak and in a lot of pain. The casita had a propane tank, and it was the only thing I could quickly sell to get some fast cash. I told them that if they sold the propane tank for me, I would give them half the money. Agreeing to help, they carried off the propane tank as I writhed around in pain.

Time stood still as I anxiously awaited their return. When they finally showed up, they gave me 120 pesos, which is about 12 dollars. A globo of brown tar heroin cost 30 pesos. I limped down the hill in the back of the neighborhood, looking for Marcos. Dragging my ass back to the casita after I bought the dope was like hiking the miracle mile, but by sunset, I felt normal again. The pain subsided, and the euphoric healing made me forget the ten hours of agony that I had just experienced. I saved a globo for a morning "wake up" shot and tried to figure something out. I knew, in an academic way, that I had really fucked up by selling the landlord's gas tank; I also knew that I was still broke and that once the last fix wore off, I would be sick again.

I knew that time had run out for me. The sickness of withdrawal was catching up to me and would soon be on my back. This is the infamous "monkey" that junkies refer to when their habits get down on them. I had run from it before; I had felt its painful arrival in my previous detox experiences. Now on my own in Mexico, isolated and with no lifeline, I felt backed into a corner. I needed heroin to function and had no idea what I was going to do. I had never been a violent person, and by this point I had lost a lot of weight. My choices were very limited, and there was nothing else I could sell from the casita without making things worse than they already were. I hoped that it would be awhile before my landlord noticed that the propane tank was missing.

The next morning, I woke up knowing that I was broke again and that my last fix was in my hand. Because of the slight detox that I had experienced the day before, my tolerance had slightly decreased. This was a good thing for a junkie with his last fix in his hand; it meant that the dope would have a stronger kick to it and keep me longer from the pains of withdrawal. The neighborhood roosters crowed as the sun rose. I shot up the last globo, sat outside on the steps adjacent to the casita, and smoked a cigarette. I felt utterly hopeless. Little did I realize that this routine would turn into a morning ritual over the next few weeks, a ritual in which I would sit and wonder how the fuck I would make it through another day.

After contemplating some bullshit thoughts, I went downtown and tried, without luck, to make some collect phone calls to anyone who might accept the charges and send some money. Everyone either hung up on me or didn't accept the calls. I don't remember the first person that I asked for money on the street, but it was on Avenida Juárez near the bridge. I had never begged for money, never asked anyone for anything on the street. I had always been a workingman; I had worked since I was seventeen years old and had always paid my own rent and been self-sufficient. I had sunk to a new bottom. Of all of the lows that life can offer, being reduced to begging on the street is one of the lowest. That afternoon, I realized that even if I were sick and dying on the sidewalk, people would just step over me and keep going. On the streets of Juárez, those who got too down-and-out stayed down-and-out. The only way I was going to survive was to struggle through and do whatever it took to scramble up enough money to maintain my habit. I knew that if I didn't act fast, I would soon be sick again. And this time, the world would walk over me, not caring whether I lived or died. Juárez is like that. If you fell off into the gutter and reached up for help, most people would walk past you without a second thought. I knew this to be true because I wasn't the only desperate mendicant out there on the streets.

A few people gave me some change, and I started to feel some hollowed-out hope. Maybe if I kept it up, just maybe I wouldn't have to be sick that day. The situation was desperately insane, but I was on automatic pilot, in survival mode. Not really sure what to do next, I found a discarded Styrofoam coffee cup in the gutter and started holding it out to the passing pedestrians. Some threw change into it, but most people just kept going. I didn't like the cup method, because it was too obvious and low class. One run-in with the police and I would end up being harassed, robbed, or jailed. I decided to throw the cup away when the cops finally walked by and gave me a funny look. A dope-sick junkie holding out a cup near the international bridge was nothing new to the Juárez police. This is probably why they didn't say anything to me the first time they passed me. Or maybe I was spared a run-in with them because they were over on the other side of the street. Nonetheless, I knew that they had seen me, I knew that they had taken note, and I knew that they would be back.

Soon after that, I tossed the cup away and just started asking people for money. I knew that the only way to get what I needed was to talk to people. So on that first day of my life as a panhandler, as the sun set and I started to feel the sickness coming on again, I desperately walked up and down Avenida Juárez, asking people for change and telling them that I needed it for rent and food. I don't remember exactly what I said, but I told some of them that I needed it for rent at the Plaza Hotel, where I had stayed before. Any fact that I could mix into my lines added some credibility to my act. My hope began to increase as I accumulated a pocket full of change. Every so often, someone would give me a dollar bill or even *un billete de veinte pesos* (a twenty-peso note)— the equivalent of two dollars. Avenida Juárez has numerous currency exchange houses (*casas de cambio*), and I felt relieved as I cashed in my change (*morralla*) for paper money. I don't know how I did it, but that evening I was back at the casita with enough money to fix, and even had enough to fix the next morning. I also had enough extra to buy some cigarettes and a fast breakfast: a piece of baked white bread, like a roll, and a banana—*una pieza de pan blanco y un plátano.*

The next morning, I sat on the steps again, wondering how the fuck I could do it all over again. A wave of fear washed over me as I realized that not doing it again would mean sitting down and waiting to get sick. I knew that I needed to keep my habit going to feel normal, so I pushed myself to get up and start walking and talking. The first people I approached and asked for money were a group of beer deliverymen who were unloading their truck at a *tiendita* (little store) at the bottom of the steps. Delivery crews were unpredictable: sometimes they would give you five or ten pesos, other times nothing. As I walked down Avenida 16 de Septiembre that morning and my pockets began to slowly fill with change, I felt as if I had taken a dive into cold and dirty water. Once you have taken the plunge and are immersed in it, it doesn't feel so cold and dirty anymore. In other words, I started to become comfortable with panhandling. By then, having fully crossed the line, I was infused with a sense of hope and even security each time someone handed me money. Even though I didn't walk very far from the casita that day, by noon I had enough for a fix. After I scored and shot up, I went back outside again and asked everyone I saw for some change. By that evening, I had enough money for my nighttime fix and my morning wake-up fix.

I continued this routine through the end of summer. By then, my sense of time had become totally distorted. I lost track of what day it was and really couldn't have cared less about it. Every day, I would get up, shoot dope, or go buy some dope and then shoot it, and then hit the streets again, talking to people and getting the scraps of change that I needed in order to survive. My rent at the casita was still paid up. I had paid six months in advance, at fifty dollars a month, back in May. My most pressing concern was to maintain my drug habit and keep myself alive.

I ate a lot of burritos, bananas, and bread. I also drank a lot of soda. It was hot on the streets of Juárez in high summer, and the sugar from the soda gave my strung-out body the energy I needed to push on. I continued to lose weight, but tried to eat every day. Of course, when you are out on the street and your pitch to passers-by is that you need money for food and rent, people tend to want to give you something to eat. This is especially true when you happen to be panhandling inside or around a restaurant or burrito stand. Soon I knew many of the taco and burrito vendors on the Avenida 16 de Septiembre, and they would let me hang around and ask their customers for change as long as I didn't act like a complete idiot and bother them if they refused to give me any. I built up a pretty good relationship with some of the food vendors, and they sometimes gave me an order on the house when business was good.

This was the way to survive on the street, and I discovered that most people out there were not violent felons and murderers; they were just normal people living hand to mouth and trying to make it through another day, another week, another month, and another year. Being out on the street meant learning to live within the whole spectrum of pain, pleasure, and acceptance. Learning how to accept rejection and the word no was always a mental battle for me, especially when the stakes meant that I could get sick from heroin withdrawal.

On average, when I worked the streets of west Juárez, close to the casita, about one in every twenty-five people would give me some money. This was a process that involved extended dry spells, then someone would give you a few pesos or, if you were lucky, a dollar or two. There was always a lot of uncertainty, but I knew that to give up panhandling would be something like suicide. Surrender was not part of my vocabulary, and I believed that I had no choice. I often hung around the Del Río minimarket on Avenida 16 de Septiembre. It's a busy corner, and people often pulled up in front of the store in their cars. I talked to numerous people on that corner, but I would also walk up and down the avenue and the nearby back streets to try talk to as many people as possible, asking them for change.

The Del Río sold a lot of beer. An ice truck left huge blocks of ice in front of the store every morning, and two or three people worked there at the same time. One worked the beer cooler, keeping it stocked and picking away at the fresh ice. I didn't drink beer, since it sped up the withdrawal symptoms and also made me too sloppy to panhandle. For me, the stakes were high, and getting sloppy would mean waking up dope-sick. Most of the people that I approached on that corner were fairly respectful, even when they refused to give me anything. At that time, for a junkie, Juárez was probably a lot safer than large American cities like New York or Chicago. I couldn't imagine doing what I did in Juárez in one of those other cities. The people of Juárez have heart. They know what it is like to live in real poverty, to live at rock bottom with no running water for a shower and no heat in the winter. They gave because they knew what it was like to be out there with nothing. There is a sense of community in Juárez, however fragmented and impoverished. People knew how difficult life could get. I noticed that the poorer folks, who had just a little bit, often gave more than the wealthy. Not too many rich people frequented that corner, and those who did tended not to flaunt their wealth.

Getting careless or having a bad day meant waking up sick. There were times when I woke up without a morning fix. This was always a nightmare: if I didn't get some heroin into my veins by eleven or so, the withdrawal symptoms would really start to kick in and slow me down. When that happened, I would soon become too weak and debilitated to work the streets. I could not let that happen, so on the mornings when I was dry (without heroin), I had to hit the pavement extra early in order to get some money. Around Colonia Postal and the west-side barrios, people in general didn't have much money, and early mornings were an especially difficult time to panhandle. In fact, on some really dead days, there was no money on the street. On those days, I collected aluminum cans and sold them to a junkyard that was located a bit behind the Del Río. At the junkyard, I watched people cash in huge bagfuls of cans and pickup trucks loaded with various types of metal. Scrap metal is a big business in Juárez, and people who know about it and have access to scrap make it their mission in life to make as much money from it as possible. For me, collecting cans took too long and certainly didn't pay enough to support my dope habit. Though when I did collect cans, I usually made a little extra money by panhandling at the junkyard and ended up leaving with enough to for a fix.

When panhandling was slow, I made money doing odd jobs around the neighborhood. There was a bar up the hill from the Del Río on the Avenida 16 where a guy arrived every morning around nine to clean up the mess from the previous night's fiesta. One morning I asked the guy whether he needed some help. This turned into an occasional deal in which I would help clean the whole place and earn twenty pesos. It would usually take about an hour or less, and since a globo cost only thirty pesos, I could usually fix right after I left there. There was another scrap yard that disassembled cars and buses, and the folks around there sometimes gave me small jobs and often just gave me some change when there was no work to do.

Soon, I didn't want to work because those part-time jobs didn't pay enough money for the dope I needed. Time was precious when the clock was ticking its way toward another heroin withdrawal. I sure didn't have the time to play around, trying to perform various odd jobs in order to support my habit. Working the streets, I had to learn how to manage my time around the needs of my addiction. This proved to be absolutely critical later on, when the stakes were even higher.

As my Spanish improved, my panhandling lines made more sense to the public, and I started to make more money. I developed a routine: "*¿Discúlpame, si puede ayúdame para mi renta?*" ("Excuse me, can you help me with my rent?"). I didn't like to panhandle in downtown Juárez, because there were too many tourists and police. It was better to maintain a slow and steady income in the barrio than to take the risk of getting locked up for twenty-four hours or returning empty handed. Downtown Juárez offered decent opportunities for a panhandler, but the problem was that there were already a lot of panhandlers working those streets, and the cops would notice me and know that I was strung out from my stature and the track marks on my arms. That would mean an instant trip to Las Piedras (the local precinct; literally, "the stones"). The barrio around the casita offered me the opportunity to make about twenty to twenty-five dollars a day. When they gave, most people would give a few pesos. Others would give five pesos, and occasionally, some especially generous person would give ten or twenty pesos.

THE NEW NORMAL

After a while, I stopped hanging around with other junkies. I made money alone and liked to shoot up alone. Pepe and Víctor were my closest shooting partners, but I had no extra time or money to look for them or share my dope with them. Sometimes I stopped by Pepe's to shoot up, but this usually happened when I was feeling sick and couldn't make it home. I shot up at Pepe's only when there was no dope around the casita and I had to walk to Altavista to pick up. Pepe's was on the way back, and it was easier and safer to shoot up there than to risk the walk back through the neighborhood with dope in my pocket. When times were really tight, I would give him the cotton and maybe five pesos for letting me use his place to fix. There were also many days that I would walk past his place and just wave if I saw him. I usually didn't have much time to spend hanging around, and most of the people that I talked to were the pedestrians I asked for money.

Because I had already established solid connections with the local dealers by this time, I was known throughout the barrio. Since I gave the dealers steady business and paid cash, they liked me. Because they liked me, the other junkies didn't mess with me. Beyond this, the only thing that kept me alive was my ability to talk to all kinds of people. I certainly didn't speak perfect Spanish, but I knew how to talk to people. I also knew many of my neighbors, and some of them invited me over for enchiladas and coffee, and stuff like that. The neighbors (*los vecinos*) all seemed curious about me and at least wanted to meet me and find out what the heck I was doing there. Some of the neighborhood guys would even joke with me and say that if I weren't on the shit, I could get myself a good woman and settle down.

I visited Marcos once in a while. Marcos sold dope, but he was not a big-time dealer. He did it just enough to support his own habit. We were friends and practically neighbors, since he lived right down the hill from the casita. I think he liked to practice his English with me, although it was already good because he used to live in LA. I got to know Marcos and his family well. I was his steady customer when he had dope, and because his place was the connection closest to the casita, I would always check there first. Sometimes when I went there to cop, I would fix there and sit around smoking cigarettes with Marcos, talking about the neighborhood and other things. Talking with other junkies was a form of information sharing that kept me up on which dealers had the best dope and what tricks the cops were using lately. Marcos had a strung-out sister-in-law who panhandled in El Paso. I met her later on, and we shared panhandling stories. She was also from California. Marcos had a lot of kids for a junkie, and they were always running around and playing outside around his place. Some of the kids even held the dope for him and ran it out to the customers. His wife worked somewhere in Juárez, and she didn't shoot up. I think she smoked reefer and just dealt with the fact that Marcos was hooked on heroin. His wife accepted that that was the way it was.

At this point, things were running fairly smoothly, but one morning I woke up dope-sick. I was feeling like crap and had only five pesos in my pocket. I walked down to Marcos's to try to get a fix on credit, but he didn't have anything. So I walked over to Polo's to see whether he would give me a globo on credit, but he wouldn't do it. I ended up walking the back streets of the neighborhood, asking everyone I saw for some change. My nose was runny, my insides were on fire, my ears rang, and my whole body was starting to hurt. I eventually scraped up thirty pesos and walked back to Polo's to buy a fix, but when I got there, he was sold out and waiting for the new batch of shit to be delivered. As I sat outside, other junkies began showing up, looking for dope; before you knew it, there were nearly twenty dope-sick tecatos hanging out in the street in front of Polo's, all of them just as miserable as could be, waiting for the big delivery. Then, suddenly someone shouted out, "*¡Caballos!*" and everyone scattered. I went with some of them into Polo's neighbor's casita. We all crammed into the little one-room shack, which was built out of pallets and tarpaper, and the police trotted by on horseback. Some of the other junkies took off on foot. We could hear the horse hooves pounding away, down the brown dirt roads, at a slow gallop, in pursuit. A *camper* sped past, creaking and crackling as it bounced over the rugged terrain. Soon after, it quieted down again.

Polo was another small-time dealer; like Marcos, he sold to keep up his habit, and his business kept all the junkies around him happy and content. A lot of those guys had known each other since childhood, and for them, the fear of being strung out created a need to establish a supply of dope that was sufficient to maintain not only their own habits, but also the habits of a good part of the neighborhood. In a way, the network seemed like a collective, but Polo and his lieutenants were clearly at the top. The incident with the cops had made me forget how sick I was. The dope finally arrived, and all the junkies bum-rushed Polo's door for their fix. At the door was a guy taking the money and passing it back as he and his compadres counted out the globos and passed them on to the customers. This helped keep a semblance of order in the midst of chaos.

I finally got out of there with my one globo and dragged my sick body back to my casita to get well. One thing about shooting up when you are real sick is that no matter how bad you feel, you cannot rush; one mistake can start the nightmare all over again. As I pulled back on the plunger and watched the blood back up into the syringe, I knew it was almost over. I slowly pushed the injection into the vein; one finger over the hole and a quick removal of the needle brought a temporary sense of accomplishment. A few seconds later, a brief euphoria flowed through my whole body, and I soon felt normal again as the liquid cure did its job. My runny nose and the nauseating stench of my sweaty, dope-sick body all became a distant memory. I rinsed the syringe with water, chewed on the cotton as if it were a piece of gum, and thought about smoking a cigarette. It was early afternoon, and I was ready to go out and panhandle some more. I couldn't let tomorrow morning be as painful as this one had been.

It was painful lessons like these that made my lifestyle as a junkie so diligent and methodical. Taking even one step out of my daily routine, for any reason at all, could result in painful consequences. A morning fix is a survival ritual for any heroin addict. When dealers dry up, finding a fix becomes a mission, and the mission is easier to accomplish when you're not going through withdrawal. It is also much easier to panhandle when you're not dope-sick. Most people don't want to give anything to someone who looks totally desperate, obviously strung out, or sick. Appearance is everything on the street; if someone appears to be halfway together, then people are more inclined to want to help that person with a few pesos or so. When I panhandled on the street, no one ever called the cops on me. This is not to say that the police never shook me down, but during the months I spent at the casita, my run-ins with the Juárez police were minimal and only once expensive.

I had a garden hose in front of my casita, and the neighborhood kids who often frequented the steps that led up to my little one-room house used to use it to get a drink of water and cool off. They weren't really kids at all, but I call them that because they were younger guys who weren't strung out on heroin. That didn't mean that they didn't use drugs. I would often catch them sniffing glue and smoking reefer on the steps. At the top of the steps was a mesa with a school and basketball court. It was nice to play ball up there because the view made it seem as if you were playing on the rooftop of a very tall building. You could see much of Juárez, and the mesa had a panoramic view of El Paso that spanned the area from UTEP to downtown. My casita was broken into once, but the only things missing were several rolls of toilet paper. This might have been because the window was the only way that the thieves could have gotten in or out.

One night, I caught one of the kids from the neighborhood snooping around the place. Maybe he just wanted to use the hose to get a drink of water. He looked in the window and smiled at me. I must have been in a bad mood that night, because I grabbed a metal pipe and chased him down the steps. I think I scared him more than anything else, and he picked up a good-sized rock and held it up as if he were going to throw it at me. We both ended up walking away, and the next time we saw each other, we never mentioned the incident. Another time, one of the older paint sniffers, a guy named Frankie, asked me whether it was all right if he used the water hose. All in all, I usually got along fine with the neighborhood kids. One night when a bunch of them were sitting on the back of the hill that led down into the barrio,

I asked them whether they had any change that they could spare. One of the leaders gave me ten pesos. I suppose that if they really didn't like me, they wouldn't have given me anything.

One day in late summer, the landlord's family was at the casita when I got home. They were moving their furniture out. The American guy told me that they knew that I had sold the propane tank and that they were kicking me out because I was a thief. Rather than argue, I just told them that someone else had stolen the tank, and I packed my clothes and left. The furniture was theirs, and the only thing I walked out of there with was one large and one small duffle bag of clothes. I had had a good day panhandling and was holding a few globos, so I just got the fuck out of there and went to the neighbors' place. They let me use their bathroom, and I shot up and walked away smoking a cigarette. My favorite Mexican cigarettes were Delicados and Faros. These are filterless cigarettes, something like Camels.

I had been kicked out of the casita, and I didn't really have a clue where I was going. The only people I knew in Juárez were the Álvarezes, Laura's family, in Felipe Angeles. Because I had gotten to know them when I was living with Laura, I hoped that they would not turn me away. Laura let me stay that night; I slept on the kid's bed while her daughter slept with her. The next day, Laura dropped me off at the international bridge on her way to work, and I walked back across and into the United States. The ride to the bridge got kind of funny when she put her hand on my leg as if she wanted to fool around. In my condition, the last thing I was thinking about was sex. She wished me luck as we separated at the bridge. I wasn't sick yet, but I knew it was only a matter of time before I would begin to suffer from withdrawal. I had shot up the last of my dope that morning at Laura's, so as I walked across the bridge, I knew this run was over.

The work is good because it helps you pass the malilla.

During the late summer of 1999, I landed at the Rescue Mission of El Paso. The mission is located right across the river from Colonia Felipe Angeles in Juárez. After Laura dropped me off at the bridge, I walked to El Paso and checked into the mission. Upon my arrival, I completed an intake interview with a counselor there named Klaus. Klaus ran a recovery program at the mission, so I admitted to him that I was strung out and would surely be sicker than hell by morning. That night I slept fairly well, but the next day, the withdrawal caught up with me. An ambulance took me from the mission to Providence Memorial Hospital. An English doctor in the emergency room there told me in disgust that in his country, junkies got locked up in jail and had to kick cold turkey. While he seemed to think that I deserved the same treatment, he did give me something that calmed me down for a while. I called Klaus, and he picked me up in front of the hospital. Whatever medicine they gave me temporarily relieved my withdrawal pains, so I was able to eat dinner at the mission, attend a recovery group, and sleep that night.

The next day, I was sick again, and I took another ambulance ride, this time to Thomason Hospital. The doctors there gave me another shot of some medicine that enabled me to sleep that night. That evening, the mission sent a van to pick me up and take me back. The next few days were hell. I couldn't sleep, my whole body hurt, and I got up in the middle of the night and took a shower just to calm my aching bones. The medicine that the hospitals gave me helped me ride through this withdrawal because it allowed me to eat and sleep during the first two days. That reprieve had given me enough energy to fight through the rest of the withdrawal. It normally takes about a month to withdraw and begin to feel somewhat normal again. I didn't leave the mission at all for the following week and slept only about two hours a night. During that time, I limped around the mission like a senior citizen. I felt old, my bones hurt, and I didn't have any idea what my next move would be.

A few days later, one of my friends from Juárez showed up at the mission. It was Marcos from Felipe Angeles. I knew Marcos from the days when I had lived with Laura and hung around with Víctor. Marcos and I had shot dope together, but compared to me, he looked clean and in good health. Marcos was happy to see me, and he helped me sort out some of the madness and confusion that I was going through. He told me that he had detoxed cold turkey at the mission before and that I should just take it easy for a few more days. Once I felt better, he would see whether he could get me a job working with him. Marcos worked construction, and it seemed odd that as sick as I was, I was actually looking forward to the prospect of working as a helper on a construction crew. The idea gave me something to aim for, something that could get me up and out of that place, something that would put money in my pockets. Marcos encouraged me to eat and to force myself to push on through this stage of my withdrawal. I still didn't have all of my energy back yet, but the thought of doing something new gave me the drive I needed to keep on going. Yet I knew that before I could go to work anywhere, I needed to be able to at least accomplish the daily routine required by the mission.

The Rescue Mission is the kind of place where people never plan to end up. Life just throws them for a few rounds, and they take a fall and wind up there. Once, back when I was a truck driver for North American Van Lines, I picked up a small shipment at what later became the mission; a local moving company had used the building to store furniture. Since I had been in the building before, I sometimes felt a sense of déjà vu or an uncomfortable sense of being a traveler in time or a sense that I had somehow missed the passage of time. It was funny that as a truck driver, I didn't know that the Mexican neighborhood across from the old warehouse would later have such an impact on my life.

The Rescue Mission was a good temporary place to get myself together, but sleeping in a dorm with 150 snoring men, showering communally with them, and living with them every day was not what I had come to El Paso and Juárez to do. The mission is an enclave for the border's social refugees, an isolated and fairly self-sufficient community in an older industrial-agricultural complex on the Rio Grande, an island straddled by railroad tracks and highways. It has its own chapel, kitchen, and rehab program. The mission houses mostly men, but there are accommodations for women. Often, especially when the weather is cold, the place fills up with homeless people sleeping on the floor and in the hallways. As they say in the mission, the mission is what you make of it. I was too weak to argue with anything about the mission. When Marcos showed up there and mentioned the possibility of work, I saw that as my way out. As soon as I felt that I was able, I told Marcos to get me the construction job.

WORKING CONSTRUCTION WITH MARCOS

My first day on the job with Marcos was tough. I was still weak from withdrawal. In the morning, the two of us walked from the mission, past trains and cars, to downtown El Paso, which seemed a good distance to walk, and keeping up with Marcos was intensely difficult. Once we arrived downtown, we waited on the corner with some of the other guys from the construction crew. Pretty soon, a pickup truck pulling a small flatbed trailer showed up to collect us. Marcos jumped in the back, and I followed. Some of the older guys hopped in front with the driver, and I could see them talking and joking around with one another. It was obvious that this crew had worked together for some time and that I was the new guy. I had never worked construction before and had no idea what I was getting myself into.

One of the first things that we did was to stop and pick up bags of cement from Jobe Concrete. The bags were heavy, but I carried what I could. We arrived at the construction site, a vacant lot in west El Paso, and piled out of the truck. There were two large rock walls flanking the lot. Our job was to complete those stone walls, and my role was to mix cement, or *mezcla*, and keep the builders supplied with both rocks and cement. I had never really worked with a wheelbarrow and shovel before, so all this was new to me. The physical intensity of the work soon made me forget about the withdrawal symptoms; I think the adrenaline rush of keeping up with the other workers and the anticipation of earning a paycheck was what kept me going that first day.

Working with Marcos was motivating. He had a machinelike drive about him and a good work attitude. After working construction for most of his life, Marcos knew how to get the job done. I knew the boss valued his labor by the way they interacted. Marcos was often sent to the smaller jobs, where skill and precision were especially important. On my first day, Marcos stayed with me and taught me how to mix the cement and bring it to the masons, or, as we called them, *maestros* (masters). Marcos knew that I was going through the final pains of heroin withdrawal, and he encouraged me to embrace the pain and get into the work. He assured me that pretty soon the worst would be over and that I would feel better. On the streets of Felipe Angeles, Marcos had been one of the leaders of La Quinta. His work ethic, positive attitude, and ruggedness matched his empathy for my situation. This is what made him a good leader as well as a good worker.

The work was physically demanding, but I did my best to keep up. The first thing we did was to make a cement pie. We dumped cement and sand in a pile and used our shovels to mix it into a mountain of sand-cement. We mixed the cement and sand really well, made a large round pie out of the pile, and poured water in the middle of it. The pie was like a round sand castle with walls that held in the water. Then, once the water started to soak in, we walked around the pile, shoveling the sand on the perimeter into the center, eventually making a mountain of wet sand and cement. Once the mixture was complete, we shoveled the muddy concoction into the wheelbarrows, which were lined up, waiting to be loaded. Making a cement pie is something that one person could do alone or that two or three people could do together, depending upon the size of the pie. Sometimes, to save time, the whole crew would build a massive cement pie in the morning, and it would supply enough cement to allow runners like me to keep the masons supplied with rocks and cement without having to stop and mix another pie. If there is such a thing as a man's job, this is it.

I knew what it meant to work hard from my time in the moving business, but this type of work was as hard as the rocks we were moving. Marcos explained what we were doing as he hustled around the cement pies with his shovel. I followed along, did what he did, and was soon sweating like crazy. There was always a large thermos of water, and we used a water hose to mix cement and drench our T-shirts and bandanas in order to stay cool. When you work directly in the sun, a baseball cap and a bandana are necessities. A sombrero would have been better, but we moved around so much that wearing one might have been awkward for that type of work.

I assumed that mixing cement and taking it to the masons was all that I was expected to do, but I also had to bring them the rocks that they used to build the wall. This might not have been the most difficult part of the job, but it sure wasn't easy. A dump truck would dump a load of large rocks, and we would pick up the basketball-size stones, load them into a wheelbarrow, and take them to the masons. You had to be careful not to get your fingers caught, and constant vigilance was an absolute requirement. During my first day, the trip from the rock pile to the wall with a wheelbarrow full of rocks was trying. When the rocks were too big to lift into the wheelbarrow, I broke them up with a large sledgehammer. I don't know which was harder, pushing a wheelbarrow full of rocks or one full of mixed cement. About halfway through the day, I slipped into a trance and worked like a machine. Marcos was with me, and when he saw me dazing out, he reminded me to drink some water. He kept telling me that work was the best way to get through the malilla, or withdrawal. I felt I had no choice but to tough it out and work my way through it.

That afternoon, we packed up and headed to another job site. The second job was to reinforce a slope below a house that was built on the edge of an arroyo, where water flowed after it rained. This seemed pretty crazy to me; we were working on the slope, shoveling sand and dumping rocks into a large hole that would itself be covered with still more cement and rocks. I worked extra hard that first day in order to prove myself to the boss. At four o'clock, I was quite relieved when we packed up the shovels and wheelbarrows and called it a day. Marcos and I rode in the back of the pickup truck, which dropped us off in front of the mission. Marcos had worked for this company before, and the boss was used to him crossing the border and staying at the mission while he was working. I didn't realize it at the time, but when I signed onto the payroll of this fly-by-night construction outfit, Frank Duran Construction, I did so as an "independent contractor." Later, this came back to haunt me because I ended up owing all kinds of taxes to the IRS. It was awful to realize that I made less than five dollars an hour for backbreaking manual labor and would subsequently end up giving much of it back to the IRS. However, at that time, all I could see was a chance to make some money and get out of the mission. Our *jefe* (boss), Frank Duran, seemed like a fair guy as long as you showed up on time and worked hard. He paid us every Friday and didn't bother us about our personal issues.

After Marcos and I got back to the mission, we ate dinner and cleaned up. The hot water from the shower felt good, but my whole body felt as if it had been run over by a freight train. The lingering withdrawal symptoms didn't help, but what would have usually been a sleepless night filled with withdrawal pains was replaced by a night of sound sleep.

The next morning, Marcos and I were up for early breakfast at the mission. Early breakfast was for clients who worked and needed to be out the door early. The mission was really good about this, and even gave us a bag lunch to take with us. As the two of us walked down West Paisano toward downtown, I knew that I was not going to be able to work as hard as I did the day before. I did a good job of denying the pain of opiate withdrawal, but the soreness I felt from the previous day's work wracked my whole body. I don't know how I managed to walk fast enough to keep up with Marcos, but I soon found myself waiting once more on the same downtown corner, waiting for the pickup truck to arrive. I admitted to *Jefe* Duran that I was in pain from yesterday's work, and he assured me that the pain would eventually go away, and when it did, I would be in real good shape. He told me that when he started working construction, he went through a deliberate process to build himself up by loading dump trucks full of rocks by hand. I don't know if he was pulling my leg or not, but the pains of the first days on the job were something with which he seemed to empathize. That day, *el jefe* put me to work with a younger guy named Juan, who seemed to get a good laugh at my pathetic condition. Juan, who spoke some English, worked circles around me while explaining how to do the job. I learned a lot about mixing cement and running rocks from him, and we got along pretty well. The work became less fatiguing when we began to teach each other words in Spanish and English. By the end of that second day, I was a wreck. That afternoon, I limped into the mission, took a hot shower, ate dinner, and slept like a rock.

Hard work took my mind off dope, and Marcos told me that I should stick it out and become a construction worker. As I slowly became stronger, I learned to manage the pain. Just the thought of having a steady income, after having spent most of that summer on the street, kept me going. The whole situation seemed desperate and kept me from questioning whether I should keep working. I felt as if I had no other choice. I knew the job was bullshit, but the experience of begging for money on the streets of Mexico had reduced my self-esteem to the point that I felt trapped in this new job. Even so, after two weeks with no money in my pockets, I was ready to try anything to regain some sort of control over my life. But our first payday brought a whole new set of changes that altered the situation even further.

After working for a week, pushing through withdrawal pains and sore muscles, I had high hopes for a new start. That Friday after work, Marcos and I set out with our paychecks in hand, bound for a night on the town. Just getting my paycheck cashed was a problem for me because while I was living at the casita, I nodded out at Pepe's one day and lost my wallet. Pepe's place was a shooting gallery, and when it comes to drugs, money, and junkies, shit happens. I remember the day well because although I had only a few pesos, I lost all of my IDs. Thus, the only form of identification that I had was a copy of my birth certificate. After I checked in at the mission, one of the first things I did was to order a replacement Social Security card. With no photo ID, legitimate check cashing was virtually impossible for me. Fortunately, one of the guys from the construction company cashed my check for me after I endorsed it. To me, the money from that first check looked like a free pass to indulge in all the things that I had been deprived of over the past couple of weeks. The first thing Marcos wanted to do was to eat a normal meal at a real restaurant instead of the cafeteria at the mission, so we went to a nearby Mexican restaurant and stuffed ourselves with tacos. While we were at it, we also had a couple of beers to relieve the past week's tensions. After we walked out of the little café on Paisano, we could have gone back to the mission or to any one of a thousand other places. But after talking it over, we walked across the bridge into Juárez.

In Juárez, Marcos suggested that we get a taxi. It was a good idea: it saved time and reduced the risk of being stopped by the cops. After a quick taxi ride, we were on the streets of Altavista, copping chiva and some new jeringas. Then we walked up to Pepe's and fixed. Pepe's place had a bathroom with nothing but cold running water, so as the dope numbed me, I took a cold shower and washed off the sweat and grime from that day's work. Cigarettes tasted good again, and all the pain of the past two weeks suddenly disappeared. My muscles didn't ache, and I no longer felt sore. I often refer to junkies as *los perros de la calle* (street dogs) because once they start using, it's like cutting loose, hanging out, and just letting things just happen. Once we were good and high, we bought razors and shaved. Maybe if the cops saw that we were clean-shaven, they might not suspect that we were using heroin. We hung around Pepe's for a few more minutes and then walked to Felipe Angeles. At this time, my friend Víctor was locked up somewhere, so we hung around the neighborhood and fixed. That night, we found a nice tree to sleep under. It was late summer, and the nights were getting cool. In the middle of the night, Marcos woke me up to give me a blanket that he had borrowed from some people in the neighborhood.

We hung out and got high in Felipe Angeles all weekend. On Sunday morning, we made plans to go back to the mission and spend another week working. By Sunday afternoon, I was walking back across the bridge to El Paso. Marcos didn't exactly tell me what his plans were, but he did say that he would meet me in the morning at the mission. I went back to the mission that night and got a few weird looks from everyone there who knew that I had just gone through heroin withdrawal. I didn't really think much about it and just went to my assigned bed and slept it off. The bureaucracy at the mission practically ceases during the weekend, and since the staff members didn't expect us to leave for the weekend, they hadn't reassigned our beds.

Marcos showed up on Monday morning, and we made it to early breakfast and left the mission with our brown-bag lunches. Although I never asked Marcos, I figured that he had probably just waited until the time was right and the Border Patrol was looking the other way and then just waded across the river from Felipe Angeles to the mission. Our bag lunches usually included recently expired sandwiches from the local Good Time convenience stores, which the company donated to the mission. Marcos and I worked that day, but when we returned to the mission, we were called into the front office. The director of the Rescue Mission, a woman named Juanita, knew all about our situations, and she got directly to the point. She had read the reports and roll calls and had put the pieces together. We got kicked out of the mission for twenty-one days but had the option to return, shower, and eat at certain designated times. We lost our beds, but were still entitled to the meals and showers; we had to be off the property by ten every night.

After being told that we had to leave, we went back to the dorm, packed our bags, and hung around the backyard of the mission until ten. Then we walked down West Paisano to a large concrete drainage tunnel near the railroad tracks and made camp for the night. Marcos had a watch, but I could gauge the time by the sound of passing cars as it intensified during the morning rush hour. The next day at six, we walked back to the mission, took showers, ate early breakfast, and left for work with our bag lunches. We were allowed to leave our duffle bags in some lockers at the mission, and they gave us claim tickets so that we could prove that they belonged to us. It felt kind of weird to have a job working construction and yet be sleeping under a bridge.

Anyway, it turned out that sleeping right next to the railroad tracks, practically next door to the mission, was not as bad as you might imagine. Trains can be noisy at times, but if you're really sleeping soundly, you never hear them. I knew I wouldn't be living under the tracks for too long, and the experience gave me a certain sense of freedom, limited as my circumstances were. Marcos and I camped in the drainage tunnel all week, but as soon as we got our paychecks that Friday, we took off for Juárez again.

Sometime after the first fix of that weekend, Marcos and I parted company. Although my bags were still in the locker at the mission, I was determined to find another apartment or get another room in Juárez. There would be no more living in drainage tunnels for me. In Juárez, I managed to find a room for fifty dollars a month. I had met the landlord, Martín, while wandering the streets of Colonia Postal after I shot up. I had approached him in hopes of getting some change from him, but after running my lines about my housing situation, which were then quite truthful, he said that he had just the place for me. Since I had just been paid and had money on me, I asked him to show me the place. It turned out to be a room with a shared community bathroom, both with outdoor entrances. The room was definitely a big improvement over the drainage tunnel near the mission. Martín was a religious type, a Jehovah's Witness, as well as a Mexican Army veteran.

Two weeks as an employee of Frank Duran Construction had been a physical roller-coaster ride for me. For the most part, I had finally sweated out my physical dependency on heroin and managed to get myself in half-decent shape in the process. I imagined that Martín had no idea that I was a tecato. This was probably because when I was living at the mission, I was a weekend warrior: I used dope only on the weekends.

RETURN TO JUÁREZ

Over the course of the next week, I continued to work construction, removed my bags from the mission, and settled into my new room. The job became even harder: I dug large trenches for huge rock walls every morning and ran cement all afternoon. Because Marcos was such a valuable employee, he ended up staying at the boss's house in El Paso instead of in the drainage tunnel. The nice thing about working construction was that I knew that as long as I showed up every morning on that downtown street corner, I had a job. My new room was good size, and the house had only two other tenants. Each room had an outside door off a passageway that led to the front gate and the street. The house had a shared bathroom with a shower and cold running water. It was located on the corner of Segundo de Ugarte and Calle Ombu in Colonia Insurgentes, or Las Canchas ("The Courts"), as it is known in Juárez. The room was furnished with a bed, a shelf for my clothes, and even a lock on the door! My biggest investment there was the purchase of a clock radio. Since I was working construction, I needed to be up and moving early in the morning.

The move into this neighborhood offered possibilities for new friendships and relationships. If I hadn't been on the fast track to being strung out again, I might have developed meaningful relationships with some of my neighbors. The thing about this place was that is was located on the other side of my old barrio, which was located just down the hill from my old casita in Colonia Postal. My new street, Calle Ombu, was located off the 16 de Septiembre, just up the hill from the neighborhood where I had spent most of my summer learning to panhandle. This put me right back among the same people and places that I had known the preceding spring. During my first few days and weekends in Las Canchas, I learned my way around the footpaths and backstreets that connected my new neighborhood to my old neighborhood. Soon, I was quite comfortable with the new room, or *cuarto*.

I was grateful for my new room. My landlord lived in Colonia Postal, right around the corner from where Polo dealt heroin. My new room was isolated, and I didn't know my neighbors. But their presence helped ward off any cat burglars who might have considered breaking in and cleaning me out. Although there wasn't much of anything to steal, they wouldn't know what was inside until they broke in. That Monday, I got up for work feeling better about having a place of my own to return to when the day was over. There was no kitchen, so I was back to eating on the street. Vendors sold burritos near the bridge every morning, three for a dollar, so I never really worried about not being able to afford food. My biggest problem was that I started using heroin after work.

When I walked home from work, I often stopped at Marcos's or Polo's to connect so that I would have something to do when I got home. I tried to budget my paycheck so that I could buy enough dope to last all week. Attempts to live as a functioning addict never, ever work for a junkie, and they are one of the biggest self-deceptions that heroin users believe as their addiction begins to rapidly take over their lives. Among dope addicts, the real beginning of the end is when they start shooting up in the morning. This starts a cycle in which they wake up needing a fix. A nighttime user may be able to make it through most of the day without fixing, but a morning shooter usually won't last past noon without a fix before withdrawal pains consume them.

While I lived in Las Canchas and worked construction, I quickly progressed from a nighttime user to a morning user. The first time that I shot dope in the morning while working on the construction crew, I felt like Superman. The rest of the workers must have thought I had lost my mind. I ran wheelbarrows full of large rocks and worked like a man possessed. One day, they took me off rock running and put me on the jackhammer. As long as I had enough dope, I worked as if I were made to build rock walls. Of course, the problem with this was that I had to buy enough dope every night for that night and the next morning. Consequently, every day after work became a mission of supply and demand as I searched for the supply to feed my increasing demand.

For the most part, finding dope wasn't a problem, but there were always times when the supply line was dry. After a few weeks of this routine, I began to physically break down. I lost weight and became increasingly dependent on heroin. Since my tolerance was increasing, I had to use more dope to feel okay. One day at work, I began to feel withdrawal pains during the late afternoon. These pains soon became an everyday occurrence. Sometimes the jones got so bad that digging a trench became a nightmare. One day, I was using a pickax to lift rocks out of a trench that I was digging for a wall foundation, and the more I worked, the faster I began to withdraw. I tried my best to finish the job, but the ground was full of large rocks. I broke two old pickaxes trying to get those little boulders out of the ground. By the time the boss came to pick me up at the end of that day, I was just sitting there feeling miserable. Withdrawal pains and construction work do not mix well, and the constant expectation of nonstop hard labor was starting to get to me.

One morning, I was told that work was slowing down and that I wasn't needed anymore. They told me to show up that Friday for my check, and that was the end of my career in the construction business. By then, I was strung out again and really could not handle the work anymore. I had worked great during the morning, but every afternoon my body needed more heroin in order to function. Without it, I was worthless. Had I known that I would end up paying so much in taxes on my earnings as an "independent contractor," I probably would have walked off a lot sooner. Independent contractors just don't work for five dollars and seventy-five cents an hour. I picked up my last paycheck and took it easy that weekend. I knew that when the money ran out, I would be broke again. At least I wasn't living at the shelter. I suppose that getting out of the Rescue Mission and finding another place to live was what I had really wanted at that time. The transition from the casita to the cuarto had brought me full circle to being strung out again. By the time I left the construction job, I had gained back almost everything that I had lost upon leaving the casita. Everything, that is, except the view.

The cuarto did not have a view; it had a window that looked onto a dirt-and-gravel road called Segundo de Ugarte. The window offered some sunlight, which added a little life to the drab, unpainted concrete walls of my fairly large room, which was otherwise lit by a single bare bulb in the middle of the ceiling. A raggedy old curtain covered the window and obscured the room from passers-by. From the front of the house, the window was at ground level, so anyone attempting to look inside would have to stoop down to do so. My door faced the rear of the house and led to a small, enclosed backyard patio, where a cement washboard, or *lavadero*, mounted on a cement table, was set up next to clotheslines. The married woman from next door washed her family's clothes there, and for twenty pesos, she would do my laundry as well. I had the same sheets that I had used at the casita, and my landlord gave me a few blankets. The patio was surrounded by a cinder-block wall that supported an elevated terrace, which supported the house next door. On one side of the small backyard, a narrow passageway led to a metal door that opened onto the street. On the other side was a passageway that led past the other two rooms, the bathroom, and the shower. This walkway led to the main entrance, a barred metal gate. I had keys to both entrances and the door to my room. The narrow alley ran next to my room, between the cinder-block building and the cinder-block wall that supported the elevated terrace. The alley was a good way to come and go early in the morning so that I would not bother the neighbors and raise their suspicions about my wanderings. After a while, I realized that they didn't really care about what I was doing. As long as I respected their space, everything was cool.

The street in front of the cuarto led to Las Canchas in one direction; in the other, it tapered off into a series of footpaths that led over some small steep hills into Colonia Postal. I got to know these footpaths pretty well, since they were the shortcuts that I used when walking to and from the local dope connections. As I mentioned before, the municipal police patrolled these pathways on horseback. One morning, right after I moved into the room, I walked to the store to get a soda and stopped to talk to two younger guys in the neighborhood. I froze when I heard the heavy hoofbeats of the caballos rapidly rounding the corner. The two guys that I was talking to ran down a gully into an area where it was difficult for horses to follow. I calmly sat there and watched it all. The cops asked me what I was doing there, and in my broken Spanish, I explained to them that I had just moved in and lived right up the street. I told them I was on my way to the store and stopped to talk with those guys. The caballos let me go that time, but as my health deteriorated and I started to take on the identifiable physical characteristics of a junkie, it became harder to talk my way out of these kinds of encounters with the police.

When all of my money was gone, I started a panhandling routine much like my previous one. As my Spanish improved, I made more money. On Calle Ombu, a few houses up from my cuarto, there was a small family-owned store. I regularly asked for change outside that store and sometimes asked the owners for change as well. They were nice people, and they usually gave me a soda and five or ten pesos. One day, I saw a car parked in front of the store with two policemen in it. One of the cops was the store's owner. He gave me some change and told me to be careful. I talked with both of them for a while, and they told me that panhandling the way I did was okay, but that if I ever stole anything from them, they would get me.

I continued to hit that neighborhood store up for change, but I always went in and asked politely. Most times, I didn't leave empty handed. Panhandling in the upper *dieciséis*—Avenida 16 de Septiembre—neighborhoods of Colonia Insurgentes and Las Canchas was tough. Most folks there didn't have that much money to begin with. After I learned my way around, I would panhandle my way down the whole 16 de Septiembre from El Centro to Colonia Insurgentes. On some days, the money came easy; on others, it was difficult to get anything. My regular route weaved through the most lucrative places. As I got to know some people, they would invite me inside for coffee and sweetbread, and often they wanted to sit and talk for the whole morning. I didn't mind this so much, but socializing cut into my time and reduced the amount of money that I could make. If I panhandled persistently, I could make between thirty and fifty pesos an hour; however, there were times when I made much more or much less.

During my travels through the neighborhood, I met a shopkeeper named Freddy, who became *un buen amistad conmigo*, a good friend. Freddy owned a house that was built over his deli and small market. He spoke English fairly well and said that he used to live in New Jersey. Freddy usually gave me a soda and a piece of *pan blanco*, and I always found small jobs that needed doing for ten or twenty pesos around his store. Freddy's was a regular stop for me, not only because we got along well and talked a lot, but also because I could hang around in front of his store and ask the people there for change. Sometimes, a morning in front of Freddy's brought enough money to go directly to one of the connections and score for that day. Another nice thing about Freddy's store was that Freddy was a federal cop who ran the store as a side business. After a while, I got to know his family. One day, I even helped them paint their living room. Another time, I arrived and found Freddy dressed in uniform with his rifle. He explained to me that they were going to raid a marijuana field somewhere in Mexico and that he would be gone for a couple of days. Even when his family worked the store, they always welcomed me and were very generous with stuff like sodas and bananas. When the store was real busy, I helped them stock the shelves and clean. Even on the worst of days, I could always count on at least five pesos, either from Freddy or one of his customers, just for showing up.

While at the Rescue Mission, I had picked up a Spanish-English dictionary and a few English-language books for Spanish speakers. I used these books to hustle some extra money by giving English lessons and telling everyone that I was an English teacher who had worked in Durango, Mexico, and had subsequently been stranded without any money in Juárez. Occasionally, a family that ran a *desponchadora* (a tire-repair shop) in Las Canchas wanted me to teach them some English. They usually gave me about twenty pesos, a cup of coffee, and a burrito or *pan dulce* for teaching them a few words and talking with them. Soon, I was known throughout the neighborhood.

The name Las Canchas derives from the basketball courts that are located on the edge of the neighborhood, just before Avenida 16 de Septiembre descends into the Arroyo de Las Víboras. The basketball courts themselves were always busy and were surrounded by small taco and flauta stands. There was one gordita stand that regularly and generously served me free coffee and gorditas. I didn't want to wear out my welcome there, because panhandling on that corner always brought decent results. At various times, residents of that neighborhood helped me out with some change and a meal, and I remember countless cups of coffee and long stories about someone's *hijo* (son) or *hija* (daughter), past marriages, and events long past. I heard many stories about journeys to the United States and family members in places like Denver or Chicago. Strenuous as it was to maintain a heroin habit and panhandle on the streets of west Juárez, I always found it within me to stop and get to know people. Marcos from the mission always told me that once the Mexican people embraced you, there wouldn't be too much to worry about.

ARREST

One thing that did worry me was the ever-present danger of getting busted by the police and missing a day's income from the street. Getting busted meant withdrawing in jail or waking up sick the next day, having to go out and panhandle while trying to hold back the runs. As I said before, it's harder to panhandle when you're sick from withdrawal, because people are less likely to help you when they see you down, and being dope-sick brings you way down—down and out. One afternoon during the fall of 1999, I walked down a neighborhood footpath and into a trap set by the caballos. They stopped me and saw the track marks on my arms. I was weary and slim, my clothes were dirty, and they knew that I was strung out and an easy target. The cops detained me in an abandoned little house and rounded up a few other unlucky souls while I waited there. I had fixed that day and still had about twenty pesos in my pocket, but luck just wasn't with me. They loaded us into the paddy wagon, *el camper*, and drove us around most of that night. We bounced around in the back as the *camper* made its rounds down by the river and through all kinds of neighborhoods. New prisoners, or hostages, were loaded and sometimes unloaded and released in exchange for small fees. I watched as a young woman, who definitely looked strung out, bought her freedom for fifty pesos. I didn't have enough money to buy my way out, so I had no choice but to ride it out.

Eventually, we arrived at the Juárez municipal police station that served the west side at that time, a station aptly known as Las Piedras.

Assimilations

Rocks, concrete, and metal bars made the holding cells a very uncomfortable place to be. They detained me for twelve hours, and knew that I would be sick from withdrawal when they released me. I sat on a cement bench and slept very little. The next morning, I wasn't too sick and managed to enjoy a significantly large plate of rice and beans with a warm drink called *champurrado*. I couldn't wait to get out of there, but it was awhile before they let me go. There was nothing great about being in a dungeon-like holding cell with a bunch of dope-sick junkies, all passing around and sharing a plastic two-liter bottle of water with the label torn off it.

When I was finally released, I was a wreck. Somehow, as sick as I felt, I managed to scrape together enough change for a fix. After a bus ride across town, I connected and dragged my ass back to my little cuarto in Las Canchas, where I brought myself back to life with one injection. Mishaps like that usually meant living through at least fifteen to twenty-four hours of hell, so avoiding the police was a priority for any active junkie on the street. It would have been worse if I hadn't had a roof over my head. The best way to get over the whole awful experience was to shoot up, relax, smoke a cigarette, and take a nice cold shower. I usually stayed clear of the police, but anyone who lives the life of a junkie is always subject to the fate of the street. My friend Víctor often said that he never worried or cared about the cops because when it was his time to go, there was nothing anyone could do about it. While this was true, I didn't see any sense in making it easy for them to mess with me. Thus, I always walked on the sidewalks instead of in the middle of the street, and I took the road less traveled whenever possible.

THE JUNKIE CODE

My network with other street junkies meant everything and nothing at the same time. One morning, I woke up dope-sick with hardly any money. It was slow going, but I finally scrambled together enough for a globo. I dragged ass down to Polo's and got the stuff, but didn't have a needle, and by then I was too weak to keep going. In front of Polo's, I asked whether anyone had a jeringa. Someone passed me an old 1 cc insulin syringe. It was so worn out that the lines and numbers were worn off it. I sat down on an old milk crate and pressed the dope onto the bottom of an old soda can and managed to load the syringe with some water that was floating around there in a clear plastic bottle. After quickly prepping the dope and the syringe, I finally found a vein. As my blood flowed into the old needle, a sense of relief passed through me. Within minutes, I could smoke a cigarette and share dope stories with the other junkies.

Dirty and unhealthy as it is, the need to fix and maintain a habit is commonly understood among most dope addicts. Hard-core heroin addicts understand what it is to be dope-sick, and they usually won't mess with another junkie who is suffering through those painful moments. Usually, junkies get burned because they trusted others who weren't dope addicts—for example, cokeheads or crackheads. This doesn't mean that one junkie would not rob another. Although most dope addicts had used other drugs on their journey to heroin addiction, to be strung out meant that there was no time for the pettiness of lesser highs. Heroin is the lifeblood of a dope addict, and as the addiction progresses, everything about life becomes centered on acquiring it. The pain and the fear of withdrawal keep this perpetual cycle in motion, and anyone who hasn't reached that stage of addiction can't fully understand it. Those who had been strung out knew how painful it was. That is why it is so easy for a true dope addict to walk into a shooting gallery full of strangers and just shoot dope right in front of them or even share their works.

Nevertheless, dope costs money, and managing a habit on the street is a twenty-four-hour-a-day job. Those who dealt black tar heroin at that time in Juárez did so to make a profit, support a habit, or both. Dealers don't care whether you're sick, and a lot of junkies assume that they can get fixed for free just by showing up and hanging around. Those who make this painful misjudgment are mostly inexperienced and younger junkies on their first little chippie, or minor withdrawal. These junkies sometimes wander to a dealer's while going through withdrawal pains and expect some empathy, or a free fix on credit, only to be turned away at the door. Some of them hang around, begging other junkies for a fix. But unless the veteran junkies know them well, this usually turns into a painful lesson in what the dope game is all about.

Most experienced junkies have a routine, and it doesn't usually involve sharing their dope with anyone. I shared dope with some of my friends, but usually as part of a larger reciprocal interaction; I was living with them and their families, and our survival in active addiction was at stake. For the most part, if a junkie is sick and trying to get something from you as you pass by, he or she is not much of a threat. After all, unless they have a gun, sick junkies going through withdrawal can't fight very well; they are likely to be in too much pain to physically rob anyone. Any junkie going through withdrawal would rather sell a gun and fix himself. At least, I know that that's what I would have done. After all, most dope fiends on the streets of Juárez, living at that level, do not have access to getaway cars, and they are often too exposed and vulnerable to be going around robbing other junkies for a fix. Yet when junkies congregate and dope sickness is present, you always have to be careful.

One morning, around six o'clock, I showed up at Polo's real early, and he came to the door with a rifle in his hands. I thought to myself, "This dude is crazy," and he definitely was. Polo let me in and sold to me, then crawled back under his blankets and told me that the next time that I showed up so early, it would cost me five pesos more. The rifle looked like something from the turn of the century, and I wondered whether it even worked. I surely didn't want to find out. Polo slept across the street from where he sold, in a little one-room shack that looked like a shantytown house from the Hoovervilles of the Great Depression, as did many of the little houses in Juárez. There were a couple of other people in there sleeping on the floor. He had a woman with him who looked strung out, yet this wasn't surprising, since a lot of female junkies get tight with dealers so they can string their habits along. That Polo had a gun wasn't surprising, since he sold dope. But I expected him to have a pistol instead of a rifle. Although a lot of dope passed through Polo to the neighborhood junkies, Polo wasn't a big-time dealer. He sold dope to maintain his own habit and keep those around him happy. The only other time I had run into a firearm in Juárez was when one of the neighborhood kids pulled a small pistol from his pocket to show it off and try to sell it to me on the steps leading to the casita. It was a .25 automatic, similar to the one I carried when I lived in Hartford and worked as a truck driver. I didn't much care for guns, and after a friend of mine was gunned down in Hartford, I knew that the best way to stay alive was to stay away from guns and the problems that they provoked. This was another reason why I panhandled and talked to people to supply my habit. I knew that if I carried myself like a violent psychopath with a drug habit, I would quickly end up either dead or in jail.

Polo's place was the connection closest to my cuarto, and many junkies from the upper dieciséis of the west side bought from him. He was very street-centered compared to Marcos, who always dealt from within the familial space of his household sphere. Since I preferred to buy from Marcos, I usually planned my panhandling route so that in the late afternoon, after I had made my mendicant rounds, I could stop by his place, cop, fix, and talk about what was new on the street. Marcos was in constant contact with the neighborhood junkies, and because he spoke English, he would run down the latest on hot spots, other people who were dealing, etc. The other nice thing about Marcos's place was that if the police were near, he would invite me inside to wait until they left. Sometimes we fixed in his kitchen and smoked cigarettes as we listened to the trotting hooves of the police horses pass by. At other times, it was the rattling metal of a *camper* as it jolted along the rutted dirt roads.

If neither Polo nor Marcos had dope, which happened occasionally, I needed to go to another connection, such as one in Altavista or Felipe Angeles. This always meant a risky and time-consuming walk. After my previous bad experiences, just the thought of getting busted while walking home from a dealer with dope in my pocket was enough to make me leery. Sometimes, it was better just to hold off and wait until the local dealers replenished their supply rather than to risk the walk. For those times when the *malilla*, withdrawal sickness, was taking hold, the journey had to be made. Buses ran through Las Canchas and into Altavista, and I soon became familiar with them. Taking the bus saved time and reduced the risk of getting caught in the open.

A bus ride also made the pain of withdrawal a tiny bit easier. One bus that ran past Freddy's would drop me off in Altavista, a block from Pepe's and two blocks from the dealer. After a morning of scraping up change in the neighborhood, I would finish off my rounds by doing a little panhandling around Freddy's while waiting for the bus. The ride to Altavista would act as a short break from everything. As I looked out the bus window and watched an occasional *camper* or squad of caballos go by, I knew that if I had been out there walking, I would have been an easy target for those patrols. I often smoked on the bus, and the music on the buses always made the ride interesting. Each bus seemed to have its own personality, depending on the driver and the passengers. Once I got off the bus, I would walk straight to the connection. If I were feeling good, I would return to the bus stop and catch the bus back to my cuarto. It would drop me off about a block and a half away. If I felt bad, I would stop at Pepe's to shoot up. If I went to Pepe's, I would start panhandling once I left there. This saved time, and if I got lucky, it meant more money for that day.

The only drawback to catching the bus back to the cuarto from Altavista was that I was vulnerable on the street while waiting for the bus at the bus stop. There was a *tiendita* on the corner by the bus stop, and I often bought a soda and talked with the old woman who ran the place while I waited. The real moments of peace came when I finally made it back to the room with the dope. I would usually shoot up and listen to my little clock radio. The local college radio station played jazz in the mornings, and it was relaxing to listen to and smoke cigarettes.

After those little breaks, I would usually head out for an afternoon of panhandling on and around Avenida 16 de Septiembre. Sometimes I would walk almost to downtown and back to Colonia Postal or Altavista to look for Marcos or another dealer. During these panhandling runs, the best of days meant making enough to eat and to buy some dope for that night and the next morning. Food was never a problem. I befriended a few of the taco and burrito vendors on 16 de Septiembre, and they often just gave me a free order and a soda while I stood there and talked to them about life on the street. They didn't always give me free food, and sometimes the only reason they gave a free meal was because I had once been a steady customer. No matter how bad it was to support a heroin habit as a panhandler, I always had ten or twenty pesos to buy something to eat at the end of a day on the street.

There weren't very many other Americans around this area, but occasionally I ran into one. Once, while panhandling at a Del Río minimarket on the 16 de Septiembre close to El Centro, I met an American guy buying a bunch of tequila to take back to the States. He gave me thirteen dollars! This was like striking gold compared to the usual two or five pesos that I usually got from the people that I approached. Most Americans, however, usually laughed at me or made some smart-ass remark. This was probably because they didn't know the depression of poverty, much less what it was like to be a tecato living on the fringes of society. Most local people from Juárez understood poverty and its dynamics. This is why, if they had some change to spare, they would usually give a few *tostones* (half pesos) or pesos to someone in need, without questioning the ethics of such an act. In short, they didn't question the source of the need when it was evident that the need itself existed. They knew that this was a matter of survival, and many of them knew the hardships such a struggle entailed. Life as a junkie supporting an addiction took everything and then some out of a person. Caught in the carelessness of my habit at the cuarto, I had fallen behind and forgotten to pay two months' rent.

Discúlpame señor, si puede ayúdame.

My landlord, Martín, was a nice guy and all, but like any other landlord, he wanted to get paid. I left the cuarto in early December 1999. Martín gave me an ultimatum that I knew I couldn't comply with, since I already owed him a hundred dollars in back rent. I packed my bags and tried to fit everything I had in them. Leaving the cuarto on Segundo de Ugarte didn't seem like a big deal. With money in my pocket from a few good rounds of panhandling, I was confident in my ability to *conseguir* (acquire money) on the street. I used a successful line that went something like: *"¿Discúlpame señor (o señora), si puede ayúdame con algún cambio para pagar mi renta y comprar un boleto para regresarme a Nueva York de camión? Era un maestro de Ingles en Durango, México, y estoy aquí en Juárez sin dinero."* (Excuse me sir [or madam], can you help me with some change so that I could pay the rent in my hotel room and buy a bus ticket to return to New York. I was an English teacher in Durango, México, and I am here in Juárez without money.)

My Spanish wasn't perfect, but it was good enough to communicate and get my message across. Most people probably didn't believe me, but some of them gave anyway. By this time, I was making about twenty dollars a day, on average, as a panhandler. It was enough to support my habit and keep me going. I couldn't blame Martín for wanting the rent money, but when he told me that he had found my birth certificate under the bed and would give it back to me only after I paid him, I knew that he would never see that money, and I couldn't have cared less about the birth certificate. "Go ahead," I thought, "and steal my identity. Who would want my miserable life anyway?"

While living in the cuarto, I had often contemplated death and was occasionally disappointed when I woke up in the morning still alive.

During the last few days in that room, I stayed awake at night reading both the Old and New Testaments of the New International Version of the Bible. Although not particularly religious, I was searching for some sort of answer to the insanity in my life. Someone from the mission gave me the Bible, and it had sat in my room for some time. One day, bored after shooting up, I began reading it. Living on the street one day at a time allowed me to fully appreciate the little things in life and to realize that destiny is often beyond the control of those who attempt to manipulate it. On the street, I began to develop trust in a God that would carry me through my daily battles, no matter how extraordinary they were. For the trials that faced me that cold December, I sure needed some support.

After leaving the cuarto, I headed downtown, where I checked into a room at the Burciaga Hotel. The hotel became my new home. It was located on Calle Ugarte, right down the street from the Plaza Hotel, where I had stayed upon my arrival in Juárez. The rooms were a lot nicer than the cuarto. They had color televisions, hot showers, and clean bedding and cost 130 pesos a night. I knew that I would have to panhandle more diligently if I were going to stay there. I don't know how I did it, but I managed to pay the rent and support my habit for most of December and part of January. Living like this was more stressful than the laid-back lifestyle in Las Canchas. There was no way I could skip out on the rent at the hotel. Plus, I didn't know any dope dealers in downtown Juárez. This meant that I had to panhandle early in the morning, take a bus to Colonia Postal or Altavista, connect in the late morning or early afternoon, and then return to the hotel to fix. I would hit the streets again until around eight or nine o'clock and return to the west side to buy enough dope for the next morning's wake-up fix.

Settling into this routine wasn't too difficult, but it involved some significant adjustments to my daily patterns. The first thing that changed was that I had to hit the streets before the downtown police patrols mobilized for the day. I could usually panhandle right around the front of the hotel until the bicycle cops started prowling around. Generally, they didn't really bother you unless they saw you consistently begging for money. Then they would shake you down and see what you were all about. If they caught on that you were strung out, it usually meant either paying a bribe or taking a trip to the local precinct for a twelve-hour stay.

One day, I crossed to El Paso to try to make some phone calls. As I crossed the bridge, I started panhandling. To my surprise, in less than ten minutes I made five dollars! On a bad day in Juárez, it often took two hours to make that much. After I passed through the customs checkpoint and walked into El Paso, I began panhandling on South El Paso Street and made a few more dollars in a matter of minutes. This discovery precipitated a territorial shift in my panhandling, and I eventually brought in four or five times more money than I had made in Juárez. By the time I got back to the Burciaga Hotel that day, I had enough for the rent and a few globos. At seven the next morning, I was back in downtown El Paso, trying to make some more money. I located a nice bus-station parking lot on the corner of Sixth and South Oregon Streets, which fit rather nicely with my line about being stranded and needing money for a bus ticket back to New York. Soon after that, I even began carrying a bag of clothes around with me to validate my story.

One of the biggest problems with living at the Burciaga Hotel was that if the rent wasn't paid by one thirty in the afternoon, they checked you out and removed your luggage from the room. I had a problem with the hotel staff members about this one afternoon when they put my bags in a storage room behind the counter. An idiot desk clerk wanted to charge me double for a room that night. This little argument was resolved when the staff agreed to let me rent another room and I paid a few extra pesos for that day's rent. From then on, I arrived promptly every day around one to make sure that my rent was paid on time.

The increased income from panhandling in El Paso made the hotel's daily rate of 130 pesos seem reasonable. Soon, the people at the hotel got to know me, and they knew that I would be there every day with the rent. Sometimes I even tipped the cleaning women a few pesos, and they kept my room clean and made the bed fresh with new sheets everyday. I often had them skip my room because I had dope stashed there and didn't want the maids to find it. Nothing ever was missing from my belongings at the hotel, and while I lived there, I slowly started to accumulate more clothes. The room was decked out with 1960s-style furniture, including a wooden pole lamp and a long triple dresser with two large mirrors attached to the back. My room was carpeted, and the heat worked fairly well. Since it was cold outside, I was glad that I had left the cuarto, which had neither heat nor air conditioning. After a while, I accumulated *un chingo de* pennies, or a lot of pennies. Eventually, I had thousands of pennies spread out across the top of the dresser and the drawers full of clothes. Renting a hotel room enabled me to make more money on the street because a bathroom with hot water allowed me to stay clean and well-shaven. Not that I couldn't manage with only cold water, but on those cold December mornings, the last thing I wanted to do was wake up and take a cold shower.

The problem with living so far from my dope connections was that timing and reliable transportation were essential for the maintenance of my habit. I usually scored from places that I was already familiar with; the only adjustment I made was that I took the bus there and back to downtown every afternoon. By this time, I was using heroin three times a day: early in the morning (always the best fix), in the afternoon after the bus ride, and in the evening before bed. Usually, although not always, I would go back out onto the streets after my afternoon fix to hustle up some extra money. It was always smart to have as much extra emergency money as possible: this eliminated the chance of becoming sick in the event of unforeseen circumstances or a change in schedule.

On some afternoons, I would go back to El Paso and work the downtown area and make twenty or forty dollars. Some evenings, after I returned to Juárez, I walked up 16 de Septiembre and panhandled all the way to Marcos's or Polo's. This occasionally brought in enough extra income to pay for not only the next day's rent, but also the next day's dope. Panhandling or scrambling didn't run that smoothly every day, but if I maintained a steady schedule, I was able to sustain my lifestyle. It was crucial to have a wake-up fix ready for the morning and not to oversleep or get lazy. The hours between seven and noon were the most critical for making my daily income, and a slow day meant more panhandling later in the evening.

After a while, I learned which days were the busiest on the street. Monday and Tuesday were always the slowest days, and sometimes Wednesday as well. Thursdays through Sundays were good days to be on the street because there was a lot of money flowing then. But by Monday morning, people were broke again. Saturday was the best. On a good Saturday, I would panhandle up and down El Paso Street, working one side on my way to the plaza, and the other side on my way back toward the bridge, and would walk away with as much as fifty or sixty dollars. I think the main difference between panhandling in Juárez and in El Paso is that in Juárez, most people hand out coins, while paper money is more common in El Paso. That is not to say that I collected only paper money in El Paso; sometimes I found myself walking around El Paso with both my pockets bulging with change.

Finding a place to cash in my change was also a project. Some establishments wanted change for their customers, and I regularly supplied them. One of them was a Chinese restaurant on El Paso Street; another was a cosmetics-supply store on the corner of El Paso and Paisano. Some casas de cambio also became regular stops for me. It was always a good feeling to convert coins to paper money and walk back to the hotel for another day. Cold and rainy mornings meant a slow rate of acquisition, but the key to success and survival in panhandling was persistence. If I gave up, there was a painful and uncertain forecast for my future. Messed up as the whole thing was, I found stability in persistence.

As I got used to living in downtown Juárez, I panhandled the areas around Calles Noche Triste and La Paz. This crowded section of El Centro was like a maze filled with various street vendors and small shops. I found safety in the constant crowds of people and was able stay close to the hotel. I always made more money in El Paso, but working in El Centro during the late afternoon kept some money coming in and let me explore the downtown area. My Spanish improved, and it became easier for me to negotiate with people. I preferred not to panhandle in El Centro because of the grinding poverty and the presence of so many other panhandlers. In El Centro, I usually walked from one small business to another and explained my situation to anyone who was there. Some people were cold and didn't want anything to do with me; others welcomed me in and offered me coffee, soda, tacos, and possibly five or ten pesos. After a few rounds in this area, I knew which places produced the best revenue, and developed trivial relationships with the people whom I spoke to regularly. They often joked with me about how things were going, and the more that folks understood the insanity or desperation of my situation, the more they opened up, talked with me, and became willing to give me a free order of flautas or a few spare pesos. I suppose that many people in Juárez feel a sense of benevolence toward dislocated and unfortunate people on the street, but when it comes to actually doing something to help someone, knowing that person or having a daily interaction with him makes it easier for them to give whatever they can without compromising their own situation.

Panhandling, as I considered it, involved a lot of walking and talking. When I worked El Paso, I stayed mostly in the Segundo Barrio area. This neighborhood was safe for panhandling; although it was located near downtown, it was outside mainstream, commercialized American society and there was a constant flow of people coming and going between Mexico and the United States. Segundo Barrio has several bus stations, and there are always new people moving through them. This was important for the places that I frequented: I could not ask the same people for money for a bus ticket every day. Realizing that I had no intention of ever buying a ticket, and they would eventually have stopped giving.

I didn't panhandle like a beggar sitting with a hat or cup in his hand. Instead, I constantly moved around, approached people, talked to them, told them my situation, and hoped that they would help me out with some spare change or something. When I worked the streets of Juárez, I told people that I needed money for food and rent at the hotel, a story that really was true. I never mentioned my drug habit, and as long that subject never came up, I had a truthful scenario to advocate for. In El Paso, I used a different approach. The hotel line didn't work in El Paso, because if I said that I needed money for a room, people would advise me to go to the Rescue Mission or the Opportunity Center for the Homeless. Those places were dumps, and I would rather live at the hotel, or in one of the barrios, than in a shelter again.

In El Paso, I never told anyone that I was living in Juárez. Most Americans would not have been able to understand why an American citizen would want to live there; moreover, helping them understand me would have been contradictory to my primary mission. What would I have told them? That I was living in Juárez because the heroin was cheap and that their generous contribution would allow me to maintain my lifestyle as a junkie? Most folks around the bridge would have just laughed and not given me anything. So instead, I used the line that I was from New York and had lived in Mexico for five years, teaching English. I told them that a bus ticket to New York cost $350 and that I only had $100. This line seemed legitimate enough both to American citizens and to Mexicans coming and going across the bridge. Of course, as time passed, the local people started noticing me and became aware that my routine was just another hustle to stay alive.

The Segundo Barrio and downtown El Paso are very busy during the daytime. Pedestrian-bridge traffic from Juárez is the primary economic lifeblood in and around the El Paso Street and Stanton Street neighborhoods. To make any money in those areas, I had to be able to speak and understand Spanish. My experiences in Juárez had prepared me just enough to be able to communicate in Spanish. By now, I knew enough to understand and be understood within the context of panhandling and the brief encounters it required.

I soon became aware that I wasn't the only junkie hustling a living out on the street. One morning as I was working Oregon Street, I approached a few people and went through my usual panhandling routine. They told me that they would like to give me something, but they had already given their spare change to someone else. Further up Oregon Street, near the Catholic church, I noticed a scraggly, skinny-looking American guy in a baseball cap, desperately begging from everyone who passed him. I thought to myself, "What a pathetic sight." Judging by his desperation and demeanor, he was obviously a junkie in the early stages of heroin withdrawal. Most people gave him a nasty look and walked around him. They tried to stay out of his way and avoid him as much as possible. His Spanish was not good enough to be of any value in establishing even the most minimal connection necessary to win over someone's sympathy. But I didn't feel sorry for him. He was here taking money out of my pocket by just existing. As pedestrians shunned him, his tone became resentful. I was used to this feeling, but had always managed to hide it and use its energy to muster up the courage to keep trying after a depressing and continual cycle of rejection. I later befriended this guy, but at the time, I just watched him with a mixture of pity and disgust as he made a mockery out of the art of panhandling.

When I worked the streets, I was always very careful to choose the people that I would approach with my story. After a while, it became easy to pick out people who would be likely to give. On those especially slow mornings, when pedestrians were scarce, you had to approach them with respect and tact. This is why I always started my introduction with the word *discúlpame*, which means "excuse me" or, more literally, "forgive me." I never just bluntly asked for money right away, even though most folks probably guessed that that was what I was after. To watch another panhandler ask everyone for a quarter so that he could go get a burrito was, to me, like hearing fingers scratch a chalkboard. I tried to talk to that beggar on Oregon Street, but he told me to get lost and stop bothering him. I kept going about my business and got as far away from him as possible. If people on the street associated me with him, they surely wouldn't give me anything.

Later on, when I got to know that guy, I found out that his name was Gary and that he slept in downtown El Paso, often outdoors, and traveled back and forth to Juárez to supply his habit. Gary never ventured outside the downtown areas of the two cities, and his dealers resided in either El Paso or the Bellavista and El Centro areas of Juárez. His life seemed to be a constant struggle as he negotiated the area and interacted with its people. After regularly seeing him on the streets, I often wondered how he survived. In comparison, I felt lucky to be able to continue in my routine and enjoy the comfort of the hotel as well as the consistency of the networks and patterns that I had developed.

Learning Spanish was essential to success on the street, and anyone without it was always at the mercy of a translator. I generally didn't like people to know that I was addicted to heroin, and I didn't let strangers into my business. I ran alone as much as I could, and even people I partially trusted represented a burden, because money was always tight. The only times I actively sought the help of other junkies was when my regular sources were dry. Bringing another junkie into my routine usually meant that I had to give him a fix in return for his knowledge or assistance. When I did this, I usually got someone like Marcos or Pepe to help me. It was always a pain in the ass when the regular sources didn't have any dope; it usually involved a longer than usual walk to an unfamiliar neighborhood and a considerable risk of getting busted. By December 1999, I had become a loner, and my improved Spanish enabled me to negotiate the simple necessities of my daily routine. Nevertheless, being an American on the streets of Juárez always meant that I stood out, and so trying to remain inconspicuous always required extra effort.

Every morning that I walked across the international bridge that December was quite windy and cold. Sunrise offered only a faint possibility that it would warm up later in the day. I was grateful for the warmth that the hotel offered. However, staying at the Burciaga Hotel meant working the streets seven days a week. One morning in El Paso, I was walking down San Antonio Street around nine; as I spoke to an older couple, about six or seven El Paso Police officers on bicycles singled me out as they were riding by. The police were likely just beginning their daily patrol. Their group was composed of one lead officer and a half a dozen rookies. The leader looked me over, then turned around and rode toward me on the sidewalk. The rookies followed. He asked the usual questions: "What are you doing here?" "Is he bothering you?" and "What were you saying to them?"

I wasn't surprised that I stood out to the cops. My old baseball cap, overlapping jackets, dirty pants, and skinny figure gave me away. The bicycle cops surrounded me, and the leader asked me for my identification. At that time, the only ID that I had was a ragged copy of my birth certificate that I kept in my inside jacket pocket. As I reached for it, the leader immediately unsnapped his holster and grasped the handle of his pistol. I told him that I was just going for my ID, and he told me to move slowly. The whole bunch of them looked real tense, as if they expected me to pull a gun out of my jacket and start blasting away. I couldn't believe it! The cops seemed relieved when the only thing I pulled out was the ragged copy of my birth certificate. The rookies gave me puzzled looks. The leader asked me some more questions, and I told them what I told everyone else: that I had been living in Mexico and was currently trying to get money for a bus ticket back to New York. Since I had a New York birth certificate, they reluctantly believed my story and advised me to go to the Rescue Mission, saying that the mission would probably buy me a bus ticket. The bicycle patrol then gave me directions to the mission and even escorted me halfway there. After that, I knew that I would have to be on the lookout for bicycle cops, so I stayed closer to the bridge and strayed less into the downtown area. I made more money in the Segundo Barrio anyway, and it was easier to blend in there.

A JUNKIE'S CHRISTMAS

As the holiday season approached, there always seemed to be enough money on the street to keep me alive. My friend Marcos was dealing consistently in Colonia Postal, and the dope he sold was pretty good. By then our relationship verged upon actual friendship. When I arrived at his place, usually twice daily, to cop my dope, he always welcomed me inside. Sometimes his wife fixed me a cup of coffee as we sat and talked. It was around then that I met his strung-out sister-in-law, who also panhandled in El Paso. She told me that she made between $150 and $200 daily. This was the most that I ever heard of a panhandler making. She said that she worked the parking lots of the Cielo Vista and Basset Center shopping malls. At that time, I considered myself lucky if I made between $60 and $80 daily. I knew that I could never match her income or attempt her type of hustle because she spoke both Spanish and English fluently, having grown up in California, and her line that she needed food for her babies always brought out the best from those inclined to give.

It was nice to be tight with Marcos and his family; our friendship enabled me to continue my routine without having to worry about the supply side. Because I was a steady and regular customer on good terms with Marcos, he made sure that I got a good deal, selling to me at a rate of six for five: that is, when I bought five globos for 150 pesos, he threw in the sixth for free. I also got this bargain from the other dealers, since this was normal in the Juárez drug game. Such incentives enabled street-level dealers to move product faster and resupply more often, which provided them with either a larger surplus for their own personal use or additional profits, depending on whether they used. Marcos always sold out at least twice a day, and his increased volume was likely the result of a good connection.

Marcos never paid off the local police; he wasn't really considered a lucrative dealer. Everyone knew that he was strung-out and dealing only to support his own habit. This also meant that going to his place was risky when the cops came around, because the cops would often shake down the customers in an attempt to collect a bribe or make a bust. The cops didn't come around Marcos's place too often. I think this was partly because the neighbors resented them, and partly because the neighborhood was full of young kids. Lots of neighbors with lots of kids, added to police harassment, make for a bad mix in an extremely impoverished neighborhood. This may be why, when the caballos passed through, they usually picked on the junkies and alcoholics who were just hanging out in the wrong place at the wrong time.

The 1999 holiday season gave me a break because, in the spirit of the Christmas, my family accepted my phone calls again. A couple weeks before Christmas, I called my family and told them that I wanted to return home for the holidays. They sent me $450 for a bus ticket. There had been a report about the discovery of a mass grave in Juárez that was supposedly full of drug addicts. My folks had been worried that I was one of them. Because I never intended to ride the bus to New York, or anywhere else for that matter, I used the money to take a vacation from panhandling. My circumstances didn't allow me to feel anything at all about it. While working the streets, I had developed a predatory sense that didn't allow me the luxury of normal human feelings. I viewed people as objects that enabled me to continue living my crazy lifestyle. I had adopted a twisted logic—kind of like a salesman who sells a product without care or consideration for the customer. The street routine had hardened my consciousness so that I didn't allow myself to feel. This was also a safety mechanism that helped me cope with the constant rejection and degradation involved with approaching people and asking them for money. I loved my family and always felt a special connection to them, but I was so far and away from them and into my habit that isolation seemed natural.

So I took a short vacation from panhandling and stayed at the hotel during the Christmas holidays. The large sum of money enabled me to buy a larger quantity of dope than usual. Marcos sold me a gram for forty dollars, and this was enough to last about two and a half days. During my vacation run, I ended up buying a few more grams because there was nothing better to do. I sat in the hotel room, watched television, and shot up.

On Christmas day, I went to Marcos's and gave his kids a bunch of sodas and chocolates. Marcos, aside from being a dealer, was also one of the few people that I shot dope with. We spent Christmas getting high, joking, and telling stories. The extra money had permitted me to take it easy, but by the third gram of heroin, Marcos told me that he couldn't get grams anymore. I usually bought the six-for-five deal from him, and would sometimes get that deal twice a day. But when I started buying grams, it messed up his whole routine and left him with more globos to sell individually. After all, I was one of his best customers. Buying the grams also hurt me because I used more and my dependency increased. Going back to globos meant going back to the familiar hustle on the streets.

The money didn't last long. Rent, dope, and meals ate away at it rather quickly. My short vacation from the street life was both good and bad: it kept me off the street during Christmas, but it also made me lazy. By this time, my family realized that I wasn't leaving Juárez, and the next phone call ended something like, "Don't call here again!" I planned on continuing my lifestyle for as long as I could. It had been quite awhile since I had last felt the pains of opiate withdrawal, and I wasn't in a hurry to experience them again anytime soon.

C'mon, we don't got all day!

On New Year's Day 2000, large wet and slushy snow-
flakes covered the streets of downtown Juárez, quickly melted, and created icy pools of water. The street in front of the hotel bustled with
people as the buses passed and sprayed slushy water all over the sidewalks. People filled the nightclubs, and it was a good day to get lost in
the crowd. I had spent New Year's Eve watching TV and enjoying the
last part of my little vacation. Soon I would be back to my usual routine, panhandling money for the rent or a "bus ticket back home." After the holidays, there was a little bit less money on the street, but I
managed to pick up where I had left off. My routine worked, the rent
got paid, and the dope kept flowing. The next couple of weeks seemed
like a blur, and I started to think about kicking heroin once again.
There is always a voice in the back of every junkie's mind that reminds
them that the run cannot last forever. I was tired of asking people for
money, and I wanted to find a way to move beyond life on the street.

One morning in late January, I found what I thought was a chance
at another life. Panhandling on the corner of Sixth and El Paso Streets,
I ran into someone from the Victory in Jesus Men's Home. He handed
me a flier and talked to me about starting over again and living without
dope. I was vaguely familiar with church-based recovery from reading David Wilkerson's *The Cross and the Switchblade* but had never considered entering such a program. I wasn't even aware that such places
existed in El Paso. I put the flyer in my pocket and thought about it
that night. It had been some time since I was offered the chance to try
something different. Lalo, the guy who gave me the flyer, said that he
was an ex-junkie who had found a new life. He convinced me to take

a chance on the program, and his description of my lifestyle really hit home with me. That evening, after I copped enough dope for that night and the next morning, my mind was made up. I decided to leave the hotel and go into the Victory in Jesus Men's Home in El Paso. I would withdraw, cold turkey, from heroin, again.

The next morning, I shot up and left the room, bound for El Paso. I left all of my belongings at the hotel, just in case the program didn't accept me and I ended up returning. All the clothes, the pennies on top of the dresser, and the dirty needles remained in the hotel room. The only things I carried were the clothes on my back. When I arrived at the corner of Sixth and El Paso Streets, I called up the recovery home. A voice on the line told me that someone was leaving to pick me up and that I should just wait there on the corner. Lalo must have been glad that he had reached out and helped someone on the street. It felt as if time was standing still as I waited for the people from Victory in Jesus. Finally, a pickup truck with three people in it showed up. They asked me if I was ready to go, and the next thing I knew, I was sitting in the back of the pickup and riding up East Paisano and Alameda Streets toward the east side of El Paso.

The Victory in Jesus home was located on Grimes Court, near Alameda in east-central El Paso. It was a midsize, single-story home that housed about a dozen guys. Lalo turned out to be the assistant home director. The main director was Pastor Donny Marcelino. Whether he was a real pastor was beyond me. My first day at the home proved to me that it was a structured rehab. Since the other guys in the home told me that they had detoxed, there was no doubt in my mind that the Victory in Jesus Men's Home was all about kicking the heroin habit and beginning life again. The "detox bedroom" had a set of bunk beds and a large closet filled with used clothes of various sizes. On the other side of the home were two bedrooms for the other residents, each with three bunk beds. At maximum capacity, the home could accommodate about sixteen people. The center of the home was a den with a fireplace, and a living room that had been converted into a makeshift chapel. Adjacent to the two center rooms were a kitchen and a side room with a few tables. The enclosed back porch had been converted into an office, and the pastor lived in a small apartment next door.

I spent my first day at the home exploring the place and talking to the pastor. I knew I would be sick as hell the next day, so I enjoyed the outdoors as much as I could while the remaining heroin in my body wore off. On that first day, I shaved, showered, and ate what I could. The guys in the home, the "brothers," rummaged in the donation closet and found some clothes that fit me. I didn't understand what Christian homes did beyond helping people detox from heroin. Once I caught on that I wouldn't be allowed to smoke, and that prayer was to be a part of everyday life, it felt awkward and weird. I decided that I would put up with whatever was necessary to make it through the pending withdrawal. I knew that once the sickness set in, I wouldn't be able to eat or sleep for a while.

The next morning, I woke up feeling icky and more anxious than ever. The raunchy food smells coming from the kitchen made it even worse. Shortly afterward, the diarrhea kicked in and I vomited relentlessly. I knew that this was going to be an ugly withdrawal: I had been using about twelve globos a day, and sometimes even more. I had been on a long run since my last real withdrawal, at the mission the year before. After twenty-four hours, I was painfully immobilized and too sick to move. I couldn't hold any food down, and everything about the home and my new "brothers" seemed like one great big blur. Some of the guys told me that if I ate something, I would get better sooner, but I threw up anything I ate. The food just wouldn't stay down. The only thing that eased my suffering was a hot bath or shower. My life revolved around the bedroom and the bathroom.

By the second day, my ears were ringing constantly and I kept hearing the sound of crackling Rice Krispies. The brothers put a bedpan next to my bed in case I couldn't make it to the bathroom, which was located on the other side of the home. A guy named David showed up and moved into the detox bedroom with me. David didn't seem sick in comparison to what I was going through, and the pastor, along with the other guys in the home, told him that helping the sick was God's work. Then they put him to work cleaning up after me. I had a few mishaps in which I had vomited all over the place, and my bedpan practically overflowed with diarrhea from one of those moments that I barely could hold it for it two seconds. I catnapped while I withdrew, experiencing dreamlike visions and hallucinations in which I swung on a rope from a pole, descended long distances, and caught myself with the rope. I was practically delirious with mad visions that added to the painful moments of my physical reality. I remember lying on the floor of the detox bedroom and listening to the home's routines of meal calls, *talacha* (chores), and prayer services for what seemed like days. Finally, someone opened the door to the room and said something like, "Yeah, he's still alive in there."

After the first week, I still couldn't sleep, but I had begun to get to know some of the brothers. The first thing I was able to eat was oatmeal. When the home residents left to perform their daily routine, a big lumberjack-looking Anglo by the name of Green stayed behind and looked after me. Green was from the border town of Del Rio, Texas, and he seemed very sincere in his walk with God. He stoked up the fireplace, which warmed my weary bones during that cold January detox, and he mixed up some oatmeal. One of the home's residents was a large talking parrot, and between the parrot's rantings and Green's spiritual support, I found enough peace within the space that they gave me to pull through the withdrawal. This was one of the worst ones that I had ever been through, almost as bad as my methadone detox in upstate New York, two years earlier. My roommate, David, although detoxing himself, was well enough that the pastor assigned him to work with the other residents and also to look after me. When David and the others were gone, Green, who had seniority, was left behind to watch over me and the home.

Green and Lalo were the pastor's most trusted servants. Lalo's duties involved supervising the rest of the guys when they were out working on the street. The home tried to be self-sufficient through its economic activities, which involved the sale of candy on the street and the daily cleaning of a large cinema complex with seven theaters. Pastor Don was an ex-convict who had been a junkie and a dope dealer. He sized me up early on and decided that I should rest in and around the home for the first three weeks. It was during these weeks that I pieced myself back together and tried to eat a full meal and get a full night's sleep. I was bedridden most of the first week, but by the second week, I was strong enough to sit in on church services. The first time that I left the home was in a van that took everyone from the home to the local church, which the residents attended. I sat through that first service practically cringed up on a metal folding chair, dazed, every bone in my body aching, while I listened to another pastor sing hymns in Spanish as he strummed an acoustic guitar. The pastor of the church, Hector Urbina, was from Honduras. Although we never spoke, he seemed like a nice person. That first church service was painful, but the cold evening air and the ride in the van were a nice change from the home.

Notwithstanding the pain, I tried to keep up with the daily routine of the home and get to know the other brothers. My roommate, David, was a heroin addict who panhandled by holding up a sign at the edge of a highway off-ramp. He told me that he made more than a hundred dollars a day with that routine. Judging by how active he was during his withdrawal—out in the yard and doing housework and all—I don't think that he had progressed too far into his habit. When I mentioned this to Pastor Don, he joked that David must have been shooting up coffee. Sometimes dealers, especially in the United States, cut Mexican brown tar heroin with instant coffee.

Don grew up in the Segundo Barrio of El Paso and mentioned that at one time, he was one of the biggest dealers in the neighborhood. Lalo, the assistant director, had lived at the home for a few years. Lalo was from one of the neighborhoods close to the home, around Alameda in central El Paso. Like most of the guys in the home, he was a tecato. Green, David, and I were the only Anglo-Americans in the home. Everyone else was either Mexican or identified himself as Chicano or Mexican American. I never considered myself an Anglo, or racialized white American, and I got along with all the guys because I spoke some Spanish and had lived in Juárez. Most of the brothers in the home had kicked heroin and knew the pain and uncertainty of it all. After a while, we all bonded in our own ways, and the home became a refuge from the realities of the lives we had lived before we got there.

Life at the Victory in Jesus Men's Home improved my Spanish. All church services were conducted in Pastor Urbina's Honduran-accented Spanish, and after a while, I even memorized the hymns, which were in Spanish as well. Once in a while, someone would show up to the home and give a workshop in English, but Spanish was the primary language of the church as well as the home. Green spoke church Spanish rather well for a beginner, and David, who probably identified himself as being the most Anglo among us—he admitted to once having been a skinhead—even began to learn a few words. Much as I liked to identify myself as Mexican or a hybrid assimilationist, Marcelino and Lalo put me to work with David and Green when I was strong enough to help with the daily work responsibilities of the home. I don't know whether this imposed racial segregation was the result of their experiences in the segregated Texas prison system, or whether it was merely an attempt to provide David and Green with some increased fellowship. The two of them seemed disconnected from many of the guys in the home, and the survival of the program depended on our ability to work together, as I would soon find out.

INDOOR AND OUTDOOR
JOBS FOR THE LORD

Despite the constant church services and Bible-based meetings, the home depended on donations and any revenue generated by residents. No matter how important religious things were, money and its production determined the survival of the home. Every morning at five, everyone except Marcelino met in the front room of the home for coffee (our equivalent of a morning fix), a pep talk from Lalo, prayer, and tool distribution for the morning's tasks. As mentioned, the home held a cleaning contract for a large cinema complex in El Paso. The twelve theatres there were trashed by the public every night. Every morning, the guys from the home loaded a bunch of hundred-foot extension cords and two leaf blowers into the home's van, which took everyone to work at the cinema. Lalo was the ringleader for this operation, and during his morning pep talks, he either presented something about church and recovery or briefed us about the day's activities, depending on what kind of mood he was in.

The cinema complex was huge. Once we arrived, I was assigned to work with David. The cinema had its own mops, brooms, and other cleaning supplies, and we soon became familiar with them all. The first time I went with the cleanup crew, I sat there in the cinema lobby near the popcorn stand, still dazed and weak from withdrawal. Since I was too weak to be of any real use, David worked enough to take up the slack. For my first job, I picked up the large trash from the aisles while David used the leaf blower to push the leftover popcorn and garbage down the sloped theatre floor toward the screen. Once all the trash was down front, I swept it up and put it into large plastic garbage bags. Then David mopped the floor, and the theatre was done. We did half of the theatres in the complex, and two other guys did the other half. After a while, we developed a routine, and as my strength increased, we switched tasks. I enjoyed mopping the floors and soon was able to clean a whole theatre by myself. When Lalo noticed how well I was doing, he split us up. But in those early days, David and I developed a decent work relationship and joked around as we worked.

Restoring a trashed cinema complex to a state in which it was presentable for another day's business involved a lot of work. Carpets needed to be vacuumed and swept, bathrooms had to be cleaned, and candy counters and windows had to be washed. While at the home, I worked every facet of the cleaning operation. This was one of the best parts of home life because it got us out and moving every morning and had us working together. The work gave us a sense of meaningful accomplishment. Sunday mornings were extraordinarily difficult. Besides being a church day, Sunday followed the busiest night of the week for the cinema: Saturday. Because we had to be at the church early on Sunday morning, we began at two thirty in the morning, finished the cinema complex by six- thirty, returned to the home, and quickly dressed for church.

When I had arrived at the home, I didn't have any clothes except for what I was wearing. While I was at the home, the brothers helped me build a small wardrobe. It was important to wear nice clothes to church, so in due time I assembled an assortment of shirts, slacks, and other hand-me-downs, which I accumulated by rummaging through the donation piles. As my appetite improved, I volunteered to work in the kitchen as a dishwasher. This meant increased access to food both before and after meals. The director didn't seem to mind, since I was so emaciated that some of the residents doubted that I would make it through the withdrawal. By my fourth week there, my appetite had grown and I had begun to sleep better at night. The daily routine of cleaning the theatres got me back into some sort of physical shape. With time, I started to gain weight, and everyone saw that as a sign of improvement.

As the days turned into weeks, I followed the daily activities as best I could. I had never been very religious, so I always felt like an outsider at church services; churchy things seemed somewhat out of touch with reality as I knew it. We, as residents of the home, were constantly told to be patient, but there didn't seem to be any plan for establishing improved lives of our own beyond the domain of the home. The director would tell us that it was our destiny to be men of God, future pastors, spiritual leaders, and warriors for Christ. I had trouble buying into it all, but I wanted to believe that there was something more to life than what I had experienced so far. I suppose that in my own way, I interpreted what they said and formulated my own sort of metaphysical understanding.

One of the other revenue-producing activities of the home was to sell candy in public. We walked the length of entire avenues, business districts, and industrial parks in El Paso, going door-to-door from business to business, approaching people as we went along and sold them candy. I worked with Green on these missions, and he told me that he used to be a vacuum cleaner salesman in Del Rio. Not knowing my history as a panhandler, he endeavored to teach me how to sell candy. The director told us to tell everyone that the candy was for a women's home that we planned to open. This line worked well with our stories of being junkies and sinners who had been saved by the Lord. We walked all day, from downtown El Paso to Sunland Park on Mesa Street. We approached people, walked into businesses, and preached our lines. It was good practice for me as I improvised, lied, negotiated, and practiced my Spanish. Green was a sincere Christian, and he often prayed for people. I quickly realized that some church members prayed for people, while others preyed on them. We sold most of our candies every time we went out. When we got tips or donations, Green often suggested that we splurge for burgers at Jack in the Box.

I often thought that Green was too sincere for the home and that the people there took him for granted. He had spent a few years in the home and was a model client. He had never done drugs and certainly wasn't a junkie. He talked about how he used to indulge in porn and drink alcohol a little bit. I think that Green was searching for somewhere to belong and that he felt a sense of purpose at the home. But some things seemed odd. Green had inherited some money from his family, and the home director managed it for him. Also, the home director and assistant director drove his new pickup truck around as if it was theirs. I never really questioned what the people at the home did; I was too busy worrying about my own situation. I thought that if Green didn't have a problem with his arrangement with the home, then why should I? Green was so sincere and so faithful to Pastor Don and Lalo, and he truly believed that he was doing the Lord's work. However, he seemed a little slow to develop any suspicions about people's ulterior motives, especially when those people seemed to have a divine connection.

I enjoyed selling candy on the streets of El Paso. The experience kept me sharp at hustling people out of some money. I never did see anything resembling a women's home around the home or the church, but I always did my best to spice up the story by telling everyone that we already had the silverware and the furniture and just needed to add a few more beds.

I suppose that Pastor Don and Lalo had good intentions for all the guys in the home, but it was beyond their capacity to guarantee everyone a successful outcome. One day, the pastor brought David and me into his office and tried to convince us to sign a commitment of indentured servitude. He explained to us that in biblical days, slavery was a form of sincere servitude, and he told us that he wanted us to think about it. However, by March 2000, I had grown tired of the daily routine at the Victory in Jesus Men's Home. One morning, after we had returned from cleaning the cinema, I was shooting basketball on the street in front of the home when I noticed that I was too heavy to play ball the way I used to. Not long afterward, I decided to leave the home. My strength had been restored, and I felt ready to go. Marcelino and Lalo tried to talk me out of leaving. They warned me that I would backslide, but my mind was made up. I wanted more freedom than the home offered, I felt ready to leave, and staying at the home seemed like a waste of time. Marcelino was upset to see me go; in fact, he told me that I was rotten. After he said that, I knew that it was time to go. I packed my stuff in a large doubled garbage bag and walked out to Alameda Street to catch the bus.

BACK TO THE MISSION, BACK TO WORKING VARIOUS JOBS, BACK TO USING

From the bus terminal near downtown El Paso's San Jacinto Plaza, I walked down West Paisano and checked into the Rescue Mission. Juanita, the director, was pleased to see me in such good physical shape. When I told her that I had been living at the Victory in Jesus Men's Home, she seemed a bit encouraged by my development. Green used to describe the church at the mission as a "worldly" church, a church that was connected to the state. That didn't make any difference to me. With a base at the mission, I could look for work and improve my own economic situation, something that had been denied me at the home. The mission was still the same crowded and depressing place that it had always been, but I was willing to put up with it for a while if doing so would allow me to improve my situation. Being healthy—that is, not withdrawing—made living at the mission easier to accept. I was clean, but during my first weekend out on the street, I used my old routine to panhandle about forty dollars. With or without a dope habit, I still needed money if I was going to look for work on the street all day.

During my first few days back at the mission, I stopped panhandling and sincerely looked for work. Luckily, at the front desk was some of my mail that had arrived since my last stay. Aside from the junk mail, there was a letter from the Social Security Administration with my new Social Security card. Card in hand, I went to the Texas Department of Public Safety and picked up an ID card. With these documents, I found work through a temporary labor agency, or staffing service. I never liked those kinds of places. They act as middlemen, supposedly providing a service by lining up willing workers with willing employers, yet they take money out of the worker's pocket and reduce meaningful pay to a minimal wage. Everyone at the mission told me that this was the best way to get my foot in the door at a company, so I decided to take a chance with them.

The staffing service sent me to a company called Stone Container, which was located in an industrial park near Hawkins and I-10. The workday began at seven in the morning, but the company advised workers to arrive around six thirty. The mission had a van service, which dropped us off in the morning, but we had to catch the bus back that afternoon. To be at work bright and early, I woke up earlier than the regular mission wake-up time, ate an early breakfast, and left the mission with a bag lunch. On my first day at the container company, I noticed that I was part of a small group from the labor service. The foremen at the company told us that there was an OSHA (Occupational Safety and Health Administration) inspection coming up and that they wanted us to clean the factory and warehouse and have them ready for inspection. I spent the next two weeks sweeping the factory and warehouse floors, cleaning grease-covered machinery, and removing cobwebs and cardboard dust from the ceiling. I worked diligently and tried my best to show Stone Container that I was a hard worker. Boring as my job was, I pushed myself to keep on working throughout the day. I watched as others from the staffing service were promoted to the assembly line. I continued to push a broom and perform jobs that no one else wanted, such as cleaning grime from corners of the factory that had not been touched in years, all the while trying to look enthused and hardworking. Quitting time was at three thirty in the afternoon, and then I caught the bus back to the mission.

I deposited my first paycheck at the mission. The mission had a system in which clients could save money, have a place to live, and eventually move out on their own. My third week at the container factory didn't go well. I was getting sick and tired of doing never-ending cleaning chores while other guys from the labor service got jobs on the production line. The people at Stone Container kept talking about the upcoming OSHA inspection, which seemed to me like some big lie designed to keep me scrubbing and sweeping—possibly to keep the turn-over from the staffing service perpetual. One day, during the middle of that week, I was cleaning out the scrap-cardboard bundling area when I hurt myself on the job. The freight trains used large air-filled cargo separators, which were kind of like very large balloons made out of du-rable paper. I was supposed to break them down and throw them out. I had never done that before, so I decided to pop one of the table-sized balloons with a long thin board. When I hit the bag with the board, the board didn't break the bag. Instead, it snapped back, practically broke my glasses, and gave me a fat lip. This little mishap slowed me down that day, and I think one of the managers may have watched it on one of their surveillance cameras.

By the end of that day, I was anxious to get the heck out of there. Five minutes before quitting time, I went to the bathroom to wash my face and check out my condition. It wasn't bad, but it wasn't good: the frames to my glasses were bent, and I knew that I would need a new pair as soon as possible. When I walked out of the bathroom, one of the managers from the container company told me to report back to my agency. This was their way of getting rid of me without having to take any responsibility. I was somewhat glad, because I just couldn't see myself making a career out of cleaning the factory, and the noise from the place was really starting to bother me. The whole time I was at Stone Container, I didn't have a meaningful interaction with anyone. In short, the job sucked, and the people didn't or wouldn't like me, no matter how hard I worked. When I left that afternoon, I optimistically told myself that there had to be something better in store for me.

My paycheck that Friday was pretty good; it was for the one full week I had put in at the container company. It was the most I had made while working a real job in quite a long time: about $450. I wasn't working anymore, so I caught the bus across town to the staffing ser-vice to pick up my check. Another guy from the mission was pick-ing up his check too, so we rode the bus out there together, cashed our checks, and decided to each get a quart of beer and celebrate. I went to the Cielo Vista Mall and bought myself a Walkman and a couple of CDs. By the time I made it back downtown, the alcohol had numbed up my system and I was feeling pretty good. Good enough, in fact, to walk across the bridge to Juárez and take a tour of my old stomping grounds. As soon as I got to Juárez, as if on automatic pilot, I caught the bus to Pepe's in Altavista and scored six globos for the price of five. I shot up a few of them and gave a couple to Pepe and his brother Víctor. I was feeling pretty good, so I decided to go for a walk and get a soda.

When I woke up, six hours later, on a street corner in Altavista, I was lying in someone's front yard with my feet sticking out onto the sidewalk. My headphones were still on, but my Walkman was gone. All the cash, everything in my front pocket left from my paycheck, was gone. Surprisingly, my wallet was still in my back pocket, probably because it had been between me and the ground as I lay there. Thankfully, there was twenty dollars in it.

I knew that I had messed up big time. Feeling high and stupid, I walked to my old casita in Colonia Postal and hung out with one of the kids who lived next door. I gave him one of the CDs that I had bought and then wandered toward the bus stop, smoking cigarettes and enjoying the effects of the brown tar heroin. I felt down and out as I walked back to the mission that night: practically broke, unemployed, and as stupid as ever. Fortunately, no one there suspected anything, so I crawled into bed defeated. That weekend, I stayed in El Paso and panhandled on the downtown streets near the bridge. I didn't get sick, but I did have a small hangover. If you use heroin only once or twice, you haven't established enough of a habit to go through full-scale withdrawal. Usually, the next day is more like coming off a night of binge drinking. The following week, I looked for work again. I also picked up my last paycheck from the labor service, went to Juárez, and bought a new pair of glasses.

Over the course of the next week at the mission, I panhandled and delivered advertising flyers to neighborhoods on El Paso's east side. The delivery job paid thirty dollars a day, and it felt nice to walk through those areas. I didn't realize that people in east El Paso lived in such beautiful homes. The incident in Altavista did not stop me from using when I could, even though I knew I had been lucky not to overdose. One evening after delivering flyers, I went to Juárez and fixed.

While rummaging through my belongings, I found a phone number that one of my candy customers had given me while I was at the Victory in Jesus Men's Home. I had forgotten all about the conversation, but after looking at that number on a small piece of paper and considering my situation, I decided that anything was worth a try. When I was selling candy for the home, I told a woman from an art store that I had moved paintings while working in the moving business. She gave me the number of a local mover she knew who might be interested in hiring someone with experience. At the time, I thought nothing of it and stashed the number away. Now I decided to call. The guy who answered the phone had a distinct New York or New Jersey accent. I told him who I was, how I had gotten his number, and what my moving-and-storage experience had been. The guy's name was Joe Huggins, and he ran a small moving business in El Paso called At Your Service Moving and Shipping. Joe seemed like a happy person, and I felt that I had made the right move by calling him. He told me that he would pick me up at the mission the next morning.

Sure enough, the next morning as I stood outside the mission in anticipation, a small truck with a box that advertised "At Your Service" on the back pulled in. Joe yelled something like, "Come on, we don't got all day!" and then broke out in a laugh. Joe was a pleasant guy who seemed happy with life and what it was doing for him. He was the first person that I had encountered with that kind of mindset in quite some time. We hit it off right away. Joe knew a lot about the moving industry, and so did I. We were both from the same part of the country: the tristate area of the Northeast. And we both had spent years as over-the-road truck drivers in the moving-and-storage business. Joe seemed like sort of a hippie, so when he asked me how I had managed to wind up at the mission, I just told him the truth. Joe was the kind of guy that you just knew you could trust with the truth, no matter how messed up it was. It felt good to be working for someone I didn't need to hide my past from.

Working for the men's home and at the factory had whipped me back into decent shape, and I was able to put in some good days of work with Joe. Joe taught me as much as he could about his business in a short time, and pretty soon he mentioned that he was going to help get me out of the mission. The only drawback was that without a valid driver's license, I could earn at most $250 a week. That was okay with me; most of the work was easy, and Joe, unlike the people at the container factory, didn't pressure me to work nonstop. I had a lot of autonomy as an employee of At Your Service, and the job seemed well suited to help me reestablish my self-esteem after all that I had been through.

THE IRRESISTIBLE PULL OF JUÁREZ

One of Joe's close friends, a guy named Henry who was like Joe's second father, helped me find a furnished apartment in El Paso. It was a nice place, located on Harrison near Dyer in a complex called the Shamrock Apartments. I couldn't have asked for a better place: the kitchen had a table, the living room had a sofa, and the bedroom had a bed and a dresser. I even bought a TV with my next paycheck. The spring of 2000 offered me a chance to turn my life around, but somewhere in the middle of this rebound, I believed that it was all right to shoot dope again, if only on the weekend.

It must have been around May when I decided to go to Juárez one Saturday and get a hotel room. The weather was warmer, and going out seemed like a good way to spend the weekend. Going to Juárez and getting a room always meant another shot of heroin. I rented a room close to Chito's, the bar in Bellavista, near El Centro. Chito's son Tommy was around and showed me where to cop close to the hotel. The hotel was an older place that had large cement balconies supported by pillars. It had the faded look of a building that had been around since before the Mexican Revolution. Since times were good for me, I treated Tommy to a shot of dope and did only one globo myself. Tommy knew me, and we talked about women and doing dope. He warned me not to do a lot, since I could easily overdose. After my last experience, when I woke up lying in the street, I knew that I needed to take it easy. After shooting up, I went to Chito's and hung around, shooting pool with the girls who worked there, smoking cigarettes, and enjoying the high. The next morning, I shot up again, and it felt deceptively nice to go though the familiar experience of waking up and fixing. That Monday on the job, I sweated a little more than normal. By the end of the day, I was just tired. I returned to Juárez the following weekend and did the same thing. This was the start of a weekend ritual for me.

On one of those Sundays, I went to Felipe Angeles to hang around and cop a last-minute fix before returning to El Paso. The main dealers in Felipe Angeles were two brothers: Perico and Kiko. They, along with most of the junkies in the neighborhood, knew me, and I had often copped dope from them in 1998 during my first summer in Juárez, when I lived with Laura. That afternoon, I bought a used bicycle from some junkie in Felipe Angeles and rode it back to El Paso. Just up the hill from Perico's lived a junkie I knew named José. José's place was convenient for shooting up right after I copped from Perico. During those weekends, José always was happy to see me because he knew I would kick him down a globo for letting me fix at his place.

After a while, José and I got tight, the way junkies do when they need something from each other, and it wasn't long before I started to venture over to José's on weekdays after work to fix on the side. My new bicycle enabled me to move around rather easily. I rode it to work every day. It wasn't long before I was riding it to José's place in Felipe Angeles to shoot some dope and then pedaling back to my apartment in El Paso. The ride back to my apartment was uphill from the bridge, but the numbing effect of the dope, plus the fact that I was in pretty good physical shape, allowed me to make the journey without a second thought. During all this, I started to become increasingly dependent on heroin again.

One morning I shot up before work, and I remember Joe giving me some odd looks that day. As with the construction job, the moving business was intensely physical and required a lot of energy. Whenever I was under the influence, I always worked like a programmed machine. The only giveaway was that I smoked an unusually large number of cigarettes, even while working. I kept up my new daily routine, riding my bicycle from my apartment to work and then, after work, to Juárez in order to fix. I became reliant on my friend José, in Felipe Angeles, because I could ride out there and shoot up at his place with no hassle: he lived a stone's throw from the dealer.

One evening while pedaling back to El Paso, I was stopped and inspected at the bridge. The U.S. Customs agents must have thought it odd to see a middle-aged American man pedaling a black, spray-painted bicycle over the border everyday, if they had even noticed. But my bike stood out. It didn't have any fenders, the handlebars were elevated, and the stem that elevated the seat was extended and welded to the frame. The bike was a custom-made high rider, which suited me because of my height. In my jeans and baseball cap and with a bandana around my forehead, I must have looked like a possible smuggler. That evening, they stopped me and gave me a thorough inspection. I was surrounded by eight customs officers with nothing better to do; they brought over a drug dog to sniff the bike over, but the dog couldn't find anything. One officer, perhaps in desperation, started to fondle the bike as if there had to be something there. They deflated the tires even after the dog had not found anything! After a while, they turned to me and asked me whether I had anything on me—as if I would've told them. When the whole ordeal was over, the agents walked away disgusted, and I picked up my very well inspected bicycle and pushed it the nearest air pump, at the corner of Paisano and Mesa. After reinflating my tires, I once more made the uphill journey back to my apartment.

I liked scoring in Felipe Angeles for a number of reasons. I could easily have ridden to any number of neighborhoods in Juárez and scored from any number of small-time street dealers. However, the ride to Felipe Angeles paralleled the river and offered a smooth grade. All the other neighborhoods I knew in Juárez were in hilly terrain and could be reached only after extensive uphill pedaling. The ride alongside the Rio Grande on Juárez's west-side border highway was flat, smooth, and relatively fast to travel by bicycle. I was known in Felipe Angeles because of my friendship with Víctor and my past relationship with Laura, his girlfriend's sister. I could shoot up at José's, which was practically next door to the dealer's, and eliminate the risk of exposing myself on the street by carrying needles or dope in my pockets. Another nice thing about riding the bike along the border highway was that the Juárez municipal police were less likely to stop me there than on the backstreets of the other west-side neighborhoods.

When I carried globos around with me, I kept them in my mouth. Brown tar heroin is usually wrapped really good and tight in plastic and then covered with a couple of layers of aluminum foil. A well-packed globo was essentially airtight and waterproof. They looked like little balls, about one-quarter the size of a marble, and rested comfortably between the gums and the top lip or cheeks. If you wedged them in there real good, you could talk with ease without anyone suspecting that you had something in your mouth. Some junkies lined up six or seven globos in their mouths, kind of like braces going around the upper gums and resting over the front teeth. People who carried that much usually didn't do much talking, but with practice, they could be elusive and pass a shakedown unless the police searched the mouth, which I saw them do occasionally when they searched suspected junkies downtown. Also, if worse came to worst, you could just swallow the dope and avoid getting busted. Pretty soon, I was riding my bike to Felipe Angeles every day after work. I got hooked again.

My boss, Joe, must have suspected that something was up, and I could sense his disappointment. Though he wanted to help me out—and had helped me considerably so far—he was no dummy, and he quickly caught on that I was using again. No doubt, this hurt my chances for advancement, but Joe kept me on board, and I showed up for work on time every day. I also had more experience in the moving-and-storage business than most laborers in El Paso. So even when under the influence of heroin, I still worked harder and had more knowledge of his operation than practically anyone else but him. Most of all, Joe still trusted me.

As time went on, however, my habit progressed, and I started feeling withdrawal symptoms at the end of the workday. This slowed me down considerably. It wasn't long before I began taking chances, sneaking dope around with me and shooting up in the mornings. Once this started happening, I knew that it was the beginning of the end for my job with Joe and his moving company. But Joe never gave up on me. He was good hearted. As the daily afternoon withdrawals set in, Joe expected less and less from me. I never stole from Joe and was always honest with him. Eventually, I told him I was going to try to detox again, and I rode my bicycle out to the Victory in Jesus Men's Home.

The home took me back in like the prodigal son. My return reassured them of the rightness of their beliefs. They had told me that I would be back, and there I was. I showed up there first thing in the morning and found the home director outside. He smiled when he saw me, as if he knew I would return. I had some dirty clothes, so I spent my first day there doing laundry. Before the effects of my last fix wore off, I took a shower and ate. By that night, I had started to feel the withdrawal pains, and they became worse as time wore on. Sometime after midnight, I got up and sat in the chapel area of the home. I couldn't sleep, and my whole body felt as if it were starting to burn from within. As I sat there, one of the brothers came up and asked me if I was okay. Perhaps, I thought, he was trying to give me some spiritual advice. I was shocked when he made a sexual pass at me. Of all the times and places for something like this to happen. I couldn't fuckin' believe it! There I was, going through heroin withdrawal in a church home, and some guy was trying to make a play at me. I brushed off his advances and decided then and there that I wasn't going to stick around the home.

The next morning, I packed my bag and dragged myself back to Juárez on that old bicycle. Although the brothers at the home might have been saved, it was clear to me that some of them still had problems that the Victory in Jesus Men's Home wasn't capable of addressing. I decided not to make their problems my problems—God knows, I had problems enough of my own. I rode my bicycle down Alameda Avenue into downtown El Paso. As the withdrawal pains began to get worse, I knew that time was running out and that I didn't have much choice in the matter. I rode to Juárez, sold the bicycle for 100 pesos, and fixed. Later that afternoon, I caught the bus back to my apartment and looked for something else that I could sell for my next fix.

¿Curastes, güey?

It was nice to have an apartment to go back to, but I had fallen behind on the rent and knew that at the rate I was going, I would never be able to pay it. I sold my color TV and VCR and went down to Juárez to fix again. By July 2000, everything I had built up had quickly disappeared. Finally, I just walked out of the apartment with a duffle bag full of clothes and some books and papers. I never returned. I knew that I was hooked again and that life in El Paso had become too much of a hassle. I didn't have any connections there anyway, and the dope was cheaper and better in Juárez.

I went to José's and explained to him that I was homeless. He told me that I could sleep where he stayed. It wasn't much more than a few cushions on the floor of the small brick shack next to his mom's small house, but it was better than sleeping outside. José and I were shooting partners by then, and I always kept some jeringas stashed around his place. I knew that staying at José's meant going back to the streets and panhandling in order to keep my habit going. In my condition, there was no way I could go back to work at Joe's. As long as I gave José some of my dope, I could stay there. It didn't take long for me to forget about everything that I had walked away from once I was strung out again. José and his family were used to the sudden changes that the junkie lifestyle produced. Both José and his brother Víctor had been strung out for quite some time.

José's mom lived in the main house with his sister. It was a small place, not much larger than my old casita. José and Víctor slept next door in a brick shack that had a blanket for a door. Living at Jose's was like camping. The roof and the walls were just capable of blocking the elements; the roof leaked during heavy rains, and a couple of plastic buckets were needed to keep the whole place from flooding. On the other side of José's mother's house was a small *jacalito*, a little shack made of pallets and wood. José's other brother slept there with his wife and their two children. The front of the compound sealed off by a concrete wall with an iron gate; the rest of the yard was surrounded by a fence made of discarded pallets.

José's mother's house had running water in the kitchen and bathroom, but our showers were taken with buckets. After a few weeks of living there, I found a motel on South El Paso Street in downtown El Paso that charged three dollars for a shower, which included the use of a clean towel. During the day, when I was out panhandling in El Paso, I would often stop and take a shower at this motel as part of my daily routine. Sometimes I skipped taking a shower, but the deal with the motel shower was convenient, since I always carried a duffle bag full of clothes with me when I was panhandling. Because my panhandling routine involved the line about getting a bus ticket, I needed to stay presentable and keep a packed bag with me to legitimize my story. As José and I got tight as shooting partners, he taught me some more lines in Spanish to help me out during my panhandling routine. The nice thing about living at José's was that there were dope dealers right next door, just down a small steep hill.

It wasn't long before I was living with my habit and performing the same panhandling routine that I had used when I stayed downtown at the Burciaga Hotel. José's mother and sister offered to wash my laundry every once in a while for fifty pesos, and when panhandling was good, I'd buy used clothes in the Segundo Barrio. Lots of little shops and street vendors sold used clothing, and some of my favorites were on Sixth Street. I panhandled in Felipe Angeles, but only when I was on my way to the bus stop or walking around, passing time after a day on the street. Living at José's was about the same as living on the street because I never knew when my situation would change. I always worried that his family would kick me out, and there were times when his other brother, the one who wasn't strung out, seemed to despise me.

It was kind of messed up that as a panhandling junkie, I made more money than he did as a full-time factory worker in one of the local *maquiladoras*. When times were real good, I would give José's mom some money. Pretty soon, she got used to seeing me around and cooked enchiladas and tamales for us. José's older brother, Víctor, who was also a junkie, showed up, and pretty soon the three of us were all camped out in the little brick shack, trying to support our heroin habits. As a panhandler, I always made at least fifty dollars a day, so there was always enough dope to go around. Yet José and Víctor were no slouches. José made money by stealing, doing odd jobs, shining shoes, and working as a coyote (smuggling people across the border). Víctor did practically the same things. He had jumped the fence and worked in a produce field somewhere in the United States for a few months. That was where he had been when I first showed up. When Víctor got back, he was in pretty good shape, but he started shooting dope on his first day back home. A few days later, he was just as sick and strung out as José and me.

A TOUR OF FELIPE ANGELES

I got to know many of the people in Felipe Angeles when I panhandled there. It wasn't long before I developed relationships with some of the local merchants, similar to the ones I had made the previous summer in Las Canchas. Every once in a while, someone would recognize me and joke around, "Hey, Nueva York," and we'd have a good laugh together. For example, on the main street of Felipe Angeles there was a tiendita owned and operated by a guy named Benny, who was from Veracruz. Benny lived with his son and daughter in a house behind his store. He was a friendly and talkative guy, and the first time I met him, I was out on the front porch of his store panhandling from his customers. He came out and gave me a couple of American quarters and offered me a soda.

I made Benny's store one of my regular morning stops. For breakfast, I often had a soda, a banana, and a pan blanco. After a day of panhandling, I usually stopped at Benny's to buy cigarettes and some last-minute snacks before fixing. A soda always raised my blood pressure just enough that I was able to hit a vein, and Benny's was my usual soda stop before fixing. I was glad for the camaraderie we had developed. Benny often gave me credit on food, cigarettes, and sodas when I was broke. Another good thing about Benny's store was that it was a refuge for me whenever the police rolled through the neighborhood, whether by *camper* or on horseback. When time allowed, especially on my good days on the street, I would hang around Benny's and just nod out, drink sodas, smoke cigarettes, talk to him, and teach him some words in English. Benny also helped me learn more Spanish. This type of interaction was constant with most of the people I knew in Juárez.

Benny's store had a delicatessen, and after a while, I got to know the people who worked there. Benny knew I was a junkie, but we developed a friendship and are still friends today. One of the main reasons for this was that I never stole from him, and when his son or daughter was working the cash register, I think that my presence may have added a measure of safety, especially when the store was busy.

After a long day on the street, I would go to Jose's for the night, fix, and sleep. Most mornings at José's were all about *la cura* (the cure for our sickness). We always woke up sick with the malilla, and doing a wake-up shot was part of the survival ritual. Usually, the first thing José asked me when we hooked up was, *"¿Curastes, güey?"* (Did you fix and get well yet, man?) When two junkies spend a lot of time together, they often get careless and forget how much discipline is needed to maintain a dope habit. Sometimes when I had put a few globos away for the morning, we would wake up early and shoot them before sunrise or, worse yet, finish all our dope the night before and wake up the next morning without anything to cure us from being dope-sick. After a while, I always kept twenty or forty dollars stashed away for these kinds of emergencies, but there were a few times when I had to go out and hustle up enough money for a fix while I was dope-sick.

Half the battle of surviving as a junkie is not getting sick to begin with. José tried to make our seemingly miserable existence as pleasant as possible, and every morning he made sure we had coffee or champurrado to drink as we smoked those first cigarettes after that blissful morning fix.

When it came to hustling on the street, I always made more money in El Paso, but sometimes I stayed in Juárez. On a couple of occasions, I did this because the bridge was closed because of a bomb scare. Most of those days, I would wander in El Centro or in Felipe Angeles, trying to wheedle money out of people with my fabricated story. I didn't make as much money in Juárez, but it wasn't as exhausting to panhandle there as in El Paso. When I panhandled in El Paso, it was like going to work: every moment was focused on making as much money as possible so that I could return to Juárez and take a break. The stress of being on the street and enduring constant rejection required the restful space that the needle and the nod provided.

Once in while that summer, José, his nephews, and I walked down to the river and went swimming. We usually went in the late afternoon, when important tasks like panhandling and fixing had been taken care of. Many people from the neighborhood swam in the Rio

Grande, and there was a small beach-like area across the river from the ASARCO smelter. One day the kids were catching *cangrejos* (crawfish) in the river with a large screen. They placed the screen at the bottom of the river, and the running water filled it with crawfish and small stones. We swam and waded downriver and eventually wound up in the area near the Rescue Mission. On those hot summer days, the river was refreshing. We never thought about how polluted the water must have been, and swimming in the river was a good way to reduce the tension and stress of everything else. When we got back to José's, we washed ourselves off with buckets of clean water. José and the kids cooked up the crawfish, but I didn't eat any; they seemed too small to eat, and I just wasn't into it. Swimming in the river was one of the few experiences that made me feel alive. It brought a sense of youthful enjoyment into the struggle to survive.

In Felipe Angeles, there is a burrito stand on the main road that runs through the colonia. At the time, the name of the establishment was Los Monchis, and it was another of my regular stops. The folks at this small street-side restaurant remembered me from when I had hung around Víctor during my first days in Juárez. Víctor had introduced me around the neighborhood as his *cuñado* (brother-in-law), and the burrito stand had been one of our regular stops. Now when I went there in the morning, the guys who worked there often asked me where Víctor was: "¿Adónde anda Víctor?" because they knew we were tight. Panhandling around the burrito stand in the morning usually included being offered a breakfast by a customer, and if I ever enjoyed anything like home-cooked meals during the summer of 2000, most of them came from Los Monchis.

Another regular stop for me was a small neighborhood grocery store on the corner, just a few buildings down from the burrito stand. The owner's son spoke some English and liked graffiti art, and we became friends after I wrote his name in graffiti letters. He usually gave me a free soda when he was running the store. His father wasn't as generous, but never bothered me when I panhandled in front of their store. I always showed the customers respect, and this is probably why some of them would stop and give me a few pesos. Putting together fifty to a hundred pesos on this corner, on a good day, made it that much easier to support my never-ending habit. Staying close to the connection also reduced the need to travel through downtown Juárez, where being harassed by the police was always a possibility.

As I mentioned earlier, the main dealers in Felipe Angeles were two brothers: Perico and Kiko. Their family lived just down the hill from José's. The two brothers ran the operation, but other family members also helped. The family's complex of houses is difficult to describe, but the main house was set back from the street and surrounded by a six-foot-high cinder-block wall. Across the street from the main house was a smaller house, which sat on an unpaved road that eventually turned into the small, very steep pathway that led up to José's. Perico and Kiko were large, heavyset guys, the kind you thought twice about before messing with. Perico, who lived in the small house across the street from the mini hacienda, sold most of the chiva from his place. The brothers knew me as a steady customer, and if I was sick, they would usually front me enough to get well so that I could pull myself together and panhandle. As always, it took some time to develop a dope-centered client-patron relationship with them. But the interaction progressed well, since I usually copped six for five every day. They saw me as a reliable customer, so helping me out with a fix was an investment for them. After all, I usually returned later that same day, paid them back, and then bought at least 200 pesos worth of dope.

One problem about getting a wake-up fix from Perico and Kiko was that they were not early risers, and if they had sold out the night before, they usually did not resupply until around nine or ten in the morning, or sometimes even later. Living up the hill from them had its advantages, but when they didn't have any dope, it didn't matter. When they were sold out, a small crowd of junkies gathered around Kiko's place, and their restlessness was obvious. The longer these junkies hung around, the sicker they became from withdrawal. Some would leave to score somewhere else, but most times I hung around, unless Kiko told me that there wasn't going to be anything that day. When that happened, mornings really became a problem. It meant taking a bus across town, finding some dope, and either shooting up on the street or returning to José's. Often, the only thing lost was time, but the fear of getting caught out, busted, and losing the first fix of the day always loomed in the back of my mind. For a junkie, there is safety in the familiarity of a routine, and breaking out of it means taking risks that could end up leading to involuntary withdrawal.

Aside from Perico, Kiko, and my friend Marcos, I found another connection not far from José's, on the outskirts of Felipe Angeles in a place called Las Moras. I don't know why they called it that, but that was the name everyone used, and if you said that there was dope at Las Moras, every junkie knew what and where you were talking about.

Las Moras sat on top of a larger hill, close to the area that bordered Felipe Angeles as you headed toward downtown. On top of the hill was a house where a family sold dope. The only way to get there was to walk up a steep dirt footpath or go around the back of the hill and walk through Colonia Montevista. Las Moras was inaccessible by car because it sat a ways in from the hilly unpaved roads that ran behind it.

The first time I went to Las Moras to buy dope, José brought me there and showed me where it was. He seemed reluctant to show me that connection because it was on the other side of the neighborhood, and he worried that I would shoot up without him. I shared a fix with José at least once or twice a day. If that stopped, it meant that he would have to support his habit without my help. As long as I stayed at his family's place and bought from his neighbors, he knew that I would share some dope with him.

A small crowd of junkies usually hung around Las Moras. It was more centrally located than Perico's, and next to it sat a vacant, roofless house that served as a shooting gallery. I shot up there once or twice when I was sick, but I preferred not to hang around. I never liked shooting up in front of a bunch of dope-sick tecatos, because they always begged for my leftover cooker and cotton so that they could get the residue. Many of the junkies who hung around Las Moras knew me. Some of them remembered me from Colonia Postal or Altavista. As the dealers at Las Moras got to know me, they watched out for me; I was a steady customer. But there is no loyalty among thieves. I always watched my back when other junkies were around and preferred to shoot up alone or with someone I trusted. While I stayed at José's, I trusted him as much as I could and usually scored from his neighbors down the hill.

Kiko was kind of like a *patrón* within the older *hacendado* system found in Mexico. The main family house was like a small hacienda, and they had a tiendita in front of the place that sold sodas and candies to the neighborhood kids. As far as junkies went, there were insiders and outsiders. The insiders were either cousins or old friends who had grown up there in the neighborhood. They hung around and did odd jobs, ran dope to a neighbor's house to hold it, or washed cars and painted the walls. They hung around Kiko's all day as if hanging around was a full-time job. Maybe they carried pistols and were ready to go ballistic if someone tried to rob the place. Most of them weren't even junkies; they just hung around all day, smoking marijuana and drinking beer.

After I got tight with Kiko, he let me hang around when he bagged up his dope. I was a regular customer, and I brought him a lot of business, so it wasn't long before a mutual respect developed between us. Kiko knew that I stayed at José's family's place, so he considered me closer than the rest of the street junkies. José told me that Kiko's wife had been his girlfriend years before, so they had known each other since childhood. Because Kiko knew Víctor from the neighborhood, he knew that I had lived with the sister of Víctor's girlfriend and that Víctor and me were tight.

When the supplier arrived, sometimes the guys who hung around the hacienda all day washed his car while he went in and delivered. At first, they all told me that he was Kiko's uncle. I didn't know who he was, but I bummed cigarettes from him and talked to him the same way I talked to anyone else on the street. After a while, I caught on that he was the supplier, but never made a big deal about it. I knew that when Kiko was dry and this guy showed up, the dope had arrived. I think what enabled me to build a half-decent relationship with Kiko and his family was that I was an honest customer who always respected their business. Easy as it was to get along in Felipe Angeles, I was always on my own on the street as a panhandler, always hustling for enough money to feed my habit.

COYOTES

Life at José's was very interesting at times, especially when he worked as a coyote. José was just a part-time coyote; he helped people cross the border into the United States, and I think it was a last resort for him. He did it mostly when his mom was really short on money. Felipe Angeles sits right on the U.S.-Mexico border, just across from UTEP and the Rescue Mission. I could see both of those places from José's front yard. Because of its location, many people jumping the border pass through the neighborhood. Sometimes José helped his childhood friends cross the border; other times, it was strictly business. Although only a part-time coyote, José definitely knew the territory. Having grown up right there on the border, he had been crossing since childhood. He told me stories about how guys in the neighborhood would sneak across the river, steal cars, drive them back to Mexico, and sell them to chop shops.

Every so often when I arrived in the late afternoon, there would be one, two, or even three people hanging around José's place, waiting anxiously. One day, a young woman arrived, and I thought she was José's new girlfriend. They were close and intimate with each other. That night, he told me that he was crossing her over the border. Maybe she paid him for his services with sexual favors.

One evening, José asked me whether I wanted to help him on one of his border runs. I had some dope set aside for morning, but decided to do it all that night so that we would be ready for the task. Soon, a young couple arrived with a baby. The baby was very young, four or five months old. After sunset, we caught the bus going northwest, toward El Rancho, a colonia that sits across from Sunland Park, New Mexico. Baby in hand, we got off the bus and walked down a long unpaved road. Cutting through someone's property, we started around the back of Mount Cristo Rey; a huge crucifix at the top of this mountain overlooks El Paso and Juárez. José knew where he was going, but I surely didn't. Soon, we came to a spot that overlooked Sunland Park.

It was a dark and moonless night, and the lights from the distant valley seemed worlds away. In an area next to some railroad tracks, we awaited the arrival of a train. The train was loud, and its noise broke the calm that I had always assumed to be necessary to cross the border without being detected. To my surprise, as we sat there watching, the train wheels screeched and it came to a halt. As the train sat there making groaning and hissing sounds, José excitedly urged us to hurry and follow him. He ran to the train, climbed up a small ladder on one of the cars, and motioned for us to follow. I was the last one to climb the ladder, which led to the deck of a car that carried two huge overseas shipping containers. It was an eight-foot climb, and as the young couple followed José up the ladder, I held their baby and then passed it up to the mother once she had made it to the top. The ladder led to a recessed deck area at the end of the railway car, which gave us just enough space to sit down and face the rear doors of the shipping container. The edges of the railway car concealed us.

The couple sat there huddled with their baby as José kept an ever-vigilant watch around us. I just sat there and tried to believe that this was really happening. A sudden jolt and the pounding response of the train brought me back to my senses. A moment later, the train moved a short distance up the tracks. Then it stopped again. José ordered us off the train and into the bushes at the side of the tracks. Again I went last and held the baby as the couple climbed down the ladder. As they reached up, I leaned over and passed the child down to them. Crouched in the mesquite, we scanned the area for signs of activity. José told me that *la migra* (immigration officers) searched the trains and that we had to be careful. A moment later when the train jolted to a start, José motioned for us to get back on. Following the same routine, I went last and passed the baby up as the couple reached the top of the ladder. The train began moving before I could climb up, but it was a slow pace, and I was easily able to follow. We rode a little farther, and the train stopped again. Worried, José made us get off the train again. We waited a little while longer in the bushes and then reboarded. When the train started off on its descent into El Paso, José told us to stay down and not move.

Overhead, I saw the framework of a large railroad trestle, which meant that we were crossing the river. Shortly afterward, the train stopped again, and José told us to get off. Between the Rescue Mission and the ASARCO smokestack, José motioned for us to walk toward the interstate. As we walked away from West Paisano, I watched a passing car slow down and take a long slow look at us. I was behind the group and watched as the car continued on. We made it to the verge of the railroad tracks, at the bottom of the steep slope that went up to the interstate highway, and began walking along the tracks toward the mission. We scattered into the bushes when a train suddenly approached us head-on, sounding its horn and disrupting my illusions of making a silent passage. After the engine passed, we emerged from hiding and walked down the side of the tracks, only a few feet from the passing freight cars as they hammered past, clacking away against the tracks.

Once the train had finally passed and we were almost to the mission, José guided us from the tracks to the very steep slope leading up to I-10. Instead of climbing the slope and sprinting across the freeway, we followed José into a drainage tunnel that ran beneath the highway, a tunnel large enough for only one person to crawl through at a time. The tunnel floor was covered with sand and stones, and once we were all just inside, we lay there and listened attentively to the sounds outside. An hour later, we heard a racket that sounded like a bunch of pickup trucks driving around the neighboring train yard, around the train that we had ridden in on. José said it was la migra. It made sense that the Border Patrol would search that train at that particular location, but then again, it might have just been railroad workers.

Regardless of who it was, once the noise subsided, we waited a little longer and then crawled out of the tunnel. Out in the open again, we walked behind the mission, through an underpass beneath the interstate, and onto the UTEP campus. I had often admired the large buildings of the University of Texas at El Paso from Colonia Postal and Felipe Angeles and wondered what they were. From the vantage point of Juárez, the monumental buildings of the university loomed in the distance like symbols of power.

We walked onto the campus, a place I had never been. I had no idea where we were or where we were going. José, who seemed to know his way around, led us though a large cement courtyard that seemed like a maze. The five of us passed through the university, ended up on Mesa Street, and walked toward downtown. In the distance, we saw a motel, and José talked the couple into paying for a room. I waited outside on the corner while José and the couple went to the motel office. When José returned, he told me that we were finished and that it was time to go home. He stopped and called someone from a pay phone. Then we walked down Mesa Street toward the bridge. The sun was coming up, and we were running on pure adrenaline as the shopkeepers on El Paso Street opened up and swept the sidewalks. José was in a real good mood when we crossed the Santa Fe Street Bridge back into Juárez. We caught a bus to his place in Felipe Angeles and fixed again.

As I look back, the experience seems tremendous. Yet at the time, I never gave it a second thought. I never saw any of the profit that José made, beyond a fix or two; I had accompanied him as a friend rather than as a business partner. Being a coyote was his hustle; being a full-time panhandler was mine. That afternoon, I crossed the bridge back into El Paso and began panhandling again. There was always the next morning's fix to worry about.

NEW PLACES TO CRASH

After I had hung around for a while at Benny's grocery store and the burrito stand in Felipe Angeles, I knew a lot of the people in the neighborhood. Since I caught the bus to El Centro every day, I often sat with people from the neighborhood. Many offered to rent me an apartment or a room, and I turned down a lot of offers. Most times, the rents were too high, and I was happy with my street lifestyle and dependence on José's place. But when José's brother complained about me being around too much, I knew that I had worn out my welcome. I thought about getting another hotel room downtown, but was still unable to decide.

One day, José told me that I couldn't stay that night, and we went and slept on the front porch of one of the abandoned houses in the neighborhood. I used my large canvas clothing bag as a pillow, and the night passed as usual. I think that José was sort of disappointed at the prospect of my leaving. I had shared my dope with him and helped him maintain his habit for most of the summer. By this time, the nights were getting cooler. A blanket would be essential for sleeping outside at night, and some sort of shelter would soon be a necessity.

One night, I returned to José's after copping some dope from next door, and he told me that he had found a nice little abandoned house where we could crash. It was dark by the time we sneaked in through the back door of this little house, but we had two candles and used them to fix that night. The little house had two twin beds, and we were happy to be there, inside and away from the cold. I had forty dollars on me, so I wasn't worried about the next morning's fix, and I planned to go out panhandling anyway. After settling in for the night and drifting off to sleep, we were awakened by loud, crashing sounds. The door was flung open, and flashlights scanned the room. It was the Juárez police. They had kicked in the door to investigate a report. Apparently, one of the neighbors had called the cops after seeing us enter the place. They searched us, found our syringes, and held them up as if they had struck gold. My biggest worry was making sure that I could bring my bag of clothes with me to the police station. The cops let me take my clothes after searching the bag, and José and I were soon handcuffed and sitting in the back of a police car. A three in the morning ride through Juárez in the back of a police car is a bleak experience. The city seemed lifeless as we passed various dark storefronts and closed steel doors.

The police took us to the new *preventivo*, a newly built jail across the street from the old one on Avenida 16 de Septiembre. They reviewed our cases from behind a long counter as we sat on the floor or on benches that lined the back wall. They processed us quickly and whisked us off into the holding cells. José told me that he needed some money, but I was too tired and irritated by the whole scene. I told him and everyone else who was listening that I didn't have any money. When the holding-cell cops came around, they took me out of the cell and asked whether I had any money. I told them that I did, so they took me back into the processing room, where I went up to a window and paid 150 pesos, about fifteen dollars. They gave me my bag of clothes, and I walked out of the police station at around four in the morning.

I walked to a flophouse in downtown Juárez that charged only fifty pesos a night. I didn't like the place; the rooms locked only from the inside, and people could spy into them from the hallway through small Plexiglas windows set in the walls. There was a little red curtain over each window, but it was quite useless for providing privacy. I crashed there for a few hours and then caught the bus back to Felipe Angeles. I still had some money, so I bought a set of works and went to Perico's and got some dope.

I didn't have a place to shoot up, so I went to Laura's (my old girl-friend's) house and hoped that her brother Jorge would be home. As it turned out, he was there with nothing to do. Jorge was an on-and-off kind of junkie who used dope when he could. I shot up there and gave him some dope for letting me use his room. He had a single room apart from the main house, a room that had its own doorway facing the street. Sometimes, when Jorge wasn't there, one of Laura's sisters let me shoot up in the outside bathroom. Since José and I had gone to jail to-gether, and especially since I hadn't bailed him out even though I could have, I figured that I was on the shit list with his family and wouldn't be welcome there again.

After I fixed that morning, I caught the bus to the bridge, walked to El Paso, and panhandled—one of my usual routines. Later on, when I went back to Perico's, José's brother Víctor saw me and asked what had happened the night before. He didn't seem mad, and I told him that if he had some water for us to shoot up with, I would give him a fix. As we walked away from his house, José's other brother emerged and said something aggressive to me. I snapped back at him and he picked up a rock and threw it at me. He missed, and I prepared for the worst. Víc-tor told me to come on and get out of there, and we both took off run-ning down the hill across the street from the front of their house. Víc-tor didn't get along with his other brother and knew it was best just to leave after what happened.

Because Víctor was a junkie, he knew about problems with the po-lice and didn't blame me fully for what had happened. Getting picked up by the cops was an occupational hazard for a junkie, and Víctor seemed willing to put it in the past. We shot up, and I explained to him in detail what had happened. José still hadn't been released yet. When he got out, he would be too sick to care about anything except get-ting a fix. I didn't see José until a few days later, and when he saw me, he acted as if nothing had happened. One morning, he even sneaked me into his place so that we could shoot up again, but I knew that I wouldn't be able to sleep there any more.

One good thing about approaching people and panhandling the way I did was that it allowed me to get to know lots of people. Some people opened up to me, others didn't. One lady who opened up her home to me was a middle-aged woman named Serna. Serna, who appeared to be in her fifties, lived across the street and up the hill from my favorite burrito stand in Felipe Angeles. One day, I helped her carry some grocery bags home, and she invited me in and cooked dinner for me. Serna crossed the bridge almost every day, so she spoke some English. I had first met her while panhandling on the streets of El Paso. Now I told her that I didn't have a place to live and asked her whether I could leave my bags at her house. She offered to let me stay the night. She told me that she had a daughter who had moved away and that she now lived with her mother. Serna was a real good-hearted woman and very religious. She had a two-bedroom house. One bedroom was large, with three beds. The other bedroom was where she slept. Because I had no place to go, I accepted her offer to stay.

Serna told me that she worked for a canning factory in El Paso. She rose every morning at three thirty to prepare for her trip to work. She usually got home around five in the evening. Her workday lasted twelve to thirteen hours, including the time she spent in transit. The first night that I slept there, she told me that she was going out early and that I needed to lock the door when I left. Her mother, who stayed home all day, was afraid to open the door for anyone. So when I left Serna's in the morning, I was out of there until the late afternoon.

I continued to panhandle while living at Serna's, and I came to rely on her place to shelter me from the streets at night. Serna had a lot of clothes and stuff all over the place. Aside from the living room, the rest of the house was jam-packed with all kinds of clothes, pots and pans, and other miscellaneous items. It was also a little dusty, but it was comfortable. I don't know what had impelled her to show me as much benevolence as she did, but I wasn't going to question her generosity. Even though her house did not have central heating, it offered protection from the elements as the autumn nights got cooler. When it got cold, Serna fired up the kitchen stove and cooked something.

While I stayed at Serna's, I kept my dope habit as low key as possible. I stashed my morning fix, a cooker, and a syringe in my clothes bag and usually shot up at her place before I left for the day. The only way that

I could fix was to get permission to use her bathroom to take a shower. Serna's house didn't have a regular bathroom. In an interior courtyard, there was an outhouse room at the very end of a cement passageway. Here was the only bathroom and shower. When she was home, Serna would boil water on the stove so that I didn't have to wash in cold water. Her "shower" consisted of a very large metal container that you stood in, a few pails of water, and a cup that was used to splash water over the head and body.

Pretty soon, as it got colder outside, I started keeping a candle in my bag so that when I fixed, I could melt the dope in a cooker. The best cooker was a spoon, but for preparing a fix in a hurry, the bottom of a Coke can worked better. The candles also came in handy because there was no electricity in the bathroom. I usually woke up, acted as though I were going to take a shower, and then did my morning fix. Then I left, caught the bus downtown, and walked across the bridge to El Paso. I was panhandling from the moment that I walked out her house. I brought in a little bit less money while staying at Serna's, but I didn't need that much, since I was supporting only my own habit. She never asked me for any rent. I always told Serna that I was out looking for a job, but I really had no intention of working. Sometimes, I would give her twenty dollars for groceries, and she would cook a few big meals.

CHILE PICKING

Right before I went to Serna's, while I was staying at José's, someone in El Paso had talked me into going to Deming, New Mexico, on the bracero bus for a day of chile picking. This person told me that I could make as much as fifty dollars a day, so I decided to give it a try. I took a jeringa and a globo with me just in case I felt sick. The bus was scheduled to leave for Deming at three thirty in the morning, so I got to the bracero center on Oregon Street in El Paso's Segundo Barrio around midnight. I found a large piece of cardboard to lie down on for a while. Later that morning, an announcer called out the names of destinations and the types of produce that would be harvested. Buses and vans lined up, and pretty soon I heard the call for workers in Deming. I boarded the bus and tried to relax. The bus headed west on I-10. We soon stopped at a truck stop for a bathroom break and some coffee.

It was still dark when we arrived at the chile fields. As soon as we had our buckets, which were actually medium-size plastic garbage cans, the group rushed the chile fields. As the sun rose that morning, I tried my best to learn how to pick long green California-style chile peppers—*chile California*. There is an art to picking them: you have to be able to locate them quickly on the plant and pick them two at a time. After picking them, you have to break the stems off by simultaneously pushing with each thumb while holding them upright. Finally, you drop the peppers into the bucket and immediately search for two more on the plant.

I tried to follow as quickly as I could, but there was no way I was ever going to be as fast as an experienced picker. I followed behind the group of veteran workers as we picked, and the plants were practically bare by the time I got to them. I had to search harder for the chiles than those working the front of the line, and I fumbled around too much. The work paid seventy-five cents a bucket, but it seemed to take forever to fill the first one. After filling their buckets, the workers ran and handed them up to the guys in a trailer that was pulled by a farm tractor. For each bucket, they gave us a little plastic chip, and each chip was worth seventy-five cents.

I gave it my best try, but by nine, I was looking around for a place to shoot up my morning fix. I had a small gym bag on my back that held a bottle of water and everything else I needed to fix. The only thing I worried about was where I could go to have some privacy. I told the people that I needed to take a crap, and they pointed to a couple of trees way off in the distance. "Fuck it," I thought—if they didn't mind me taking a long enough break to walk over there and fix, I wasn't going to mind either. I walked to the other end of the large chile field until I was next to the trees. I had prepared a syringe outdoors many times; this one was no different. As I shot up, I watched the chile pickers off in the distance, working their way through the endless field that spanned the horizon. I smoked a cigarette, walked back to the group, and started to work again.

There was no lunch break, and everyone in the field seemed to be working with a vigorous fanaticism that would not tolerate any interruption. The little globo that I had shot up was not enough to hold me throughout the day. In Juárez, I used two to four globos every morning. By two thirty, when we stopped working and cashed in our chips, I was feeling down and thinking about my next fix. So far, I had put eleven hours into this deal. The people handed out the cash from the tailgate of an old station wagon. When I cashed in my chips for the day, they counted out nineteen dollars and some change and handed it to me. We waited around until everyone got paid before we got back on the bus.

A few vendors had shown up, selling sodas and cold beers. Most of the people from the bus were drinking and laughing, turning the day's journey into an after-work party. To me, the beer, and even the soda, seemed too expensive to waste hard-earned money on. We reboarded the bus, and what had been a silent and sleepy bunch of people on the trip there became a very talkative and lively group on the way back. Before we left Deming, we stopped at a supermarket, and some of the people from the bus pitched in and bought a couple of cases of beer. Others bought barbeque chicken and chips. As I walked through the supermarket, I thought to myself that for the wages we had been paid, everything in this store was way too expensive. I felt cheated. I had spent the whole day picking chiles for less than twenty dollars. At that point, there was nothing to do but get back to El Paso. As I got on the bus and felt withdrawal pains starting up in my bones, I decided to sit back and just enjoy the ride to El Paso. I wasn't sick yet, but I was beginning to feel that crappy sensation that comes along just before a real bad heroin withdrawal.

As the bus journeyed through the New Mexico countryside, I accepted a beer from someone and guzzled it down. The buzz made me numb enough to participate in a conversation with the braceros. I didn't like to drink, because when the alcohol wore off, heroin withdrawal seemed twice as bad. But by then, it seemed as though everyone on the bus was drinking, laughing, shouting, and telling stories—behaving like people under the influence of alcohol. The people sitting next to me, who had given me the beer, asked the usual questions—where was I from, and so on. Someone suggested that I return to the fields tomorrow, telling me that if I kept it up, I would become more skillful and earn more money. I played along, but knew that I could never work at that type of hard physical job every day in my condition. Between the shouting, the laughing, and the music, I just wanted to get back to El Paso and get off the bus. I didn't realize it until after we arrived, but I was quite dirty from being in the field all day. While working in the field, an infection on one of my feet had become irritated and swollen.

When we got back to El Paso around five that evening, some of the guys from the bus invited me inside the bracero center for a meal. They were having burritos with red chile that day. The center also had showers, and I knew I needed one. When I put my infected foot under the hot water of the shower, it hurt like hell. The people saw the pain that I was in and got one of the staff members to look at me. After helping me bandage the sore, they suggested that I rest on one of the plastic cots in the center. The shower refreshed me, and it felt good that they wanted me to stay. But I knew I needed to get out of there and head home.

I walked across the bridge, back to Juárez, with some of the other braceros. We parted company on Juárez Avenue. By seven, I was shooting up at Jose's. It felt good to be fixed again, and the dope took away all my physical pain. The next day, I returned to my daily panhandling routine; the foot healed itself in time. Every once in a while, someone near the bridge would point to the bracero center and say, "C'mon, lets go over there and get some work." But I believed that I was better off working the streets. A fifteen-hour day picking chiles had paid me nineteen dollars; on a good morning, down by the bridge, I could make that much in one hour. I decided not to work until I was off heroin and healthy enough. Because I was in no hurry to go through the kind of withdrawal pains that I had experienced at Marcelino's the previous January, I just kept doing what had always worked for me.

RUNNING ALONE

While living at Serna's, I never considered pursuing actual work; I knew the pain it would bring me. Insane as it seems, it was easier to continue in my habit than to try to become something that I wasn't ready to be. One day, I was in a little store in Felipe Angeles when a guy from the neighborhood came in and said he needed some help clearing a vacant lot. I worked with him all day, and when it was over, he paid me 100 pesos. That kind of wage wasn't enough to support my habit. Right around then, I realized that panhandling was the only possible way to maintain my habit. Serna never questioned what I did on the street all day. She seemed grateful when I brought her groceries or gave her fifty pesos to buy some eggs and coffee.

Since I couldn't go back to Serna's during the day, I found someplace else to fix during my midday breaks from panhandling. I started catching the bus up to Barrio Magnesio to visit Marcos. Another one of his relatives had set up a bedroom in front of his place in a makeshift house built of plastic and pallets. She and her boyfriend used it as a shooting gallery. During these days, I regularly visited Marcos's, copped a few globos, and fixed before I left. I also dropped in at Pepe's from time to time, and as long as I kicked them down a globo, a new syringe, or at least the cotton, Pepe and Víctor let me use their place to shoot up. They didn't do much during the day. Pepe usually just sat around the house waiting for someone to show up and get him high. I didn't like to go to Pepe's; I associated the place with almost overdosing, passing out on the street, and losing all my money. I also hung out up at Las Moras, and that became one of my regular stops as I sought to distance myself from José and his family.

José had become too dependent on me to help him with his habit. When he wasn't working as a coyote, José shined shoes, and he would often clean my sneakers for a fix. He made good money when he hustled, but he shined shoes in downtown Juárez, and once in a while the local police would hassle him and run him in for having track marks on his arms. I knew his routine. Sometimes we caught the bus downtown together, and he would venture off on his shoe-shining mission while I walked to the bridge for another day of panhandling.

For one reason or another, José acted as if I owed him, and one afternoon we got into a fistfight over it. This happened one day when I went to Jorge's, Laura's brother's place, to shoot up. José was there, and he asked me for some dope. I told him no, and before I knew it, he snatched a globo off the table. I hit him pretty good, and he started hitting back. We rolled around Jorge's place, knocking over the furniture and anything else that was standing. I was so numb from using heroin that I didn't feel anything. When it was over, Jorge complained about the mess we made, and José and I were both a little banged up. We made up right after that, but we were never as tight as we had been over the summer. I ended up giving him a globo after all that because he was getting sick. Afterward, I started to distance myself from him and anyone else who thought that they had some sort of privileged access to my dope. I knew how to run alone if I had to, and I decided I would take care of my own habit as much as possible.

The Plaza Hotel on Calle Ugarte, El Centro, Juárez. Bus lines to west Juárez pick up and drop off passengers on Calle Ugarte. Photograph by Adam Díaz.

View across the U.S. border from Colonia Felipe Angeles, Juárez, Mexico. The University of Texas at El Paso is in the background. Photograph by Adam Díaz.

Left, behind the trees: *The steps to the casita where I lived in Colonia Postal. At the top of the steps is an entrance to a schoolyard on the mesa. Photograph by Adam Díaz.*

The casita from a pathway across the steps, which lead into Colonia Postal. Many of the neighborhood kids often congregated on the steps, especially at night. Photograph by Adam Díaz.

Polo's casita in Colonia Postal, where he dealt chiva. Photograph by Adam Díaz.

Another view of Polo's casita. In 1999, the little house was in better condition. The yard was enclosed by a small picket fence, and there was some shrubbery around the house. Today, the neighboring lots are empty, and the yard is full of garbage. Structures such as this one often serve as shooting galleries. Photograph by Adam Díaz.

El cuarto, Las Canchas. Bottom center: *The window of the room I rented from Martín on Calle Segundo de Ugarte, Juárez. Note the two entranceways on both sides of the structure and the elevated buildings on the terrace above and behind it. Photograph by Adam Díaz.*

Freddy's store, Las Canchas. I often helped Freddy out by doing odd jobs, and I used to catch the bus to Altavista from this corner. Photograph by Adam Díaz.

Puestecitos, Las Canchas. A gordita stand that sometimes gave me free gorditas de picadillo when I passed by in the morning. Behind the stands are basketball courts. Recently, many of those stands have closed because of escalating violence and extortion. Photograph by Adam Díaz.

The view down the hill from José's neighborhood, Felipe Angeles. Below the hill was one of the main connection points for neighborhood junkies. This photo was taken from the spot where I once paid a municipal police officer forty dollars for the freedom of my friend Víctor. Photograph by Adam Díaz.

Looking west at Cerna's house, Felipe Angeles. The ASARCO smokestack rises in the background. Photograph by Adam Díaz.

Front view of Benny's store, Felipe Angeles. Benny still runs the store and was still in good spirits when I talked to him in 2009. Photograph by Adam Díaz.

Another view of Felipe Angeles, looking down at the connection point from José's. Photograph by Adam Díaz.

Burritos Monchis, one of my favorite places in Felipe Angeles. It seems odd that it was closed the morning this photo was taken. It used to bustle with customers, and cars used to line up in front. Photograph by Adam Díaz.

View of Felipe Angeles from UTEP. Center: *José's family's property, above the cable that crosses the photo. Photograph by Scott Comar.*

People walking on El Paso Street in Segundo Barrio near the international bridge. Photograph by Scott Comar.

El Paso Street Bridge, also known as the Santa Fe Street Bridge. It crosses from El Paso Street in El Paso to Juárez Avenue in Juárez. Photograph by Scott Comar.

Under the Santa Fe Street Bridge. The Chihuahuan civil registration office sits in the background. Photograph by Scott Comar.

A view of the Santa Fe Street Bridge from Santa Fe Street in El Paso. The bridge was diverted to El Paso Street in the 1960s. Photograph by Scott Comar.

People gathering around a street vendor at the corner of El Paso and Father Rahm Streets in Segundo Barrio. Photograph by Scott Comar.

Sylvia's, one of my and Joe Huggins's regular stops. It is still one of my favorites. Photograph by Scott Comar.

Walking and shopping by the bridge in Segundo Barrio at Sixth and El Paso Streets. Photograph by Scott Comar.

Stanton Street Bridge, the passageway to Mexico from Stanton Street in El Paso. Photograph by Scott Comar.

People walking and shopping on Stanton Street in El Paso. Photograph by Scott Comar.

Shoppers and pedestrians walking in front of the old Colon movie theatre on El Paso Street. Photograph by Scott Comar.

Oregon Street bus station, at Sixth and Oregon. One of my frequent panhandling stops. Photograph by Scott Comar.

When it's your time it's your time.

In the fall of 2000, Víctor Vásquez returned to the neighborhood. We had been friends since my first week in Juárez in 1998, and when he got back, we hung out together like before. Víctor was like a brother to me, and when he learned about my circumstances, he offered to let me stay at his mom's place with him. Hanging out with Víctor was more appealing to me than trying to hide my habit and conform to Serna's schedule. I told Serna that I was moving to Víctor's, and she wished me luck. Sometimes I would stop by and visit her. She always invited me in and gave me something to eat, or at least a cup of coffee. She enjoyed talking to me, and she knew I would never rip her off. Living with Serna was okay, but if she had known that I was a tecato, it would have been very different. I hid my habit from her, and that is what kept us on good terms.

Life at Víctor's, in Felipe Angeles, very rapidly became problematic. Not because we didn't get along, but because Laura's sister, Víctor's girlfriend, came around practically every night. Víctor was good people, but he had just been released from prison, and he understandably wanted to spend time with his girlfriend. Víctor resolved the problem of finding a place for me to sleep by putting a foam mattress on the roof of his building and giving me a sleeping bag. He told me that I could sleep on the roof when his girlfriend stayed over. I didn't mind, since there was an outdoor public bathroom and shower next to the ladder that led to the rooftop, and I could get up early, shoot up, and hit the streets without bothering anyone.

Víctor had been locked up for a little while; he said that he had been sent to federal prison in the States. He told me that he had learned a lot of English while in prison and that he wanted to keep learning. We made a deal that he would teach me Spanish and I would teach him English. He said that he had been sent to federal prison after being captured by the U.S. Border Patrol while smuggling marijuana. Víctor said that he had fought the officers as they brought him in and that was why he got put away for so long. According to neighborhood folklore, Víctor, Jorge, José, José's brother Víctor, and Marcos from the mission and the construction job were all members of a street-gang called La Quinta. Víctor's older brothers were both in the gang, which was well known on the west side of Juárez, near the river. One of the main dope spots in Colonia Altavista stood upon a hill known as La Quinta Loma because of its affiliation with the gang. The dealers at La Quinta Loma were also involved with the gang, as were Pepe and his brother Víctor, who lived a block away from the hill in Altavista. I once saw a photo of the gang, which included many of the aforementioned members, all of them holding sawed-off shotguns, rifles, and pistols.

My friend Víctor from Felipe Angeles had earned his street reputation through his gang activities, and a lot of the people in the neighborhood probably weren't exactly thrilled that he was back. Víctor had a habit of going out very early in the morning to break into people's cars and houses. He just couldn't support his dope habit without stealing or smuggling. As he became strung out on heroin after his return to the neighborhood, I shared my dope with him as I had done with José. Víctor was very respectful of me, and if something was on his mind, he would let me know. He never expected more from me than I was able to give; he respected my privacy, what little I had; and he expected that same respect in return. His family also welcomed me, and that made living there an easier experience.

Víctor's place was actually his parents' place, which the family had built from scratch. His family was originally from Durango, Mexico, and the father was a master construction worker and homebuilder. The old man made his own cinder blocks from scratch and eventually made many additions to their property in Felipe Angeles. Both of Víctor's brothers worked construction and were very handy at home maintenance. They knew a lot about electrical work and plumbing. One morning while sleeping on the roof, I was awakened by one of his brothers as he connected an electrical line by tapping directly into the main power line in the street. Their family property contained three houses: the main house at the back; one brother's house on the right, where Víctor's brother Gilbert and his wife and children lived; and Víctor's house in the front, which was divided into two apartments: one was Víctor's and the other housed either his sister or his other brother, Gustavo ("Gus").

The family's compound was built like a fort, with a gate at the end of the driveway. The gate opened into the yard that sat between the houses. The family's vehicles were always kept within the yard at night. The father owned a Chevy El Camino, and Gilbert owned an El Camino as well as a Dodge Ram pickup truck. Sometimes when we couldn't find any dope in the neighborhood, Gilbert would give us a ride across town to connect. The family knew I was a junkie, but they never held it against me. I just had to respect them and not shoot up out in the open.

In the courtyard of Víctor's parents' property was a bathroom door and, next to it, a shower-room door. Next to those doors was an old wooden ladder that led to the flat roof. The roof wasn't entirely flat, but was slanted just enough to allow the water to drain off when it rained. I was really happy that it hardly ever rained in Juárez. In the mornings, I would climb down the ladder and fix in the bathroom or shower room. If I wanted to take a shower, there was a hose spigot on the side of the building, and I filled up a bucket of water and used it to splash water over myself, as I had done at Serna's. I never walked around dirty unless I got lazy. A woman across the street cut hair and often gave me credit on a haircut.

Víctor and I didn't hang out together all the time, because I was constantly out panhandling on the street. I made between fifty and eighty dollars a day, seven days a week, and I felt as if I didn't really have time to hang around and do nothing. I usually gave Víctor one globo a day, but if we were hanging out and I had a lot of money on me, I would share what I had with him. I didn't mind hooking Víctor up; I saw him as a friend, and the security of living at his place maintained my habit and kept me functioning so I could continue panhandling. Víctor also hooked me up when he had drugs and always gave what he could.

I usually enjoyed the peace that sleeping on the rooftop offered. I told Víctor that I would rather sleep on the roof, and I slept up there most of the time unless it was raining. When it rained, Víctor would wake me up to go inside his room and sleep on the sofa. Living on the rooftop also enabled me to get up early every morning and start another day of panhandling on the street. I was usually gone during the day, so Víctor's family saw me around only in the evening or very early in the morning. They knew Víctor and I were good friends, so they didn't seem to mind my presence.

All the same, after a month or so of sleeping on the rooftop, I questioned my lifestyle and decided to change my situation. I knew that getting sick was inevitable and that everything was going to catch up with me sooner or later.

VICTORY OUTREACH

Just after Halloween in 2000, I checked myself into another detox program. This time it was the Victory Outreach Men's Home, located off Alameda Avenue on Grimes Court, in the Ysleta area of El Paso's Lower Valley. I learned about the Victory Outreach program from a flyer at the Rescue Mission. One day while I was walking around downtown with my bag full of clothes, I decided to give the number a call and see what would happen. I was in the parking lot of the McDonald's on Paisano Street when a beat-up Dodge van stopped and the driver asked whether I was the guy who called. After telling him I was, I soon found myself bound for Victory Outreach.

I began to wonder what I had gotten myself into when, as soon as I walked through the door, a group of guys wanted to pray for me. I decided to go along with it and soon got to know most of the people at that home. The director's name was Polo, or at least that's what everyone called him. Polo had grown up in Juárez and spoke only Spanish. The assistant director was a large, heavyset, bald guy from Los Angeles, California. He was an ex-gangbanger who had found the Lord and changed his ways. The guys in the home were friendly, and as time went by, I got to know them better. I wasn't sick yet, but that night, Polo asked me whether there was anything that would help ease the withdrawal pains. I just shrugged my shoulders, since I didn't know what to say. A shot of dope maybe? Polo suggested some chocolates and some vitamins. He came back with some vitamins and a drink that he called *suero*. As Polo watched, one of the ex-junkies from the home prepped my vitamin shot and injected me in the buttock with what seemed like a large syringe. He said it would help relieve some of the pain. I later learned that a lot of the pain that hard-core junkies face during withdrawal is due to simple dehydration; suero hydrates the body and replaces a lot of the liquids that are lost from vomiting and diarrhea.

The next day, I started feeling bad. I sat around under a blanket, watching old Mexican cowboy movies on a small black-and-white TV.

I just kind of phased out for the next two days. They shot me up with some more vitamins and gave me more chocolate candies. To my relief, this withdrawal wasn't as bad as my previous one. After I had been there a day or two, the pastor from the local Victory Outreach church came by to check up on me; Polo had told him about me. His name was Felipe González, and he was an ex-junkie who had helped start the Victory Outreach church and rehab program in El Paso.

The guys in the home advised me to take it easy and stay in bed for the first week, but by the second week, I had to participate in the home activities. I quickly became friends with Oscar, the cook, and he let me drink as much coffee as I could handle. The home also had a bunch of muffins that had been donated by a local Good Time Store, and together the coffee and the muffins helped me through this withdrawal. I still had trouble sleeping, but at least the food stayed down long enough for me to have diarrhea. Oscar said that he had been a cook in the Coast Guard, and I was grateful for his cooking experience. The first job that I was assigned was dishwashing, which didn't bother me at all. I was so skinny that I looked just as bad as I had during the last detox.

This was the second major detox that I had endured that year, yet it didn't seem as painful as the first. When I told the guys in the home that, they attributed it to their rehab center being truly blessed (unlike those other, "worldly" rehab centers). They believed that God had lessened my withdrawal pains, and I was inclined to believe it as well. Most of the guys at Victory Outreach were recovering drug addicts, and many of them were ex-junkies. They had been driven them to the home either directly by drugs or indirectly by a lifestyle connected to drugs.

The assistant home director told me that although he had smoked a little weed, he had joined Victory Outreach to escape the violence of his life as a gang member in California. At the end of my first week, I still felt painfully weak, but tried my best to participate in all of the required home activities. I got up at six for an hour of prayer, attended every meal, and stayed out of bed as much as possible during activity hours. I also participated in all church services and Bible studies. Getting used to this type of lifestyle wasn't easy for me, but pretty soon I adjusted. However, I couldn't quite grasp the religious fervor that seemed to drive the guys in the home. Some babbled and spoke in tongues, some shouted out loud during prayer time, and others walked around as if they were possessed by some supernatural power. It all seemed like just too much for me, but the food was good, the people were considerate, and I wasn't healthy enough to leave. I found their church services easier to stomach than those of the Victory in Jesus Men's Home, and I began to enjoy the gospel music that Pastor Beto played.

The more I learned about Victory Outreach, the more I considered it. The only thing that threw me was the religious fanaticism that seemed to motivate everyone. I just didn't understand it enough to fully accept it as concrete truth, yet I got as close to the idea of God as I possibly could. After sitting through enough church services in Spanish, I found that I could understand about half of what was said. Thus, I decided to make the most of it and picked up a Spanish-English dictionary.

Staying at the Victory Outreach men's home may have been a great opportunity, but I just wasn't ready for what they were offering me. I stayed there until I felt that I had enough strength to get along without dope, and then I left. The day I decided to go, the assistant home director and some of the guys tried their best to talk me into staying. They told me that I wasn't ready to go back out into the world, but I refused to believe them. If anything, I just wasn't ready to live in such a rigid environment. If there was to be structure in my life, I wanted to be the one to decide how it would be formulated.

BACK AT JOE'S

When I left the Victory Outreach home that December, I had no idea where I would go or what I would do. It was not until I was on my way back downtown on the bus that I decided to get off a block away from Joe Huggins's moving company. Joe happened to be there, and when he saw me, he seemed pleasantly surprised. I told him that I just cleaned up at rehab. Joe was the kind of guy who would say, "It doesn't matter how many times you fall, just as long as you keep getting back up." I suppose that was how he viewed himself as well as me—as people who got back up. I was lucky to have a friend like Joe, and he put me back to work that day, cleaning the warehouse and helping him out with a shipment.

The last time I had been to Joe's place was after I had walked away from the apartment in El Paso six months earlier. Joe told me what had happened to all the stuff that I left behind in the apartment on Harrison. He had tried to hold it for me in his warehouse, but his old partner, Henry, told him that I wasn't coming back and pillaged my stuff, taking whatever he thought he could use. Henry later apologized to me and admitted that it was true; they really didn't think I was coming back. I just laughed and told them that if I had really cared about that stuff, I would have never walked away and left it behind. After all that I had been through, I could not have cared less about a box full of pots and pans, papers, and some scraggly old rug. Anyway, I had sold anything worth selling before I left in order to feed my habit.

At first, Joe let me sleep in an old refrigerated freight trailer that he had converted into a crash pad. I didn't mind this, because he left me the keys to the warehouse, which had a shower with hot running water. The trailer had electricity and was warm because, as an old refrigerated trailer, it was well insulated. The inside of the trailer was partitioned off into two sections, both of which were carpeted and finished with paneled walls. The rear half was used to store moving equipment. The front half was fully furnished with plush sofas, a nice television, and a stereo. Joe used it as his crash pad away from home, and I knew that he still trusted me when he was willing to let me stay there. I got used to waking up early in order to open the warehouse before Joe got there in the morning. Joe usually showed up a few minutes after I got out of the shower, and then took me to breakfast. There are a lot of small burrito stands and restaurants around central El Paso, where Joe's warehouse was located, and our favorite stops were the California Café and Sylvia's. Joe always bragged that they had the best breakfasts in town, and I agreed with him.

I stayed at the warehouse the first weekend after I left Victory Outreach, and when I had a chance, I went back to Juárez to get high and roam around a little bit. I walked over to Pepe's one night, and when I got there, there must have been twenty candles burning while they all shot dope and nodded out. Pepe was very thin, like a concentration camp inmate, but I didn't think much about it; most junkies who have been on a run for a long time lose a lot of weight. Whenever I entered a detox program after a run, I also looked like I had just stepped out of a concentration camp. Still, whenever I went to Pepe's to shoot up, I always stopped at the pharmacy and bought a couple of new insulin syringes, one for him and one for me. I shot dope that Sunday and then went back to the trailer and slept it off.

That week, I worked it off and decided I would try to stay away from Juárez for a while. In a way, I missed Mexico and life on the street. Even with as much freedom as I knew that I had with Joe, I still felt trapped by working at the warehouse and sleeping there too. I knew that Joe's idea of helping me out was the best thing that I had going for me at the time, so I decided to go along, keep an open mind, and see what happened. Joe sold tie-dyed T-shirts on the weekends, and he wanted me to help him sell shirts at the little fairs and gatherings where he set up his booth. I thought it was a nice idea, so the next weekend, I went home with him, slept in the spare bedroom that he had in his basement, and helped him and his wife, Cary, sell shirts.

The shirt business was a departure from the moving business, and Joe had set up a part of his warehouse as a place to manufacture tie-dyed shirts, blankets, etc. He had a complete coloring section with washing machines and dryers. Joe's mom had taught him how to tie-dye shirts, and he seemed content with the money that they brought in. When the moving business lagged, as it always did after the first of December, Joe planned to go all out with his shirt business, and he showed me how to tie-dye shirts, socks, and practically anything else made of cloth. He picked up white T-shirts and clothing from the Goodwill store and similar places, colored them at the warehouse, and sold them on the weekends. I gave it a try, and pretty soon I was making pretty good tie-dyed shirts myself.

As the holiday season approached, I spent a lot of time at Joe's house with his family. Joe's wife was a strict vegetarian, and Joe claimed to be one too. She turned me on to soy burgers and told me that meat was not good for people. I got used to the vegetarian diet at Joe's place, but every morning after we left for the warehouse, Joe loved to stop for breakfast or breakfast burritos. Nevertheless, I got used to eating soy and salads, and I trusted his wife's judgment, since she was a registered nurse.

While staying at Joe's, I sneaked off to Juárez and shot up a few times, but I didn't make it a habit. Joe knew a lot about the drug life, he knew me, and he joked around, sometimes seriously insinuating that if I went missing in action, he would know that I had gone to Juárez to get another fix. I still felt the desire to get high. Even though I had some misgivings about using dope, there wasn't much that could be said or done to talk me out of it. I spent that Christmas with Joe and his family, and he did his best to make me feel at home.

After Christmas, Joe told me that I needed to live at the warehouse and keep working. He agreed to pay me seven dollars an hour for all the time I put in. His goal was for me to get another place and try to start over. In the evenings, I often crossed over to Juárez and shot up at

Pepe's. I thought nothing of it. I caught the bus there, shot up, and then walked back home to the warehouse. I wasn't hooked yet, but I was beginning to become more and more obsessed with shooting heroin. It was again becoming my favorite recreational activity.

Joe's partner, Henry, surprised me soon afterward when he took me to a fully furnished apartment that he had helped one of his cronies, another guy who worked for him and Joe, put together. The guy had taken off, and since Henry had a lot of his own stuff stored at that apartment, he kept renting it. Henry told me that he would let me move in if I would pay the rent, and I gladly accepted. I felt kind of funny when I noticed that the sheets on the bed were the same sheets that I had left at the apartment on Harrison the previous July. This apartment was on Grandview Terrace in El Paso. My first day there I had the gas and electricity turned on. The water was included in the rent, which was $350 monthly. I met the landlord, and he just smiled and shook my hand. I wasn't sure about staying there, but it sure seemed as if things had turned in my favor.

Looking back, it's obvious to me that Joe and Henry were the best friends that a guy who was down on his luck could have asked for. The looming problem was that I was going to Juárez every day after work to shoot up, and after a while, I started to become dependent on dope again. I mostly went over to Pepe's because there seemed to be a constant connection at La Quinta Loma, which was a block from his place. One cold night when I went to Pepe's to shoot up, he had about fifteen candles lit because the power was out. In the candlelight, Pepe's visage looked like something from a horror movie. He was all skin and bones, like someone close to death.

After crossing to Juárez and shooting up after work, I always walked back to my apartment, which was located in central El Paso near Montana and Cotton. Increasingly, my nights were consumed by the need to go to Juárez and fix. Once in a while on those evenings, I went back to Felipe Angeles to shoot up. Víctor, my *compañero*, had disappeared again. He had been arrested and was doing time in the local prison in Juárez known as the CERESO. I knew that when Víctor was down and his habit was getting to him, he would often resort to robbery and burglary, so it was likely that he had been convicted for something along those lines. When I went to Felipe Angeles I usually passed by José's. Even though it meant giving him a fix, he would always invite me in so that I could shoot up in his room. His family had forgotten any grudges that they may have held against me, and they were behind closed doors anyway, since the weather that winter was quite cold. As this went on, I became hooked again and started to sneak globos back to El Paso, where I took them with me to work and fixed in the bathroom.

The final downfall for anyone who messes with heroin begins when they start shooting up early in the morning every day. I had soon fallen back into this pattern, and maintaining my job and my habit soon over-burdened me. I did moving jobs whenever they came in, and soon I was shooting dope in the customers' bathrooms. The dope helped me work harder. I'm sure that most customers never really thought any-thing about my lengthy visits to the bathroom.

What was really problematic was when money started to get tight and I would show up to work broke and with no dope. The whole day I would rack my brain for ways to get some extra money. I told one customer that I worked for tips; on another job, I practically demanded twenty dollars from someone who wanted us to move an old refrigera-tor, from a previous tenant, into his basement. Every day after work, I made an urgent trip to Juárez, as if I were living there again, and every night I journeyed back to the apartment.

The only thing that disrupted the pattern was when I didn't have money. It wasn't long before I started panhandling after work in order to get enough money to fix. One night it was eight o'clock before I had scraped up enough to score some dope for that night and the next day. The reason it took so long to make ten or fifteen dollars was that in-stead of working my usual area near the bridge, I had tried to panhan-dle on Montana Street near my apartment. It was cold, and people were hard to deal with at that time and in that space.

One night, by the time I had enough money, an old man in a pickup up truck offered me a ride to the bridge. That night, I went to Pepe's and fixed, better late than never. Pepe and his brother Víctor often stayed up very late, sometimes all night, because many of the junkies who went there also shot cocaine. Pepe's little shooting gallery became a daily stop for me. If Pepe wasn't around, his brother Víctor always let me in to shoot up. After a while, as always, whenever I tried to mix work with my drug habit, things began to break down. I began show-ing up late and leaving work early, sometimes around noontime. Go-ing to work dope-sick was painful. It meant going through withdrawal pains while trying to look normal. In the moving business, this was difficult, even impossible, and I would have rather walked away from the warehouse than gone to a job site feeling sick.

Some of those afternoons, I started panhandling the moment I walked off the job. By the time I got downtown, I usually had a few dollars already, and this meant wasting less time walking around and trying to talk people out of their money. One morning in February 2001, I woke up and decided that it had all become too much. I checked myself back into the Victory Outreach program.

ANOTHER SHOT AT VICTORY

Back at the Victory Outreach Men's Home in Ysleta, I just wanted to get through the withdrawal and rest. Working and maintaining a dope habit at the same time had exhausted me. One of the main reasons I checked back into Victory Outreach was that I felt that there was no place else to go. I could have gone to the Rescue Mission, but going through heroin withdrawal there would have been a lot worse than at the home. Polo, the home director, gave me the vitamin shots, and I braced myself for a few weeks of withdrawal pains. The withdrawal was difficult, but I had been through worse. The hardest part was trying to sleep at night. Many nights I just lay there motionless, my ears ringing. I tossed and turned as I tried to ignore the burning and stinging sensations deep within my bones.

By my third week there, I found myself waking up in the morning instead of listening to everyone else wake up. The Victory Outreach home had four bedrooms with two bunk beds in each room. Additional beds were stored in a garage in the backyard. A fifth bedroom was used by the home director, and this room also held the paperwork and personal belongings for program participants. Part of the sign-in process involved surrendering your ID and any other personal belongings that needed to be safeguarded. Even something as simple as mouthwash or aftershave had to be carefully looked after. One day, a guy who checked in to detox drank a bottle of aftershave and washed it down with some mouthwash. Subsequently, an ambulance took him to the emergency room, and we never saw him again. As for me, I was serious about cleaning up and just went along with everything that the administration told me that I had to do. As I felt my health improving, I decided to stay there for a while and learn for myself what this place was all about, to give it a try.

I always woke up early and looked forward to the morning coffee. The front room of the home was the chapel, cafeteria, and living room all rolled into one. Every morning, the folding chairs had to be set up for a prayer service. After that, the chairs were rearranged around a couple of long folding tables for breakfast. Then we put the chairs back into rows for the morning classes and Bible study. At about midmorning, all the chairs and tables were put away and the whole house participated in talacha, or housecleaning. Afterward, the tables and chairs were set up again for lunch, and so on. This routine continued every day except Sunday. Sunday was all about church services and fellowship with church members. Residents of the home sat in the front two rows of the church during services. The home was also supposed to provide assistance to the pastors and parishioners and help set up and clean the church.

There was a big emphasis on prayer, and I caught on right away that getting along at the home meant being an active participant in praise and prayer. At first it was difficult for me to pray at all, then, slowly, I got into it and started to pray out loud. It seemed to me as if the only thing I was doing was loudly expressing my pent-up frustrations. I also sang along with all the church songs and learned as many as I could. The singing made everything seem fun, and praying out loud helped pass the hours of prayer that would have otherwise been spent just sitting there, waiting for the ruckus to subside. At times, the prayers seemed to make sense, but I always had to laugh at myself when I spoke in tongues. All and all, participating in church activities helped pass the time in the program, but it was my development of interpersonal relationships with other members that really made the time pass by smoothly. After about a month at the home, it seemed as if I were becoming institutionalized.

Polo tried to break up the monotony by taking us out on evangelizing field trips to downtown El Paso. On these trips, they gave each of us a handful of flyers and told us to partner up, walk around, pass out flyers, and, if we felt especially ambitious, pray for someone. Handing out flyers was kind of like panhandling without trying to get money from people. Once in a while someone would donate few dollars and tell us that it was a blessing. The freedom of being allowed to walk around for part of the day was the best thing about these missions; they helped dissolve the tensions that arose from time to time within the home.

One day, we were taken downtown and instructed to return to San Jacinto Plaza, where the van was parked, at a specific time. My partner that day was one of the younger guys in the program, and I talked him into going to Juárez with me. We weren't supposed to have our wallets, but we had them anyway. This was one of the rules that were often overlooked. I think they let us carry our wallets so that we didn't feel like prisoners at the home. Some of the guys there had done time in prison, and letting us carry our wallets and identifications reduced the stigma of living in a controlled environment. Although we were free to go whenever we wanted to, most of us had no place to go that would provide the stability and support that we found at Victory Outreach. So on that day, the two of us walked over the bridge into Juárez, handed out flyers, and enjoyed the sunshine. In Juárez, we got some tacos, and I visited Chito's. Chito seemed ambivalent about us being on an outreach mission for a church. He responded to us in a "that's nice" sort of way.

We walked back to El Paso and hung around until everyone else returned to the van. Some of the guys in the home used these breaks as opportunities to shoot up, but that seemed too petty to me, so I didn't try to fix while I was in the home. After all, if I really wanted to get high, I would have just walked out. Polo also took us to play baseball at the Valle Verde Campus of El Paso Community College. This was always a nice way to relieve some stress, and I also enjoyed playing handball on the courts there. As time passed at the home, Polo trusted us enough to let us walk through the neighborhood on our own. As long as we were on time for all the home's activities, we were allowed to go for walks. Sometimes at night we walked to the local park and played basketball. All this helped me forget the drama of the recent heroin withdrawal and also put me in good physical shape.

Victory Outreach is a worldwide network of churches and men's and women's homes. The ministry recruits from within, and some of the junkies that walk through their doors eventually become pastors and home directors in one of their locations. They mentioned to me that I could possibly be sent to do outreach work in South America! El Paso didn't have a women's home, but other cities did. Some of the guys in the home would joke around and talk about how they needed one here! One weekend, we took a road trip to Albuquerque. The ride north was a nice break from our daily routine. When we arrived, we stayed at the Albuquerque Victory Outreach Men's Home. I realized how big the organization was when we arrived at a large church and saw the groups from different men's and women's homes filling the pews.

While I felt good at Victory Outreach and learned a lot from the experience, I also felt apart and distant from everything around me. By that time, I had begun to write some of my thoughts in a journal. I was feeling more confident in my spiritual journey, and it showed when I boldly sang and prayed with the other guys from the El Paso home.

I played the part that the home required me to play rather well. And then just when it seemed I had become a good example of everything that the home was all about, I woke up one morning and decided that it was time for me to go. I had become so consumed by the praying and singing that my voice was hoarse and my throat was sore. The Christian routine was wearing me out. In reality, I had worn myself out by trying to become noticed as a dedicated participant in all those church activities, yet the person I truly was deep inside didn't fully accept the act that I was putting on day after day. I had given the home a try, and now I decided to stop trying.

One morning in April 2001, I got up early, as usual, packed my bags, and walked out the front door. There was nothing to say to anyone, and I knew that talking about leaving would only upset those who would try to convince me to stay. As I reached the street, Polo came out of the house and asked me if I was leaving. I told him, "Thanks for everything," and kept walking. I walked out to Alameda Avenue, asked a few people for bus fare, and caught the bus downtown. That afternoon, I checked myself into the Rescue Mission. While at Victory Outreach, I had gained a lot of weight and restored a lot of my physical strength. Once again, I felt confident that I could start out and make it on my own.

THE LURE OF JUÁREZ OVERPOWERS ME AGAIN

I knew the routine at the mission, and the first thing I did was to go out and look for work moving furniture. Summer was quickly approaching, and I knew that the moving business would be busy around that time. I decided to look for a job with a company that could pay me what I was worth. Joe was a good guy and all, but when I worked for him, it was like working as an indentured servant. This time around, I wanted more money. I had started working in the moving business when I was eighteen years old. By the time I was nineteen, I had a tractor-trailer license and was a member of the Teamsters. A few years later I had bought and paid for my first truck and was hauling furniture across country. Since I was in such good physical shape, and I truly believed that God wanted something good for me, I was going to try to get the best possible moving job that I could find in El Paso. I found it, soon enough, at a local Allied Van Lines agent that did a lot of military and civilian moving jobs. I fit right in at Allied, and when a dispatcher asked a driver about how well I worked, the driver responded, "You got the right one, baby."

I worked every day except Sunday, although once in a while I had Saturdays off too. I stayed at the mission and took a bus to and from work. The job paid good for a moving job in El Paso, and considering the hours I put in, it wasn't long before I had more money in my pocket than I had had in years. The paychecks came to three hundred to five hundred dollars a week. I knew a lot about the moving and storage business, and the people at the company liked me enough to keep me working six days a week. It wasn't long before I was out of the mission. Yet despite all the opportunities available to me, I wound up back in Juárez, renting a room from Víctor's mom.

One morning, I had gone to Juárez to look for Víctor. I felt like visiting, and the mission was a dreary place to hang around. When I got to Víctor's house in Felipe Angeles, his family told me that he was still locked up in the CERESO. It was early in the day, and Víctor's mother asked whether I wanted to go with her to visit him. She visited him every Saturday. We caught the bus from Felipe Angeles to downtown and then transferred to another bus that took us directly to the CERESO. When we got there, we went through the check-in and waited for Víctor in an outdoor entranceway surrounded by a barred fence. There were a lot of inmates around, some trying to bum change or sell candy. Víctor's mom gave one of them a couple of pesos. But once Víctor showed up, they shied away and left us alone. I gave Víctor twenty dollars and told him not to worry about it. When I told Víctor and his mom that I was working, she offered to rent me Víctor's old room. The bus ride back downtown was refreshing after visiting the prison.

With my new job, I could have rented a room practically anywhere in El Paso or Juárez, and moving back to Víctor's surely wasn't the best decision. I was keeping a journal, and on 23 April 2001, I wrote this entry:

> Well today I am very happy. Its my 1st night back in Mexico and in my own room . . . The rent is very reasonable 35 dollars a month [350 pesos] . . . I went to visit Víctor in the CERESO and he told me about the room. So I went to talk

to his family [since the room is in their hacienda] and they painted it and I moved in. I feel very fortunate they rented it to me. It ain't much but its better than life at the mission. I will have to wake up early to make it to work but that's no problem. Take a bucket shower with cold water. Its better than showering with five guys at the same time and I don't have to smell their farts all night. And you know I couldn't stand that bed next to the bathroom either. It smelled and I hate living with those guys all dirty and smelly and all.

It seemed that I had set myself up to get strung out again. I had started shooting up after work, but I was in good shape and kept telling myself that I could control my addiction and stop after that shot. The problem was that it was a lie. My journal entry for 25 April:

> I slipped this week and it needs to stop. I need money in the bank but not in the drug dealers bank . . . I took my first bucket shower today and it wasn't that bad. As a matter of fact it was better than I thought it would be . . . I went to Angelica's house after work and she and her brother Jorge were both dopesick. It sucks because I like her and I would like her to be my novia (vieja) pero I don't know if she will ever totally clean up and I guess the same goes for me . . . Oh yea today after work I went downtown and ran into Joe Huggins. I was surprised to find out he's not mad at me no more and you know I was happy to see him again. He invited me to a party at the thirteenth floor of a building downtown and it turned out to be the El Paso Buzzards [the local hockey team] and I met the owner and director of the team and it was a'lright. We drank and laughed and it felt good to meet some new people and eat bagel sandwiches. I realized I would rather have Joe as a friend than as a boss.

I ran into a young girl named Angelica one day when I was copping dope from Kiko's and asked her if she shot up. She denied it and told me that the dope was for her brother. I think that she shot up, but tried to hide it as much as she could. From the way she looked, she probably did not use heroin that much. Her brother Jorge was a junkie for sure. After I got to know him, I frequently saw him around all the neighborhood dope spots. Angelica and Jorge lived with their mom across the river from ASARCO, at the far end of Felipe Angeles in an area known as Anapra. I used to visit them once in a while, and we spent our time shooting up, nodding out, smoking cigarettes, and talking.

I began shooting up the first day that I moved back to Juárez. I tried to keep it down to one globo a day, after work, and for the first week or so, I kept telling myself that I wasn't sick. However, it wasn't long before my body started feeling funny and my dependency on dope began increasing. On 2 May 2001, I wrote:

> Well sad to say today I am slippin into an addiction and so soon after starting my job and all. I am scared to tell anybody anything, but I need help. Maybe a few days to clean my system will be all I need because I haven't been using that much. This weekend I will try to break [the habit]. I better break because I want to go to work Monday morning clean and ready. I hope there is no work on Saturday so I will use Friday morning and that will be the last fix for my weekend withdrawal . . . Lately at work I have been feeling tired and sick and I don't want to go through withdrawals on my new job.

Renting the room from Víctor's mom had seemed like a good deal at the time. I was making good money, and the rent hardly cut into it. That meant lots of extra money for food and heroin. I didn't expect much out of life; the only things that made me happy were the simple pleasures of shooting up, drinking sodas, and smoking cigarettes. On average, I would go through two packs a day of unfiltered Mexican cigarettes. The room at Víctor's had an outside door that opened onto the driveway, next to the front gate. It had a bed, an overstuffed chair, and a small nightstand. While I was there, I learned to live out of my bags and always had clean clothes. Víctor's sister often washed my clothes for fifty pesos, and there was a Laundromat ten minutes away. Sometimes I carried my duffle bag full of dirty clothes to the Laundromat and enjoyed the reprieve that washing them offered. But I went only when I really needed clean clothes and had extra money to wash them.

Víctor's family lived about a block away from José's, but José did not visit often because Víctor's family didn't like him. Dope was easily accessible at Víctor's, and my habit quickly progressed. My room was a five-minute walk from Kiko's and about a half-hour round trip to Las

Moras. Soon, I began using dope early in the morning and after work. Consequently, I found myself repeating the same pattern as before, trying to juggle a job and a habit at the same time.

I was still in good physical shape, and working in the moving business kept me busy. But I was lying to myself by thinking that I could detox at Víctor's over the weekend. Eventually, every morning I woke up feeling sick and needing to use. At that stage, wake-up fixes become a necessity. Telling myself that I would pull out of it, I continued with my daily routine of catching the bus from Felipe Angeles to the bridge, walking over to El Paso and catching the bus to the Cielo Vista bus terminal, and then walking another mile to the moving job. There was a bus that ran from the east side terminal to a street corner near the warehouse, but it didn't always run on time and sometimes didn't show up at all. One of the guys from work offered to pick me up downtown in the morning if I could meet him at the end of an I-10 exit ramp. After work, someone from the job usually gave me a ride to the east El Paso bus terminal. From there I caught the bus downtown, walked back over the bridge to Juárez, and caught another bus back to Felipe Angeles.

This type of daily transit routine is normal for the many workers who cross the border from Juárez to El Paso and then back again each day. Every morning, the bridge was (and still is) very busy, full of pedestrians heading to work to make a living and support their families. I never felt sorry for myself after I saw older men and women walk across the bridge to find work in El Paso. These people had experienced the hardships of life firsthand. When I compared myself to others, my situation didn't seem so bad. I used these kinds of comparisons to justify my actions, forgetting that I was a junkie, an addict.

Nevertheless, at some level, I knew that I was going in a bad direction. On 15 May 2001, I confided to my journal:

> Sometimes I wonder if I made the right choice in leaving Victory Outreach so soon . . . All the extra money seems to be going down the drain. I was hoping on the weekends I would not use and would clean up my act but unfortunately its not working out that way and when I have extra money on the weekends I find excuses to use. During the weekday I don't want to go to work sick and weak and I don't want to be going through withdrawals on the job so I am using early in the morning and in the evening when I get off

work. I have trapped myself again and to keep my job and my place I must function everyday especially in the morning. This weekend coming up I will try to break for Friday night Sat. and Sunday. If I'm real sick I will use a little to get me by at work on Monday–Friday but then for the next weekend I will deny myself again. I know it sounds good on paper but really doing it is something else.

While renting the room from Víctor's mom, I developed a preoccupation with time. I always wanted to be at work on time, and my time always needed to be used to the fullest so that I could keep up with my habit. I had two clocks: a windup alarm clock and a small clock radio.

One weekend, I bought a boom box at one of the local swap meets held every weekend in the middle of Felipe Angeles. This flea market was a big event. Hundreds of people and entire families would set up small booths and tents and sell everything from tacos and menudo to clothes and tools. I liked to shoot up and then walk around and check out the interesting stands. Once in while, I bought a used shirt or pair of pants. When I eventually stopped working, I panhandled at this same flea market. But at that time, I had money in my pocket, so I explored the different booths, tried the food, and talked to the people. There were always lots of people there, and Saturday was the best day of the week for making money on the street. That's probably why the flea market at Felipe Angeles was always so crowded. Colonia Altavista also had a weekend street market, but it wasn't as big as the one in Felipe Angeles, which was held in a large open lot and extended down into the side streets of the neighborhood.

On 19 May 2001, I wrote:

> Today I bought a little boom box for $30.00 used in the swap meet they have every weekend. It's nice and when I get some wire for the speakers I will separate them and put them in each corner of the room . . . I need to get a grip on this situation and start using less . . . I am really disappointed because I am getting addicted again and I worked so hard to get this far . . . Damn smoke in my eye from this cigarro . . . Its good to be working but this job is so demanding and they are talking about long days and the fucking warehouse everyday after we do our daily work. For me to get clean again I don't know how its going to happen

but a good four day weekend is what I am going to need. Well I am falling asleep as I am writing this, and I just woke up and when I am sitting up my upper back is fuckin with me . . . Well I am getting tired of writing and all. I know I am better off staying home and that if I go downtown I will be wasting $ but I feel I should have bought some sodas and stuff. Maybe next weekend I will buy a TV set. But if I hit the cantina, I'll end up spending money on nothing.

Besides the inexpensive rent, I really didn't have a justifiable reason for moving back to Juárez. Aside from the cheap and easy access to heroin, I wanted to live in Juárez for reasons other than the superficial excuses that I often told people when they asked me why I lived there. I liked Mexico because it was different. Yes, the simple things like food and shelter were less expensive, but for me, living in Mexico represented an opportunity to experience life outside the rat race of the American way. I believed that whether or not I was a junkie, I would never have the money necessary to really own anything, regardless of where I lived. Dope numbed my sense of self so much that I stopped caring about anything beyond the daily necessities of my existence as an addict. The moving job was good for putting some quick cash in my pocket, but working as laborer would never provide me with enough money to move beyond the poverty level, especially if I had to live in El Paso. Juárez gave me enough economic breathing room to live as I wanted, messed up as I was, in a sort of societal chasm: a hidden interstice between and within the two social economies on the border. Juárez was a place that enabled me to be who I was and to persist as a junkie.

As moving season approached, the job demanded more from all the drivers and helpers. Sometimes I worked until nine at night or even later. This wreaked havoc on my body; my habit required me to shoot up at least twice a day in order to function normally, once in the morning and once in the afternoon. When I worked until nine, I experienced all kinds of misery: early withdrawal pains and the risk and anxiety of trying to find dope in Juárez when I returned there. Getting off work late, catching the bus downtown, and walking across the bridge was a real drag when I was starting to get dope-sick; and it only got worse when the local dealers were dry. This always meant that I had to stay up late and find something somewhere else on the street so that I could sleep and make it to work the next day. As before, I found myself trying to juggle my habit with my job, and in the end, the drug habit always won.

Eventually I started shooting up on the job, and that made work a little easier to handle. I often fixed in gas station bathrooms and got some angry looks from the people waiting outside to use them; constant knocks on the door signified their anxious desperation as I patiently cooked the dope in a spoon, drew it into the syringe, and found a vein.

The guys I worked with always wondered why I took so long in the bathroom. But I worked fast and had experience, so they didn't complain. Some of them knew I was strung out. They could tell from my beady eyes and my constant cigarette smoking. Most of the guys at the moving business had either directly or indirectly been affected by drugs, and heroin addiction had likely touched some them at least once in their lives. At the warehouse in the morning, one of the guys often joked with me, saying, "*¿Arreglastes?*" ("Did you fix yourself?"). When I made long visits to customers' bathrooms, many of the guys I worked with knew what I was up to. I tried to maintain my habit as much as I could, but there were still days when dope was scarce or I got caught out without enough to make it through.

On 25 May 2001, at 12:57 a.m., I wrote:

> I'm fucked up now and I cant fuckin believe I got to work Saturday morning . . . Yea lately I haven't been getting home until 8:00–9:00. I don't like working late . . . Tonite when I went to go cop la policía me pasaron en la pinche calle [the police passed me in the street] and then layed for me and I know they were hoping to take me off [rob me]. So I gave José 200 pesos and sent him down to cop 4 globos[.] Yea the same fuckin cops that were laying for me stopped him and took the money. Poor kid, he started arguing with the cops, saying that it wasn't his money. Then the sucker went and told the cops it was my money and called me down to confirm his story. What a stupid cat. What did he expect, me to run down there and say here I am yea its my money and the dope is for me? Oh and by the way I just got paid today so steal my paycheck while y'all is at it. Well, they took the money and he comes back crying, "why didn't I go down there?" and admit I'm fucked up and he isn't, yea right.

My delusional ramblings reveal how insane the lifestyle really was. I was under the influence when I wrote that entry. After all that, José and I ended up getting some dope, and I eventually made it back to the sanctuary of my room.

Most of the time connecting with a dope dealer was smooth and easy, but there were always times of uncertainty and unexpected surprises. I wanted to avoid surprises as much as possible. As spring turned to summer, my habit became worse, but I continued to work. As I became sicker and more strung out, the moving company seemed to expect less from me. By then, I was often walking off the job at lunchtime or as soon as a job was complete, and then writing my time on my time card the next morning. I expected the company to fire me, but it didn't. Things were so busy that it needed every worker it could get. Other times, I worked all day and just punched out and left as soon as we got back to the warehouse. In my mind, that was how it was supposed to be, and with withdrawal setting in at five, volunteering to work three more hours was the last thing I wanted to do. I would rather walk off the job, catch the bus, and go fix than put myself through more withdrawal pains than I felt were necessary.

Being clean-shaven was important for a panhandler in the bridge area.

The nice thing about living with Víctor's family was that when I wasn't home, they watched my room. Elsewhere in Juárez, there was always the possibility that someone would have cased my place, broken in, and cleaned me out. One weekend as I walked through the neighborhood, I was almost attacked by a group of vigilantes who accused me of stealing a radio. After questioning me, they persuaded me to walk to the door of a nearby house where they asked an old woman and someone else inside, "Is he the one?" One of them had a baseball bat, and I knew that if I fought them, I would lose. I decided to go along and only fight as a last resort. Luckily, it didn't come to that. When we got to the door, the old woman took off screaming, and a young guy came to the front door, looked at me, and told the gang, "No, it wasn't him!" The vigilantes let me go.

Down at Perico's later that day, all the guys there told me that *algunos vatos andaban buscando para ti* ("Some cats had been looking for you") because of a stolen radio. I told them that I knew all about it and that it had been resolved. Since I lived at Víctor's and Víctor had a reputation as a thief, there may have been some confusion that marked me as a suspect. The whole incident blew over, and I was just glad that the young guy at that door denied my involvement in whatever was going on.

No one from the neighborhood came around my room to start trouble with me, and Víctor's family was not one to be messed with. His brother Gilbert, who lived right next door to me, was in the Mexican Army and kept a sidearm in his house. Víctor once told me that back in the days of the local gang wars, his brother had used a shotgun against another gang. While I lived there, there didn't seem to be a lot of violence in Juárez, and if there was, I wasn't around when it happened. I usually just minded my own business. Keeping up my habit and making it to work everyday took all of my time and energy.

By late June, I was thinking about trying to detox again. I spoke with my boss at work and confessed everything. He understood my position and respected me for telling the truth. Because of a lag in pay periods, the company owed me a full week's pay, so I knew that I would have some money when I got out of whatever facility I decided to go to. A journal entry I wrote at the end of August summarizes several attempts to detox over the summer:

> If only I would have stayed off dope when I had the job. They even gave me a second chance at Allied. All's I had to do was leave the needle alone. When I went back to v/outreach in June I had the strength and the chance to get it right but I stayed 2½ days and took off with 400 pesos in my pocket and over 500 dollars in checks waiting for me at work[.] How did I ever expect to stay clean. By the end of that week I had 7–8 hundred dollars in my wallet but I also had a monster of a dope addiction holding me back. So I stopped going to work and it was an instant replay of last summer all over again. 3 wks later I was broke and living in Juárez. And to make it all worse [it happened while I was living] in Víctor's room which he wanted when he got out of jail. At least the rent was only 35 dollars a month. But I now know I would have been way better off living in El Paso and paying the higher rent and should have kept working. Not panhandling like I do everyday now. Even the money panhandling at 40–50 dollars a day could have gone for something better, but it's the drugs. They suck my pockets dry and are killing me [specifically heroin]. I am so skinny now it scares me when I look in the mirror. I should have stayed in the mission [and] saved some loot, stayed clean and maybe I wouldn't be in this mess right now. I should have stayed away from Juárez and maybe I would have been alright[.] I knew the room at Víctor's was a time bomb but I desperately wanted to be free but now I'm not free. Forced to panhandle every day to survive and support my habit its really turning worse than bet-

ter. So the end of July I went back to Victory Outreach, skinnier than before. I lasted two days and Sunday morning I was out of there. They went to church and I went to panhandle. I wish those church homes gave us medicine to take away the pain, a little methadone or something to make it through the hard days of my withdrawal from Heroin. Although I really hate to think of withdrawing from methadone one more time. But if I would have followed the program instead of relapsing maybe it would not have been this bad. There is one rehab center in El Paso that could help me but its so hard to get in and so far on the east side [that] I don't know if buses run there or not. I wish I knew someone with a car. Maybe I should call up the methadone clinic on the phone and find out what they say. I need help and I'm scared, I'm so skinny and strung out and there's no place to go . . . But anyway I'm here now and I'm all alone. So to catch up in time its getting to be the end of August and I went to Marcelino's Victory in Jesus home . . . I was skinnier when I left there than when I went in . . . I don't think I'm ever going back there . . . I went in on Mon[day] and left on Friday [.] When I got off the bus downtown I panhandled some money and went back to my room in Juárez at Víctor's moms house. I thought at least here I can have some peace. I did have a moments peace that day and I shot up a couple [of] globos, but when I talked to Víctor's mom my peace started to fade away as I learned Víctor was coming back that afternoon . . . Great, well he came and it was all good for the first 3 hours[.] [T]hen when I tried to sleep he was up all night shooting cocaine and [running] in and out [of the room] and I knew it was over for me there. The next day was worse. I didn't pay the rent and it wasn't my room any more it was his. He was out of jail and the favor was over. It was good while it lasted but its time to go. Summer is over and so is my time with Víctor's family. So I didn't know what I was gonna do and I still really don't. I went to Sernas . . . and asked her to help me[.] I was in a jam and need[ed] a place to crash for a little bit. Well here I am with her and her mother. Her mom is in her 80s and she's in her late 50s . . . I don't want to wear out my welcome here but I'm afraid it ain't going to last that long . . . Well its dark out and I will go smoke a cigarette and eat something . . . I don't know when the next entry will be if ever.

As this rambling entry tries to make clear, the summer of 2001 descended into a routine of panhandling, shooting up, and bouncing in and out of church-based rehab homes, trying to go cold turkey. After I told the moving company that I was going into a rehab home to detox, I returned to Victory Outreach but couldn't handle it. The summertime heat makes withdrawal twice as hard as normal, and because the weather was so warm, it was easier to be out on the street. Walking out of a rehab center in the middle of a withdrawal is not easy. Yet when weighed against the prospect of three weeks of pain and sleepless nights, it is an appealing option. Everything about life during those journeys from the church homes to the dealers was painful and next to insanity. I always felt hollowed out and weak; my ears rang, and my body seemed to be on fire inside. The endless waits for the bus on Alameda and the seemingly long bus rides downtown, during which I sat and tried to appear normal, were mental and physical battles. When I had money in my pocket, returning to the street for a fix was easier.

During my first walkout that summer, I had money, both in my pocket and at the company. My last paycheck was still at the moving company, and they even gave me more work. The walk across the international bridge into Juárez always gave me some extra strength when I was dope-sick. Just the idea of getting closer to the connection made my adrenaline surge and renewed my energy. I stopped that day to eat a hamburger in El Centro. Close to the bridge, there was a hamburger stand that I often stopped at after a good day on the street. It offered singles, doubles, and just about any combination imaginable. The hamburger stand also had fresh *aguas* in a variety of flavors. My favorite was *agua de melón* (cantaloupe juice). No matter how bad I felt, I knew that food would help me.

I didn't give up my room at Víctor's during those episodes. I probably knew instinctively that my attempts to go cold turkey wouldn't work. If I had managed to stay at one of the homes during those attempts to detox, I would have forgotten about everything that I had left behind. Víctor's family thought that I had taken off for only a few days. So each time that I returned to Víctor's, my room was exactly as it had been when I left, with all my possessions still waiting for me. Víctor's family knew that I always carried my bag of clothes when I left, so they probably thought nothing of me being away for a few days. I never wanted to give up having a place to live; it always felt good to arrive and put my bags down each day.

Of course, my first stop was the dealer's, just down the street. I usually had a few old needles, and if I didn't, a trip to the pharmacy to buy an insulin syringe was no big deal unless they were sold out. Shooting up with an old, used needle was painful, but not as painful as the third day of withdrawal. I always found a way to puncture a vein with the dull tips of those old, worn-out insulin syringes. One way or another, I would get that shit into my system. Those moments right after fixing during a return from a withdrawal experience were peaceful indeed. My stomach stopped churning, and the sweat and awful body odor that reeked from my pores during withdrawal were reduced, bringing me some blissful comfort. A quick bucket shower and a shave returned me to the familiar state of medicated normalcy that I had become so addicted to.

After I stopped working and began panhandling again, walking out of a rehab home during withdrawal became a dreadful experience. It involved lugging my bag full of clothes and fighting through the weak, dizzy, and nauseating sensations. My ears rang, and it was all I could do to stand up sometimes. Once when I left the rehab home with no money in my pocket, I walked out to Alameda and panhandled until I had enough to catch the bus downtown, but even waiting for the bus while dope-sick proved difficult. Sometimes, getting on the bus and sitting down was an act in itself. On that day when I didn't have any money, I got off the bus at the corner of Stanton and Paisano feeling weak and weary, but I immediately began panhandling.

Stepping off a bus into a sunny and bustling downtown afternoon when you are dope-sick is quite uncomfortable. The need to fix drove me to panhandle methodically and patiently. I knew that if I seemed too desperate, it would take longer to get the money that I needed for a fix. In my altered state, I slowly walked up and down Stanton Street, asking people for money and running my usual lines about needing a bus ticket and a place to stay. Very slowly, my pockets filled with pesos, quarters, and, occasionally, a few dollar bills. Once I had twelve dollars, I called it quits and headed for the bridge. As always, on my way to the bridge, I hustled up a few more dollars. Any extra money that I could get meant that I could buy something to eat and some cigarettes after I fixed. It's always a good feeling to have money in your pocket when you're feeling dope-sick. It means that you're that much closer to fixing and feeling better again.

Walking across the international bridge with my large duffel bag full of clothes, I forced myself to keep moving. As I crossed into Mexico, a renewed sense of energy surged through me. I had to force myself to keep going and look as normal as possible, although I looked and felt like death warmed over. The bus stop for La Ruta 10, the bus to Felipe Angeles, was three blocks from Juárez Avenue. I knew that I was almost home when I got on the number ten bus. Once I got off the bus, it was just a matter of walking down the street to Kiko's and then to Víctor's. To finally sit down with the dope, a needle, and a cooker was an incredible relief. The appearance of blood in the syringe, the push of my thumb on the plunger of the needle, and the quick rush followed by relaxation and satisfaction instantly brought an end to all the dope-sick and dizzy feelings of the previous few days. The wretched body odor would disappear, and after my stomach churned into a state of stability, I would be ready to eat.

After an aborted detox experience, getting back the strength that I needed to go back downtown and panhandle always meant forcing myself to eat. If I was broke, I got meals on credit and always paid them back that evening or the next day. Once I fixed, I went back to downtown El Paso and panhandled until seven or eight that night. Staying well always meant having money in my pockets for the next day's fix.

That summer at Víctor's, I got used to catching the bus from the bridge to Felipe Angeles. Once I got near the Mariscal, I got off the bus, panhandled in that area, and got to know some of the people there. I met a taxi driver who, for thirty-five pesos, would take me right to my front door. If I was in a hurry and had any extra money, I would take the cab. If I had had a good day panhandling, I would give the cabbie fifty pesos for the ride. It was worth it to take the cab, especially if I had fifty or sixty dollars on me, because waiting on the corner for the bus had its own risks. The Juárez bicycle police patrolled that area, and I looked too skinny and strung out. If they stopped me—and they did—it always meant trouble if they found fresh track marks.

One day, a cop stopped me when I had twenty-five dollars on me. The cop insisted that I had panhandled it and didn't deserve it. He implied that I should give some of it to him. I told him that the marks on my arms weren't tracks, but cuts from moving furniture. He finally stopped hassling me and let me go. Another time, as I walked in the same area, two bicycle cops stopped me and found tracks. They were ready to take me in, so I told them that I could give them a hundred pesos. They told me to put the bill in my back pocket and to let them search me. When they patted me down, they just reached in the pocket, took the bill, and let me go. After a few of these experiences, I didn't like to be out in the open when I was returning from a panhandling run in El Paso. And so I took the taxi when I could afford it. Most of the time, I didn't take the taxi; I usually just caught the bus. I took that cab only because I knew the driver and talked to him every day, often panhandling passers-by right in front of him. There were lots of other taxis out there on the street, but if I didn't see my friend, I just walked on and caught the bus.

THE COPS

That area of the bridge was always problematic, not just for me, but for any junkie who was unfortunate enough to happen along when the municipal police were performing a routine roundup. In these dragnets, junkies, drunks, and scraggly-looking homeless people were taken into custody and escorted down to the local precinct. One morning I was stopped only a block away from the bridge and searched. I was trying to walk around two of Juárez's finest when they decided to check me out. I had only three dollars on me, certainly not enough to buy my release, so they held me. They took me into custody because I had track marks on my arms. Most of my formerly large veins were slowly disappearing because of the constant injections. The threat of detection plus the availability of veins in other areas led me to stop shooting up in my arms. Thus, I began to shoot up in my legs, feet, and underarms.

That morning, I knew I was going into custody: once the cops learned that I didn't have any money, they sat me down on the curb and radioed in for a *camper*. As I waited, they kidnapped two more guys, probably junkies or pot smokers who were unfortunate enough to have resin marks on their fingertips, and made them sit next to me. When the *camper* showed up, it was already full, and after a short ride, we were all down at the local preventivo, Delicias. I wasn't sick yet, but the excursion set me back quite a bit.

I witnessed an interesting spectacle that morning as I sat on the floor with everyone else who had been taken into custody. The judge at the station pulled out a fifth of tequila and gave some of it to a prisoner who stood before him. The prisoner was an alcoholic who was going into the holding cells for the next twelve to twenty-four hours. The judge probably knew that the DTs, which accompany alcohol withdrawal, were bad. Although I never went through them, I know that some alcohol withdrawals are just as painful as heroin withdrawals. Of course, I knew that they wouldn't be asking any junkies going into custody whether they wanted one last shot of dope. Instead, they locked us up in a cement cell full of people, with one metal toilet that stood out in the open. I wearily watched as the alcoholic prisoner chugged down as much as he could in one turn of the bottle. When he finished his first big swig, the judge told him to go ahead and take another. The wide-eyed prisoner looked astonished as he held the bottle and then took another long drink.

While I was in custody, the cops sent me in to see their doctor. The doc spoke some English and seemed eager to practice his vocabulary skills on me. He took a little longer with me than he did with the other prisoners, but I didn't mind. I still felt high from that morning's fix, and he let me smoke a cigarette as he wrote me up. The doctor told me that I would be spending the next twelve hours of my life "with us" and to take it easy because I would soon be back out on the street. I was dirty, and the doctor sized me up right away. He knew that I was strung out and not in the best of health.

They put me in a cell that was not as crowded as the others we passed, but it still had a half a dozen people in it. I was a little upset at being there because I knew that it was just a matter of time before my habit came down on me and I would be sick. There wasn't much I could do. I kicked the bars, which made a loud, deep, pounding echo that seemed to momentarily silence the whole jail. The cops came to investigate the noise, but by then I was done. I sat there on the hard bench and waited for my name to be called. I knew that if I didn't waste my energy and didn't sleep that the dope would hold longer and I wouldn't get sick as fast. If I slept, it would be worse because I would probably wake up sick.

While I was in the cell, I met a guy from Guatemala. He didn't seem to be a junkie or an alcoholic, but he had been caught up in the morning dragnet nonetheless. Maybe the cops had picked him up because he didn't have any money and had asked someone for something to eat; maybe they singled him out because he was a foreigner. His predicament must have been desperate, caught out so far from home, yet he was one of the most talkative guys in the cell. The other prisoners tried to sleep as best they could on a cement floor, but they seemed real miserable about the whole scene. Time seemed to stand still; minutes felt like hours. I stared at the wall, then at the floor, and then at something else as I tried to keep my eyes open. After long periods of silence and nothingness, an officer would call out a name; this was followed by the sound of jingling keys and the opening of a cell door. Then the silence would return, along with an occasional comment from someone in one of the other cells.

After what seemed like a very long time, my name was called, and they opened the cell door for me. Once I started moving, I realized how crappy I was starting to feel. In my diminished state, I gathered up my belongings and walked out the door, not even knowing what time it was. From what I remember, the sun was setting, but there were still a few more minutes of daylight. It felt strange to be walking out of that place while just beginning to feel the pains of withdrawal. I walked two houses down from the police station and asked the people who lived there if they could help me out with some change. I ended up going to almost every house on that street, and the next street over, desperately trying to scrape up enough money for a fix. The more I walked, the sicker I became. But there was no other choice if I wanted to avoid the real pains of a full-fledged withdrawal. Little by little, my pockets filled up with change and an occasional bill.

Later that night, I tried to ignore how sick I was as I bought the dope and trudged back to the room. A late-night fix was just as good as any other when it meant curing me of the increasingly painful experience of withdrawal. As usual, after a few cigarettes and a fleeting moment to enjoy the rush, another day had passed.

One thing was certain from that point on: I couldn't take my mornings for granted anymore. I tried to avoid shooting up anywhere on my body that was readily visible and would give away the fact that I was a junkie. The veins in my arms were pretty spent already, but I still had a lot of untapped veins in my legs and feet. Another new preoccupation for me was avoidance of the corner by Juárez Avenue, the bridge, and the Mariscal. I avoided that corner as much as possible and stayed on the bus until it was a block or so away from that area. It was much easier to hide in the crowd on Juárez Avenue as I walked toward the bridge than it was to pass that corner when the bicycle cops were just sitting there, waiting for anyone like me to come along. I remember riding past on the bus and watching the bicycle cops on that corner. After a while, I just stopped panhandling down by the bridge. It wasn't worth getting stopped by the Juárez police.

The main reason that the cops hauled me in on that day was because they had seen me asking people for money. It wasn't worth losing a day's revenue from the streets of El Paso to make a few extra pesos down by the bridge in Juárez. Subsequently, unless I was real dopesick and had no other choice, I wouldn't start panhandling until I was a good way up the bridge toward the American side. I still made money on the bridge, but it wasn't as if I stayed on the bridge all day asking people for money. I worked the bridge only as I walked across it. Sometimes I would make as much as seven dollars a crossing, while other times I couldn't even get a quarter. The bridge was too unpredictable, so I preferred to do most of my panhandling in the Segundo Barrio of downtown El Paso. I made money in that area, and the constant flow of people allowed me some obscurity.

Although I had some run-ins with the El Paso police, they never took me into custody. The cops in El Paso would often ride up on me on their bicycles while I was in the middle of telling my story to someone. They would tell me to stay out of downtown because the people there didn't have any money to begin with. This must have made sense to them; asking poor people for money seems like a losing proposition at first glance, especially from an American worldview. However, this particular space was not totally American to begin with, and as in Juárez, poor people, when they had it good, always gave more than the rich or the American middle class. I can just imagine the comments that I would have gotten if I had tried to work my hustle on the west side of El Paso. It probably would have taken me twice as long to make half as much money. So when the El Paso bicycle cops gave me their advice, I listened and patiently waited for them to move on to bigger and better things.

Another approach they tried with me was to escort me out of town. That usually involved a pathetic attempt to guide me to the Rescue Mission while explaining to me that I shouldn't be asking the poor for anything. I always walked at least a block toward the mission before I doubled back toward the bridge. On one occasion, they passed me and gave me a funny look as they chased someone in hot pursuit. Another time, I just walked right by them when they had a prisoner in custody. Once the bike patrol caught on that I lived in Juárez, they would escort me to the bridge. This was probably an unconstitutional violation of my civil rights, but I put up with it and played along. It was better to be calm and level headed on the street than it was to be hardheaded and mouthy in a holding cell. After a while, I knew when the bike cops started patrolling and what times they policed the areas near the bridge.

I avoided them as much as possible and kept moving while I was panhandling. I believed that I would be an easy target if I stayed in one place and that as long as I kept moving, the world would move around me without even noticing me.

ANOTHER PRISON VISIT

Before I stopped working in the summer of 2001, I went to visit Víctor again at the CERESO prison in Juárez. I went alone on this second visit. I went on a Saturday, when the prison was open to visitors. The bus ride to the prison was long but interesting; it took me through neighborhoods and avenues in Juárez that I didn't know much about and had never really seen except for the one other time that I had ridden the bus out there. The bus passed the shantytown barrios and large shopping centers that consumed the landscape. I often heard that Juárez was a huge city of millions, but I never grasped the immensity of it all until after I had been through the outlying areas, which were just as overpopulated as Felipe Angeles or Altavista. In many places, it seemed that the houses overlapped and were built one on top of the other, wherever there was space.

There were a lot of buses running through Juárez, and the bus I was on participated in the usual competitive race with the other buses on the same route, passing one another recklessly while vying for the next passenger and the four pesos that he or she would contribute to the driver's daily revenue. I could see the sense of satisfaction in the driver's demeanor as he passed the bus in front of him, which had just stopped to pick up another passenger. The opportunity for the next pickup impelled him along. This battle of the buses kept the Juárez transportation system moving. There were a lot of buses in Juárez, yet the drivers didn't seem to be motivated by a desire to provide a public service as much as by the opportunity to participate autonomously in the workforce. It seemed that driving a bus, whether for yourself or someone else, offered a decent career in comparison to some of the other jobs in Juárez.

Being a junkie and living the demanding lifestyle of heroin addiction ultimately voids the possibilities for meaningful employment. I remember when Víctor told me that he gave up looking for work because he couldn't get a good job with his prison background. Knowing that he was essentially excluded from the formal Mexican economy, he often mentioned going to the States to find work. I knew that my situation wasn't as bad as his. I had never done hard time, mostly because I never saw crime as a solution to my problems. Víctor lived a volatile life, and when he applied his energy, it almost always involved some sort of criminal act. It seemed that the only way he maintained his own addiction was through criminal activity. When his family could give him money, they gave it to him with no questions, just to keep him out of trouble. They knew he had a habit, and they did what they could to keep him out of jail. Even while he was in jail, his mom visited him regularly and brought him money and groceries.

That particular Saturday, Víctor's mom couldn't make the trip, so I went to the CERESO alone. I was still working, so I had some money in my pocket. I didn't bother to stop and buy anything at the store; I knew that cash was the best gift for anyone in Víctor's situation.

When the bus arrived at the CERESO, it parked across the street from the prison in a dirt lot. Parking-lot vendors sold beverages and food, and visitors often bought last-minute gifts from them before they walked into the prison. The CERESO was big and looked intimidating, like any other large correctional facility, with guard towers, huge brick walls, and lots of fences everywhere. I walked through the front door and got in line. When I got to the front desk, I told the officer that I was Víctor's cousin; only family members were admitted for visitation. After passing through a metal detector, I proceeded to a second checkpoint, where they stamped my hand with a mark that glowed under ultraviolet light. They also gave me a ticket for my wallet and my keys and told me that I didn't need them inside the facility. With my money in my front pocket, I followed the crowd of visitors with no problems. There were thousands of visitors that day, and as I checked into the prison, I was just another link in a long chain. After walking down a series of long hallways, I found myself in the greeting area of the prison. This area, where visitors waited for their family members, was contained by a maze of tall wire fences.

As I waited, an inmate with a name tag and number approached me and asked me who was I looking for. I handed him ten pesos, a coin a little bigger than a silver dollar, and told him I was looking for Víctor Vasquez. He enthusiastically shouted Víctor's name and led me through courtyards, buildings, cell-block recreation areas, and basketball courts. My guide was persistent and loud as he searched the prison. It seemed as if finding Víctor was a crucial life-and-death mission for him. As he shouted Víctor's name over and over again, other inmates repeated his words in a sort of echo. Everyone understood what a visit meant. It was a gesture of respect to help connect another inmate with a visitor, and Víctor was always big on respect. After a few more minutes of searching, Víctor finally found me. He had heard through the grapevine that someone was looking for him.

Víctor wasn't a threatening-looking man. He was a bit shorter than me and wasn't exceptionally muscular. I could tell by looking at him that he was still strung out on dope despite being locked up in prison. He humbly approached me with a smile on his face and said he was happy to see me. The significance of my showing up and being there for him exemplified a family-like connection that went beyond two junkies who got high together. We looked out for each other like brothers, and I lived with his family. Víctor and I had met through a sort of extended-family situation: we were involved in relationships with two sisters. That made us cuñados of sorts, and although we weren't formally married to the women, the relationships had the qualities of marriage.

After the short greeting, the first thing we talked about was our habits. Víctor had been in an in-house drug rehab program that the inmates ran in the prison. He had made it through the worst part of heroin withdrawal, la malilla, but when he reentered the general population, he started using again. That was a month or so before my visit, and I remember going there with his mom around that time and not being able to see him: some inmates from the in-house program showed up at the entrance to the yard that day and told us he was detoxing.

Subsequently, it wasn't long before we decided to get high right there in the prison. There was no shortage of drugs in the CERESO, and I knew some junkies regularly went there to connect as well as fix. There were a good many inmates who were strung out on either heroin or methadone, and it seemed that junkies didn't have to worry about getting busted, since they were already in prison. You could say that they didn't have to worry about being eaten, because they were already in the belly of the beast. Finding dope there was easy, and within minutes we were walking between the *patios* (the buildings that housed the inmates) with six globos. Dope was the same price in the prison that it was on the street, six for five. The quality was equal to or better than street dope. The only thing that held us up was finding a set of works and a place to shoot up. Víctor didn't have any money, so he didn't have his own cell. Everything in the CERESO had a price, and a private cell was expensive.

Víctor knew the prison well. He led me to an open cell that had a maze of bunk beds inside. The large concrete cell was open, as were most of them on visiting days. In fact, the whole prison was open, with men and women practically moving about the entire facility. As we entered the cell, I saw a bunch of guys in there shooting dope. Junkies controlled this cell and used it to shoot up and make petty dope deals. The place was a shooting gallery, and it was busy. We rented a used syringe for five pesos; the deal included access to a cooker, water, and a small bottle of bleach. I wouldn't have used that *cuete* (slang for "needle" or "syringe") if there hadn't been any bleach, and I cleaned it out really well before I used it. I had used old works on the street, but I always cleaned them with bleach, or at least water. On the street, the general rule was to always have your own works. In prison, the rules were different, but that didn't mean being careless. Bleach was a necessity for junkies who knew anything about using dope, and the prison shooting gallery had lots of it. We shot up most of the dope right then and there. I told Víctor to keep a globo for later.

Afterward, we walked around the yard. Víctor gave me a tour of the place. The inmates lived in the *patios*, barracks-like two-story buildings. Some *patios* were in better shape than others and had areas with chairs, tables, and small hamburger stands. For the most part, they were dismal places, so we walked to a good-size soccer stadium and hung out on the bleachers. It was a good day to be outside, and the whole yard was teeming with visitors and inmates. Víctor and I smoked cigarettes, discussed life in the CERESO, and shared stories about our life experiences. As usual, we talked about what we would do once this part of our lives was finished. Víctor imagined going someplace like New York and working, making some money, and having a blonde American girl. He had gotten Laura's sister pregnant, but he didn't seem content with her. I told him that I liked morenas, and he joked about how he was an indigenous Mexican with brown skin that liked white chicks with blonde hair, while I was a *güero* (white guy) who liked brown-skinned Mexican women.

We wandered into a recreation building that had pool tables and all kinds of taco and hamburger stands. I had some money, so we shot pool, smoked cigarettes, and continued our conversation. They sold loose cigarettes, *sueltos*, so I bought a handful of them. We played pool, ate, and enjoyed the day. The place was crowded. This was probably the best day of the week for inmates to make money. Saturday was always the best moneymaking day on the street, and it was the same in the CERESO. Visiting women who had relatives or friends inside worked as prostitutes. Female inmates also took advantage of the open yard and seemed to move freely throughout the prison: gender-segregated areas seemed to be suspended, or perhaps an open-yard policy was the norm on visiting day. At times, it seemed as if there were more visitors than inmates, but it was difficult to tell who was who. The only distinguishing markers were the transparent stamps that glowed under ultraviolet light, and the little claim tickets we were given so that we could retrieve our belongings at the checkpoint when we left.

I had never visited an inmate at an American prison, but I just couldn't imagine this scenario occurring there. It was as if Saturday were a free-for-all, a stress reducer. Family members accompanied inmates to their cells, to the shooting galleries, to the bootlegger, to the chapel, to the soccer stadium, to the cafeteria, to the rec room, and to the areas between the men's and women's *patios*. People laughed, drank, ate, smoked, and talked about anything that came to mind. I suppose that in the CERESO, everyone lives for those weekend visits, when people can cut loose and try to forget about the pain and misery of prison life and the situations behind it. Prison guards seemed to be having a good time as well, talking with family members, joking, and minimizing the tension that exists between officers and inmates.

Everything seemed easygoing and loose until late afternoon, when it all came to an end. Announcements over the PA system informed everyone that visiting time was over. Everyone procrastinated as they tried to squeeze more experience from the day's visit. I gave Víctor forty dollars and wished him well. He walked me as far as he could and gave me the handshake we always did: a clasping of thumbs, followed by the locking of fingers, and then the connection of knuckles as our fists clashed against each other, knuckle to knuckle, in a punching motion. As I passed through the next fenced area, I found myself in a very long line. We waited forever in that line, which eventually started moving at a slow pace. The same thousands of people who had roamed around the prison yard all day as visitors were now impatient to leave. The guy behind me in the line held a set of blueprints and spoke an intellectual, academic Spanish. I asked him if he was a professor. He answered yes. I chatted with him to pass the time. Eventually, I made it to the counter where they shined the black light on my stamped hand. My stamp glowed an eerie blue color. Then I presented the officers behind the desk with my claim ticket, and they gave me back my keys and my wallet. As I walked out the front door of the prison, there were a few buses parked across the street, taking passengers.

I enjoyed visiting Víctor, but once the visit was over, I just wanted to get as far away from there as possible. The illusion for me was over, and despite how much freedom the inmates seemed to have inside the prison, they were only as privileged as their wallets allowed them to be. Without money, doing time at the CERESO would be a very miserable experience. Víctor told me that they gave free food to the inmates at the cafeteria; he said that each prisoner received a ration of beans, rice, and tortillas. All the other food cost money. Also, having a dope habit there surely couldn't have been any fun. Víctor never talked about how he supported his habit beyond saying that he did some odd jobs that paid him enough to get by. I think that between the odd jobs and the money that his family gave him, he barely survived.

Víctor didn't have a plan for anything when he got out. He often spoke as if being locked up wasn't really that bad. The CERESO had drugs and, on visiting days, women. Víctor's family probably gave him more money when he was inside than when he was out. Being strung out or dope-sick in there surely must have been a real nightmare. I never went back to the CERESO; two visits were enough for me. I hoped that the last visit was meaningful for Víctor and that the money I gave him would ease his burden. I knew that practically all of it would be spent on dope, but that was the way it was.

THE SURVIVAL NETWORK

Later that summer, after I had stopped working and was strung out and panhandling again, I never considered going to visit Víctor at the CERESO. I was too busy trying to maintain my own habit, which was an all-day job, seven days a week. I usually panhandled in El Paso during the morning, took a break, went to my room and fixed around noon, and then returned to El Paso and panhandled until roughly six or sometimes seven in the evening. After a day of panhandling, I usually had enough money to fix that night and the next morning. I almost always had enough money to eat, buy cigarettes, and pay some of the rent. With everything on schedule, I kept up with my habit and the days quickly passed.

I spent most of my days on the streets of the Segundo Barrio and downtown El Paso, and developed or increased a small survival network. I call it a survival network because the regular stops I made, the people I knew, and the places I frequented helped me survive and maintain myself in the midst of an insane situation. One of my first regular stops was on the bridge itself. It was the public restroom on the Mexican side of the Santa Fe, or El Paso Street, Bridge, where pedestrians cross from Juárez to El Paso. Because I almost always carried a bag with me in order to play the role of a vagabond traveler on his way back to New York, I always had clothes and shaving gear. It was important for a panhandler in the bridge area to be clean-shaven: most people on the street believed that a clean-shaven man was respectable. They also were more inclined to give to someone who looked clean. A dirty, unshaven panhandler was easily associated with alcoholism and laziness; I suspect that most people are not aware of things like heroin addiction and dependency.

Since looking presentable was important, I often shaved and washed my face in the public bathroom on the Mexican side of the bridge. I wasn't alone in this use of public accommodation; many of the border crossers destined for the United States stopped at this public bathroom to shave and get ready. The eight sinks in the public restroom were separated from the toilet section by a wall and were lined up next to one another in front of a long mirror. There was a water regulator at the end of each faucet. This meant that to turn on the water, you had to move the stem to one side or the other in order for the water to run. When shaving, this meant a constant manipulation of the sink. Shaving like this with disposable razors wasn't easy after I had gone without a shave for a week or so, and my facial hair was tough. But making myself look presentable meant more money in less time, so it was worth it.

Tourists and people of more normal circumstances must have looked at us as if we were the dregs of society. Standing in front of a sink in a public restroom on an international bridge, shaving while shirtless, I didn't really care what anyone thought. If there were other guys using the sinks, I just joked and talked with them. Mexican public employees sat by the entrance at a small table and supervised the bathroom. The table held toilet paper and a tip jar. After I shaved, washed up, and changed my shirt, I often left them a few pesos. This was important: they could have easily kicked us out, and I wasn't the only person who shaved there. Tipping the bathroom staff also motivated them to keep paper towels in the dispensers. This was important for wiping facial hair from the sinks, drying off, and cleaning my glasses; dirty glasses were problematic for various reasons.

The thing about running game out on the street—trying to get money from the general public—was that it was largely cosmetic. People judge others from first impressions. I have often heard older people describe beggars they run into as being down on their luck and having dirty clothes, etc. Yet they always seemed to justify their acts of benevolence and social acceptance by commenting, "but he was clean-shaven." Although Víctor's place had a shower room, where I often cleaned up, I sometimes used the bathroom down on the bridge in order to get an early start and get through downtown Juárez before the bicycle cops were out in full force. Timing was everything, and tardiness or sloppiness could change my day by putting me in the wrong place at the wrong time.

The Rainbow Hotel on El Paso Street rented showers. It was a flophouse hotel, and the rooms didn't have individual bathrooms or showers. Instead, they were located at the end of a long hallway. The hotel was upstairs, and at the head of the stairs was a window where you could either check into a room or pay three dollars for a shower. This was one of my regular stops, when I had the time, and I liked it especially because the Rainbow Hotel had hot water. Bucket showers at Víctor's were cold. This was no problem in the summer, but in colder weather, a hot shower was nice. Next to the two bathrooms in the upstairs hallway of the Rainbow Hotel there was a door that led to the fire escape, which descended to the alley behind the building. In the summertime, this door was kept open, and after I showered, I often sat near it and dried off. The hotel had a washing machine near the bathrooms. I often just left the dirty hotel towels right there on the washing machine. Those moments after a nice hot shower always felt good, and looking clean and feeling good always brought more money from pedestrians. The showers and bathrooms weren't luxurious; they were small, cramped, confined, and regularly used. They often had half-used bars of soap on the floor, and there was hardly enough room to dry off and get dressed. But none of that really mattered because most street people like me were grateful just to have a place that offered a hot private shower for a down-to-earth price. Without places like the Rainbow Hotel, we never would have had that.

A few doors down from the Rainbow there was a Chinese restaurant. I often went there to trade in all my quarters, dimes, and nickels for dollar bills. After a while, I got to know the people who worked there. One of the women who worked the cash register became a regular acquaintance, and she looked forward to my visits, which kept her cash register stocked with change. Like most of the people that I knew on the street, the two of us talked a lot about ourselves. I told her I lived in Juárez, and she seemed to understand my situation. The three people who worked in the kitchen were from Juárez, so my situation didn't surprise them or her. She was Korean and had probably experienced poverty at some point in her life. Almost every day, I showed up at the restaurant with my pockets full of change, which I cashed in for dollar bills. The women knew when I'd had a good afternoon, and I normally cashed in twenty or thirty dollars' worth of change. When I had pesos, I cashed them in for Mexican paper currency at a casa de cambio in Juárez or El Paso.

The Chinese restaurant featured a buffet. If I showed up at closing time, or anytime when business was good, my Korean friend usually gave me a plate and told me to help myself. Those buffet dinners were good. I don't know why they called it a Chinese restaurant. The people there weren't Chinese; they were Korean and Mexican. The food, at least some of it, was Chinese. Yet there was also an eclectic menu of hybrid dishes that included chiles in most of the recipes. Whatever ethnicity the food was, it was good. In those days, I was practically skin and bones, so the meals at that restaurant kept me going. To this day I am grateful for the consideration that was shown to me by the Korean woman and the Mexican people who worked there. Even when I was in a hurry and didn't have time to stop, she always offered me an iced tea while I cashed in my change.

If I timed it just right, I could take a shower at the Rainbow and then go to the buffet for something to eat before I returned to Juárez after a day on the street. The Chinese restaurant also had public restrooms, which made my life easier when I was in that part of downtown. I never shot dope at the restaurant or the little hotel. In fact, I hardly ever shot up in El Paso when I lived in Juárez. There were a couple of exceptions, but for the most part, I was never involved with drugs, drug dealers, or other people who used drugs when I was on the U.S. side of the border. There was no need for me to mess around in El Paso; all my connections and networks were in Juárez.

On the same block as the Chinese restaurant and the Rainbow Hotel stood a small grocery store that was owned and operated by an American guy and his Korean wife. They had been married for decades, and the wife often spoke about their sons and daughters, and their careers and relationships. I also cashed my change in at their store and developed a good repartee with them. I usually visited them in the morning before I returned to Juárez for my lunchtime fix, and this worked well for me. When following my usual practice, I worked the downtown area, made my rounds through the Segundo Barrio, and finished off at the north end of El Paso Street. Cashing in my change completed the circular path of my panhandling routine. The Korean wife worked at the grocery store most of the time and often gave me a soda when I showed up. Even when she didn't, I still bought one, both as a courtesy to her for cashing in my change and because of the heat.

The heat was always intense in El Paso and Juárez during those endless summers, and I always drank soda, iced tea, and various *aguas frescas*. You needed to drink something, or you would dry up like everything else in the desert. Since I was out on the streets most of the time, a lot of soda vendors who sold sodas and chips from pushcarts with umbrellas remembered me. Sometimes if I had only a little change to cash in, I asked a street vendor if he needed some change. Many of the soda vendors knew that I panhandled. I often worked the same corners that they did. I got along well with street vendors because I never bothered their customers during a sale. Even if the people just looked as though they were interested in buying something, I left them alone. I asked people for money only after they had purchased from the vendor, never before.

Another one of my rules of thumb was to keep moving; I never stuck around long enough to become a nuisance. I knew most of the vendors because I passed their corners every day, not because I stayed long enough to wear out my welcome. One street vendor regularly parked his cart on the corner of Father Rahm and El Paso Streets. We got along well and always made small talk while I worked his corner and the four corners of that intersection. I always stopped to say good morning. Talking with the vendors made me feel like part of the community. This was important because it was this community, this survival network, that sustained my income, maintained my habit, and kept me alive.

At the corner of El Paso and Sixth Streets was a bus station that I frequented. It was the terminal of a small bus line that served mostly western states, but also sent buses as far north as Chicago. This terminal was always a good place to work the crowd. I often hung around the parking lot and panhandled everybody and anybody who passed through. Sometimes I made good money at this bus station. The nice thing about it was that it was close to the international bridges. The bus station also had public, but very crowded, restrooms. When I panhandled there, I didn't look totally out of place with my duffle bag full of clothes slung over my shoulder. This is probably one of the reasons why I was never bothered on that corner. Many of the taxi drivers knew me by then, and after a while, the people from the bus company began to notice me. Generally, they left me alone, but once in a while the baggage handlers tried to run me off. They never did. I always persisted and easily moved between the masses of travelers.

Sometimes the terminal was so crowded that all the seats inside were taken. Passengers often stood both inside and outside the terminal while waiting for their buses. Every hour or two, buses picked up and dropped off multitudes of travelers to and from Los Angeles, Denver, and other big cities. On some days, when I needed a break, I would go inside, sit in the waiting area, watch TV, drink a soda, and smoke a cigarette. If the bicycle cops were in the neighborhood, I would wait inside the bus terminal until they left. Sometimes I panhandled inside the terminal and talked to the people who sat there waiting for their bus.

There are a number of bus stations in downtown El Paso and the Segundo Barrio, and bus companies profit nicely from the migration of people across the U.S.-Mexico border. Every day, people crossed the bridge with handcarts loaded down with suitcases and bags, on their way to visit a relative somewhere in the United States. Travelers and migrants returning to Mexico also carried loads of baggage. Some seemed joyful as they returned, while others seemed down, in a state of dejection as they slowly walked across the bridge, possibly in search of a family member waiting for them on the other side.

On reflection, the bus stations, migrants, and perpetual movement over the border created a space within which a subtle traveler could exist and panhandle. I was that ambiguous traveler, living in survival mode and driven by ulterior motives. I walked around some of the other bus stations once in a while, but I avoided the large Greyhound terminal. It was already full of homeless and displaced people, and it was too risky to panhandle there. After all, what would I do if someone called my bluff and offered to buy me a bus ticket to New York? How would I turn it down? There was no distance between me and my cover story at the Greyhound station; it was the only bus company in town that ran to New York. Instead, I preferred the regional terminals that served people traveling west. The smaller bus terminals were crowded, and the buses often left jam-packed with people. In the midst of that type of chaos, it was easier to blend in. I suspect that the local economy would dry right up if not for all those travelers constantly passing through El Paso. After all, this cross-border travel and trade and keeps downtown and Segundo Barrio economically alive.

Down by the bridge on Sixth Street there were always half a dozen pickup trucks and small vans parked and waiting for a *movida* (a small moving job). Perhaps someone had just bought some furniture, or was moving across town, or across the bridge, and needed help moving it. The guys down at the bridge specialized in that kind of work. In the moving business, we called them "moonlighters"—movers who moved furniture and household goods and were paid under the table. The moonlighters were always out there, every day. When I began panhandling down by the bridge, the moonlighters fell for my story and gave me some money. Once they got to know me, they still gave me some change once in a while, but they often joked, "Hey, Nueva York, when are you leaving?" After a while, I talked with them about what I did, and they became another part of my daily network. I never worked for them; there was no shortage of moving help near the bridge. Guys would hang around that corner all day, just waiting for a *movida* to come along. Sometimes, in the afternoon, I passed by and noticed that all the trucks were out. This was good for the moonlighters because they were making money, and if they were making money, they were happy. If they were happy, they wouldn't mess with me when I hung around their corner, approached people, and asked for money.

RECKLESS JUNKIES

My usual routine had not changed much: *¿Discúlpame, si puede ayúdame con algún cambio para comprarme un boleto a Nueva York? Estoy aquí sin dinero y me falta la feria para un boleto. Tengo cincuenta dólares pero uno boleto a Neuva York es trescientos sesenta dólares. ¿Si puede ayudarme con algún cambio o algo?* (Forgive me. Can you help me with some change so that I can buy a ticket to New York? I have fifty dollars, but the tickets cost three hundred and sixty dollars. Can you help me with some change or something?) These lines worked pretty well. My accent was now more localized, my vocabulary had improved, and I was more convincing and more able to connect with the people who crossed the bridge. However, there were difficult days in which it seemed I was in a constant *lucha* (struggle). On those days it was difficult to get the minimum amount that I needed. I suppose I was hard on myself, since I set my own quota. Returning to Juárez at noon with less than twenty or thirty dollars was unacceptable. After an afternoon on the street, I needed to have between forty and fifty dollars in my pocket. If I didn't, I fell short of my own expectations.

As I panhandled along the streets of south El Paso and Segundo Barrio, I didn't run into too many people in my same situation—that is, junkies who panhandled and crossed to Juárez to supply their habit. Once in a while, I encountered people who slept on the street, people who negotiated between the street and the local shelters, mainly the Rescue Mission or the Opportunity Center. And there were the local junkies in Segundo as well as the alcoholics and the homeless. But most of them just stayed in El Paso and didn't go to Juárez. Of course, some did, but I kept to myself for the most part, at least as far as drugs were concerned, so I didn't know too many junkies from El Paso. It seemed like the only time I got in with El Paso junkies was when I was in the rehab homes; those places were always full of junkies from the El Paso side of the border. Someone at a rehab home once told me that a lot of junkies from El Paso didn't go to Juárez because they were on paper, meaning that they were either on probation or parole and couldn't cross the border.

There was a junkie named Gary (mentioned in Chapter 5) who panhandled around Segundo and also went to Juárez to supply his habit. I had met Gary on Oregon Street near the bus station on Sixth Street. An American from someplace down South, he was strung out pretty bad. His Spanish was terrible, but that didn't stop him from panhandling. I saw him around from time to time, and we got to know each other after a while. He seemed like a mean-spirited sort, and the first time I tried talked to him, he told me to get away from him because he was trying to panhandle. In time, he approached me when he wasn't dope-sick and tried to scrounge up the money for a fix. We often talked about the best dope spots in Juárez and El Paso as well as the best places to panhandle and the best lines to use. He said he often bought dope in Juárez, but didn't live there. He slept in vacant buildings and alleyways in south El Paso and Segundo and went to Juárez only to cop and fix.

Gary was a reckless junkie who shot up in public and often carried a globo or two with him across the bridge. I knew that if I lived the way he did, I'd be in jail in no time. Sometimes after I hadn't seen him for a while, he would show up and tell me about being busted and locked up. I could usually tell when he had been locked up because he always looked healthier after a short stint in the El Paso County jail. Gary usually wore a few jackets and a baseball cap. He often looked dirty and slim. His southern accent worsened his broken Spanish. But he carried himself fairly well on the streets. When he offered to help me find a local connection, I always declined. I preferred to keep my drug affairs to myself. I was secure in my little system, and changing it meant risking and disrupting my daily flow.

I rarely included Gary in my daily routine. One morning I ran into him when I had finished panhandling and was on my way to cop. He was dope-sick, and his connection had dried up. He told me he had some money, but not enough to buy a fix. Since I had had a worthwhile morning panhandling, I told him that if he wanted to hang out with me, I would help him out. Gary didn't venture beyond downtown and the Bellavista area of Juárez, so he was uneasy about following me into an area that he was unfamiliar with. We walked across the bridge, caught the bus in Juárez, and transferred to another bus to Colonia Postal. I might have walked if I had been alone, but Gary warned me that the Juárez police knew him on sight. Instead of risking it, I decided to stay below the radar as much as possible. Riding the bus was always worth it when it meant avoiding a day in a crowded holding cell and being robbed us of my dope money.

We went to fix at Marcos's. Marcos's place was always a safe bet; if he didn't have anything, he would know where to get it. Also, Marcos had family who lived next door, and because they were all strung out, he always had dope for them. We copped at Marcos's, but because I wasn't alone, we couldn't shoot at his place. His cousin, a young guy who was an occasional shooting partner of mine, showed us a place to fix behind a neighbor's house and also helped us out with some water and a cooker. We fixed and felt pretty good afterward. As we left, some older kids from the neighborhood threw a few rocks at us from a nearby hilltop. I threw a couple of rocks back and cursed them out. Gary, who was self-conscious and felt out of place in the neighborhood, blamed himself for causing the attack. He said that we needed to get out of there and that it was his fault that the kids were scoping us out. I always felt at home in Colonia Postal, probably because I had lived and panhandled there during the summer and fall of 1999 while living in the casita.

We caught the bus back downtown and crossed the bridge back to El Paso. During the journey, Gary thanked me, but told me that he didn't want to go back there again. Whatever. We needed to get back to work panhandling so that we would have enough to carry us through the next fix. Gary liked to cop dope downtown because he thought it was safer. I couldn't see his logic; the police always heavily patrolled those downtown streets. Whenever I saw Gary in Juárez after that, he looked as though he was trying to avoid the police or had just been released from lockup. For some reason, he didn't blend in so well on those downtown backstreets, but he persisted, as did his habit.

One day when I saw Gary on the street in El Paso, he offered to share some of his dope with me. I followed him down an alley and over a fence to a place that he used as his shooting area. I didn't like the setup one bit; if someone called the cops, or a bike patrol happened along, we would have been easily trapped and busted. Gary didn't seem to care, so I prepped the works as fast as possible and hastily drew the stuff up into the syringe. I never liked fixing when I felt rushed, and this place was just too open for me. Quickly, I found a vein, pushed the shit in, and got the hell out of there. I usually enjoyed a cigarette after I fixed, but I couldn't even do that because I was in such a hurry to get out of that alley.

I never shot up in downtown El Paso after that; I always tried to fix in a secure and relaxed setting. Even fixing outside on the backstreets of Juárez was less stressful than shooting up downtown. Most of the places where I scored had nice secluded areas nearby for shooting up. Most of the time, however, I just went back to my room at Víctor's, made myself comfortable, and fixed in peace. Panhandling on the street was one thing, but using dope on the street was guaranteed to bring more problems than I wanted.

Stay in the moment, in the now.

The summer of 2001 went slow and fast. I had no major problems on the street. The money continued to flow, and I maintained my habit. One afternoon near the end of that summer, as I walked down the street in Juárez, I noticed a few guys moving a dentist's office. I stopped to talk to them and see whether they needed some help. Coincidentally, I showed up right when they were having trouble with a heavy dentist's chair. I had already made my quota for the day, and I was feeling pretty good, so I agreed to help them with the chair. They must have thought that I was out of my mind when I told the biggest guy there to pick up the chair and help me carry it. No lie—that thing was heavy. But we managed to pick it up and carry it to the truck parked out front.

After it was all loaded, I looked at the guys and asked them how much they would pay me to help unload. An older fellow answered that he would give me 100 pesos. What the hell? I accepted the offer. Before I knew it, I was riding with them across Juárez, crammed like a sardine in the cab of their fully loaded pickup truck, on my way to the new dentist's office. When we got to the new place, I hauled ass and unloaded that furniture as if I were unloading a trailer. We were done in a few minutes. When we returned downtown, I helped them finish cleaning out the dentist's office, and the older guy gave me about 140 pesos. This was a nice addition to my day's panhandling profits.

During the summer of 2001, I tried to detox from heroin three times. I just couldn't do it. The weather seemed too nice to sit in a hot rehab home and try to sweat it out. Over the course of that summer, I lived at Víctor's, Serna's, and passed a few nights at José's. On a few occasions, I spent the night on the street, at the mission, or in a hotel room in downtown Juárez.

That summer, I bought most of my heroin in Las Moras. Las Moras was a fortress of sorts. As mentioned previously, because it was located on top of a hill, it was a great place for dealers; lookouts could see everything that was going on in the surrounding area. It was also easy to fix up there. If the cops showed up, all the junkies would run in the opposite direction. For the most part, the cops rode by and didn't bother the place, but every so often, los caballos came around with a *camper* for backup and rounded up the few unfortunates who could not get away in time.

One day I went to Las Moras after I had worked the streets all morning, and the cops showed up. By then, I was well acquainted with the people who sold there and was in good standing with them. Since I was a regular customer who always paid cash, they let me in and had me wait in their living room. As I sat there and minded my own business, the cops came to the door and talked with the dealers. A few minutes later, the cops left, and I was on my way down the hill toward Víctor's. I knew a few of the junkies who hung out at Las Moras. Some of them remembered me from Colonia Postal, Las Canchas, or Felipe Angeles. After I got tight with the dealers up there, I would hang around and tell them stories about myself. One of the younger guys who peddled dope there drove a big old white Cadillac. I always joked with him about how he owned a New York City pimpmobile.

Once that summer, I walked out of a church home in the middle of a withdrawal, went downtown, and panhandled about fifteen dollars. Afterward, I bought some dope at Las Moras and sat on the side of the hill with a few other junkies and fixed myself. For a while, time seemed to exist only for the sake of finding more money to keep myself from becoming sick. As summer turned into fall, my routine became all about getting as much done as possible during daylight so that my evenings could be a time for rest and relaxation. If I was panhandling after seven in the evening, something was wrong. That summer, traffic on the international bridges moved pretty fluidly, and I often crossed easily two or three times a day. After September 11, my routine changed, but it did not change drastically.

September 11, 2001, was the day that the World Trade Center and the Pentagon were attacked by terrorists in hijacked jet airliners. That morning, I was panhandling in a bus station in downtown El Paso at the corner of Sixth and Oregon. As I moved through the crowd and tried to get my morning quota, I was stopped dead in my tracks by the mayhem on television: a jet plane flew into one of the twin towers in New York City and blew up. Shit! What a fucked-up place the world was! I was surprised and numb at the same time. That day, I finished my rounds and returned to Juárez as usual. Over the next few days, bridge lines extended back onto Juárez Avenue. Soldiers carrying M-16s occupied the roof of the U.S. port of entry. I compensated for the delays by waking up earlier. But by my second daily trip across the border, in the afternoon, I ran into long lines of pedestrians, and this really messed up my routine.

Soon after the September 11 attacks, the long lines on the international bridges helped me decide to try and detox again. On November 13, I went back to Marcelino's Victory in Jesus Men's Home, determined to kick the habit. My duffle bag was full of dirty clothes, so I spent my first day there smoking cigarettes and doing laundry. That withdrawal was not the worst that I had suffered through. I spent most of my time there dragging ass from the bunk bed to the bathroom. I practically lived in the shower or the tub and was quite thankful for the hot water. As before, once I felt better, I left the home. I stopped by to visit Joe Huggins's place on the way downtown again. Joe was happy to see me and brought me home with him. His wife cooked dinner, and it was the best food I had eaten in a very long time.

Joe and his family sincerely tried to help me again, and I stayed with them for the Christmas season. By early December, I was gaining weight and feeling good again. I helped Joe with the business, but instead of paying me in cash, he gave me room and board. The room was okay. It was in his basement and furnished. I grew used to the routine at Joe's, and time passed rather quickly. Progressive or liberal as Joe seemed, he surprised me when he hired a housekeeper from Juárez. Joe claimed to be countercultural most of the time, but emphasized a rigid work ethic in his moving business. Joe's wife was also very active, like some kind of workaholic. It seemed as if we all helped the housekeeper do the kitchen work. I think they needed the housekeeper more for babysitting than for actual housework. Joe's housekeeper was an older woman who showed up a couple of times a week. I translated once in a while and got to know her well enough to suggest a few meals that everyone might like. This was important because Joe's wife was a vegetarian. Joe was also a vegetarian, but not as rigidly as his wife. If there is one good Mexican dish that meets vegetarian criteria, I would have to say it is enchiladas. One night the housekeeper stayed at Joe's and slept in Joe's basement, across from me in another bed. We became friends and joked often. I saw her again once or twice on the bridge after I had left Joe's, much later. She didn't have too much to say to me when she saw me panhandling.

As Christmas 2001 approached, Joe told me that he had a road trip planned and that he intended to bring me along. He also mentioned taking an old road hand named Ronnie. The trip involved an airline flight to Spokane, Washington, where we would pick up a tractor-trailer, drive it to Montana, load it full of household goods, and drive it to Texas. Joe told me that he would pay me cash money for the trip, and I figured that it would be well over a thousand dollars. This made me feel pretty good because it meant a shot at some real money and a new start. Ronnie showed up a week or so before Christmas, and he seemed okay company for a moving run. He stayed at the warehouse and worked there doing odd jobs and getting shipments ready for transit. I got along with him fairly well and decided to give him the benefit of the doubt, since he was one of Joe's old running partners.

Ronnie was a good worker, for a mover, and he had experience. But he drank a lot. I suppose the fact that he was a good worker compensated for his drinking, yet the more comfortable he felt with a situation, the more he drank. The same could be said about me using dope on moving jobs, but the only time dope made me sloppy in the morning was when I had not had any. Drinking, on the other hand, makes a worker very sloppy. Watching Ronnie drink in the warehouse brought back memories of the guys I used to run into when I drove over the road. At that stage, my past as a van line driver seemed as if it had happened in another lifetime—a distant, prehistoric age, the pre-heroin period.

We celebrated Christmas at Joe's and then flew to Spokane, to pick up the truck. I enjoyed the plane ride; it was the first time in years that I had traveled that far from El Paso and Juárez. When we got off the plane, it was two in the morning. It was also cold, but I had expected as much. When we got to the moving company to pick up the truck, we were more than ready to hit the road. The truck was a Kenworth Aerodyne cabover with a 400-horsepower Caterpillar engine and a thirteen-speed transmission. The trailer was a forty-eight-foot flat floor with a one-foot drop deck. In short, the unit we picked up at the moving agency was adequate for the run we were going on. The company had prepped the truck for us, so the only thing we had to do was get in and turn the key. The paperwork for the run was on the doghouse, the dash between the seats. By the look of things, they were happy that Joe had taken the contract. In no time at all, we were on I-90, heading east.

I knew a lot about trucks because I had owned three of them, so when Joe got tired and asked me to drive, I jumped at the chance. It was snowing in western Montana, yet the snow subsided that morning. We stopped at a truck stop in the country and had breakfast. I felt lifetimes away from everything; the needles, the dope, the withdrawals, and the panhandling all seemed like a distant dream out there in the clean open spaces of Montana. That evening we arrived in Wolf Point and got a motel room. The town was quiet, and I was surprised to see Joe and Ronnie drinking at the motel on the night before the job. Nothing stopped us from loading the shipment, though, and I think the cold weather woke us up real quick. We loaded the trailer full of household goods and large pieces of machinery that had been stored in a farmhouse and barn. The place was in the middle of a large horse ranch, and there was nothing else out there. It was so fuckin' cold that if you took a shit outside, it was frozen by the time it hit the ground.

We were all experienced movers, so it took us only two days to pack and load the truck. When we pulled away, we had twenty-eight thousand pounds of furniture, boxes, and machinery in the trailer. This was good for everyone; it meant that the load would pay well, since we were just about maxed out, weight-wise. By the following night, we were in Colorado, celebrating our good fortune. We must have drunk a case of beer that night, but the next day we were back on the road.

Ronnie talked a lot when he drank. Alcohol seemed to open him up and make him livelier than when he was sober. He talked about working a truck stop as a lumper (freelance laborer who unloads freight) up in Cordelia, California, and about his Cuban wife and daughter in Miami. I could relate to his experiences because I had been to both places. When I was driving my own truck, I once spent two weeks in Cordelia waiting for a shipment going back east. I even knew a few of the people Ronnie mentioned in his stories. When I used to go to Miami, I usually copped dope somewhere in North Miami.

The Miami chapter in Ronnie's life seemed to bring out the worst in him, and he was full of resentment. For the most part, our discussions did not get too heavy. I think that for Ronnie and me, this trip was more like a vacation than work. We both had been through a difficult year, and it did not seem worthwhile to stir up unhappy memories and dwell on them. After all, this trip was supposed to be our new beginning. I planned to move out of Joe's basement with the money and get my own apartment. Joe seemed happy with the work I was doing and said that when we got back to El Paso, I could work on the clock and get paid in full for everything I did around the shop. Yes indeed, as we approached 2002, things looked better for me than they had in a while.

We made it to Houston, Texas, and delivered the shipment. The trip worked out well for all of us. As we drove back to El Paso, we relished in the sense of accomplishment that came from completing the run. But change happened slowly for me. I was in pretty good physical shape again. When I got paid, the first thing I did was to buy a new pair of glasses. I think that the trip to Montana and the idea of getting it together sounded nice, but it all seemed to fall apart after we had been back in El Paso for a while. Ronnie eventually caught the bus out of town, and I was still living at Joe's well into January. After a while, I became impatient with the situation and started looking for a way to move out on my own again.

BACK ON THE ADDICTION TREADMILL

Joe was a great guy, he really was, but working for him was not so great sometimes. He gave me a roof over my head and put a little money in my pocket, but working for Joe, or for the kind of business that Joe ran, was not a career. At best, it was a way to fill a temporary void in life and then move on. El Paso seemed full of small, mom-and-pop businesses that would give someone a job when there was work, but could not afford to pay a living wage because the business itself was constantly on the edge, or uncertain. Joe's company was not in bankruptcy, at least not yet. But it was becoming apparent that it was in debt and was not producing any significant profits. This was one of the reasons why Joe decided to work for the moving company in Spokane: to generate some quick cash and keep things going. At that stage, it didn't really matter to me what was going on with the business; I was starting to drift back into active addiction, into that illusive and comfortable place that the needle provided.

I left Joe's on January 19, 2002, and moved back into Víctor's place in Colonia Felipe Angeles in Juárez. Víctor's mom rented me a room in her basement for 500 pesos, about fifty dollars, a month. As before, I rationalized how good it was for me to be living in Juárez. In my diary, I wrote: "I am happy because I am in Juárez and an apartment in El Paso would have left me broke with no money for food or anything else." I did not realize it at the time, but this is the way an addict's mind works. I put myself in situations that I knew would easily lead to my using dope. I could have made excuses all day about why it was better to live in Juárez, but when it was all said and done, I would have walked down the street and bought a shot of dope. And, of course, that was exactly what I did.

After moving back to Juárez, I worked for Joe a little while longer. Everything I had accumulated over the previous months started to disappear. I sold my cell phone to Kiko. He gave me about fifteen dollars' worth of heroin for it, but it did not really matter to me by then. As my habit got worse, Joe depended on me less and less. One Monday, after a weekend binge, I didn't show up for work at all. By then, I was right back where I had been the previous fall. I tried to clean up and get it together, but it just did not work for me. Joe went out of his way to help me restore myself physically, but there was only so much he could do. Even if economic opportunities had been available, I was not ready to benefit from them. I think that at that stage, I didn't really want to stop using dope. I just wanted to take a vacation from it for a little while.

I tried to detox at the El Paso County Detox, which was located at Southwestern General Hospital in central El Paso. I checked in and let myself get sick for a few days, but once I felt better, I packed my bags and signed myself out. While I was there, Joe's wife came by and picked up the warehouse keys. I still worked there occasionally, but I was back to being just another junkie looking for a day's work. It wasn't long before I began to make more money running my lines on the street than I made working. But I did stop in and talk with Joe from time to time. He always used to joke that I was a hell of a good worker when I wasn't on "that shit." The nice thing about Joe was that he did not resent me and never held a grudge; he just accepted me for what I was, and we remained friends.

Southwestern General was a pretty nice place to detox. There were televisions in the hospital rooms, and only two beds per room. Each room had a bathroom and a shower with great hot water. And they gave the patients three meals a day. The food took some getting used to, after a heroin withdrawal, but for the most part, it was pretty good. For anyone really ready to detox and find recovery, Southwestern General was the kind of place that could help.

The day I walked out of Southwestern General that February, I was more weak than sick. Just carrying my bags made me feel dizzy. I did not have any money, but Joe still owed me a week's pay. I knew that I could collect my money from Joe, but I went downtown and panhandled twenty or so dollars so that I could fix quickly. It seemed as if it would be easier to deal with everything once I fixed again, once I was under the influence of heroin. When I finally picked up my last paycheck from Joe's, it gave me a break from the daily routine that had already reestablished itself in my life. Picking up that paycheck was like saying, "Good-bye and nice knowing you." For Joe and his sidekick, Henry, it was more like "good luck, and if you're lucky, we'll see you next year."

Getting used to life at Víctor's was easy; it seemed as though I had never left. Víctor, finally out of the CERESO, had talked his mom into renting me the basement. It was below the kitchen of the main house. It was not much: a room that was about fourteen by eight feet at the bottom of a cement stairway. Everything was made of concrete, and there was a ceiling light with one electrical outlet. I didn't realize it at the time, but that basement would be my home for most of 2002. It was still winter when I moved in, and it was a bit cold. Víctor's mother kept a bunch of birdcages at the top of the stairs, and the birds always sang in the morning. Sometime before April, I wrote: "I like to listen to the birds upstairs, they sound so joyful on this rainy day, they sound nice from inside those little cages. It is very cold in here and I can't wait until winter is over. The cold is always the worst here in Juárez. Most houses here just aren't made for the cold and it is very hard for the people who can't afford heaters."

This was especially so for the cement and cinder-block dwellings of west Juárez. Walking through the neighborhoods on cold nights, I often watched people gather around bonfires or barrel fires in their front yards to stay warm. Even during those nights I had stayed at José's, he had a small electric heater that he used to crank up when it got cold. One time I met a waitress who invited me over to her friend's house during that winter. When she and I went inside, her friend asked us if we were cold. We told her that of course we were, so she turned on the oven and opened the oven door. This was normal for dealing with the cold in Juárez. But it still did not erase the fact that those buildings were not made to handle the cold. Juárez and El Paso are funny like that. Half the year it is so hot that it will dry you out. I mean, it is really hot. Yet for the other part of the year, it is cold. Spring and fall pass quickly, and summer often shifts into winter after a very few days that might be perceived as fall.

Víctor was washing cars for a living, but what it really amounted to was his hanging around a mechanic's shop and washing a few cars a day to maintain his heroin habit. When I moved back to Felipe Angeles in 2002, I was working at Joe's and had money. When I stopped working, I started panhandling again. In any case, I always had money for a fix and did not really worry about getting sick. For Víctor, this meant that if he got sick, I would always be around to get him out of it. That's the way junkies who are tight work it out. But I never called Víctor out on any favors. I always supported my own habit and gave Víctor a fix whenever he was down-and-out and needed one. Aside from renting from his mom and living next door to Víctor, I never really hung out with him on the street. It was not that we were not tight; it was that I did not have a lot of time to mess around. Maintaining a habit was a full-time job. Besides, Víctor went off on some wild excursions from time to time, and the last thing I wanted was to get caught with him when he was committing armed robbery or something. I usually sensed when he had been involved in that kind of activity because he would surprise me and give me a few globos.

Sometimes after a morning of panhandling on the street, around ten thirty or eleven, I would pass by where he washed cars and offer to share some dope with him. This was cool with him because if he was having a slow day, and his habit was down on him, I would help him get well so that he could hustle that afternoon. Aside from that, I sometimes ran into him around six or seven at night, when I was finished panhandling for the day. If he had gone through the whole day without a fix, I was one of the first to know it when I got back. In any event, I made pretty good money panhandling on the street then, and giving him a fix never imposed upon my habit. In fact, I made between sixty and eighty dollars a day panhandling and was really messing myself up by using more dope than I needed to.

Víctor's family never gave me any hassle. I paid my rent on time and helped them out with money for their electric bills. I helped keep Víctor *curado* (cured) of the sickness of heroin withdrawal, which otherwise might have caused him to go out and rob someone. When Víctor was hurting for a fix, he often disappeared, ripped something off and sold it, and came back with some dope. Another reason why Víctor got into trouble on numerous late-night excursions was because he liked to shoot cocaine. Shooting cocaine intravenously creates an instant rush that is quite different from that of heroin. Heroin takes the pain of withdrawal away and creates a euphoric, lackadaisical sleepiness or painlessness that lasts from several hours to all day. Cocaine, on the other hand, causes an intense rush that lasts about five minutes, after which, the person will more than likely want to induce the rush again. This is the same cycle that crack (rock cocaine) smokers and coke (powder cocaine) sniffers go through, but people who shoot cocaine experience the drug's effects to the fullest because of its direct injection into the bloodstream.

Víctor shot cocaine only after he had fixed himself with heroin, yet once he took that first shot of coke, he was off and running. I saw this as one of his weaknesses, and I told him about it all the time. But he did what he wanted. Víctor's brothers drank beer and smoked a little weed, and when Víctor was high on cocaine, they did not like it. It made him too unpredictable. If he wanted to keep doing it, he would hit the streets and find a way to get more. I tried shooting cocaine, but I never liked it. It was a sloppy high that made me feel too anxious. It was also a waste of money. Why waste the money I needed to keep from getting sick on something that made me feel sick once the rush was over? No thanks!

After I stopped working for Joe, when I was fully strung out, I did not sit and wallow in my misfortune. There was no time for that. I used my well-developed style of panhandling on the street and made pretty good money. I knew the dealers in the neighborhood and the backup dealers in other neighborhoods, and I had pretty good credit with all of them in case of an emergency. Nevertheless, in late March, I tried to clean up again, this time at the Aliviane drug treatment center in El Paso.

FIRST TIME AT ALIVIANE

One of the most memorable parts of that experience was getting into the program in the first place. An intake nurse named Jerry was supposed to draw blood from all the new patients. I told her that there was practically no way that she was going to find any veins in my arms, but she seemed pretty confident that she would. She tied my arm and began looking for a vein with the precision of a junkie. As she looked at the condition of my arms, she told me about her experiences with junkies in San Francisco. In a few minutes, she found a small vein somewhere on one of my wrists. I felt kind of cheated: if I had known about that vein, I would have used it myself. I was impressed with her ability to strike blood where I thought there was none. Some IV drug users possess the gift of being able to shoot up another person, and Jerry was gifted in this way. Because I knew that I did not possess this talent, I dreaded it when Víctor or someone else asked me to shoot them up in the neck or something. If you tried to help a junkie fix and missed the shot, it hurt you almost as much as it hurt them just to watch them writhe around in pain as the junk was absorbed into the skin and muscle tissue. If you missed while shooting yourself up, you could still expect the dope to kick in and make you feel better. It just kicked in slower.

The Aliviane experience was kind of crazy because they gave me some methadone for a few days in order to make the dope withdrawal less painful. It seemed pretty good until the last day of methadone, when I decided that I did not want to go through that shit (withdrawal) anytime soon. However, Aliviane was so far from downtown (in Socorro) that leaving there was full of uncertainty. I left anyway and hitched a ride to a local bus stop. I ended up at a large shopping center, where I panhandled just enough money to get back downtown. I also had thirteen dollars on me, so the only thing I had to do was get off the bus and walk across the bridge. I remember that day well because when I got back to Juárez, my room was still waiting for me. Víctor's family had not really noticed that I had been gone a few days, so everything was cool. I hung around the neighborhood and spent that day smoking cigarettes and drinking sodas until about four, when I went back to El Paso and made some money for the next day's fix, the rent, and something to eat.

BACK ON THE TREADMILL

By this time, the long lines that had become a regular feature of the bridge in the aftermath of September 11 were beginning to dissipate. Traffic on the bridge never really returned to normal, but it was not as bad as those first few days after the attacks. After I scoped out the traffic patterns, the best time to cross seemed to be around nine in the morning, after most of the pedestrian traffic had crossed, and around one in the afternoon. There was no real certainty to this, and just because those times might have been better did not mean that I always crossed then. Everything that I did depended on the availability of dope and how I felt in the morning. Sometimes, panhandling from eight to nine thirty in the morning brought in pretty good money, but even on my worst day, it still brought twenty dollars minimum. Afternoons brought in at least fifty dollars, and sometimes a lot more.

By May, I had lost a lot of weight and looked as skinny as ever; the summer's heat had arrived, and clean clothes became a necessity. Cinco de Mayo weekend brought a lot of money onto the street. It also brought a lot of tourists to Juárez. The bridge was packed with people, and it took me at least an hour or more to cross to El Paso. But the money seemed good, and I never went without dope. By this time, the best dealers around Felipe Angeles were the guys in Las Moras. They had good dope, and practically every junkie on the west side of Juárez was going there to pick up. As long as I showed up and gave them my business, I was a welcomed customer. If they did not have any dope, which was rare, they would go across town and pick some up as long as I agreed to wait around for them to get back. This was always an inconvenience, but in the long run, it was better than going around the neighborhood myself and trying to find another connection. I wrote about this in my journal in May 5, 2002: "It's a junkies nightmare . . . to be withdrawing and you got the money to cop, and you walk to the connection, and you knock on the door, or whatever, and they tell you that they sold out and there's no more dope, to either wait for them to re-up, or the painful walk to another dealer." By this time, my whole life had become centered on making money and maintaining a stable supply of heroin for my habit. Yet as my world shrank, I began to reflect inward.

For some reason, I was doing more writing in my journal around this time. It may have been because I actually had some free time to write. On May 6, 2002 I wrote:

> For the most part today was a good day. When I went
> downtown to hustle I started around noon. It was as usual,
> the hustle and grind of bumming money in the street. Then
> I saw the first bike cop. I didn't look at him directly, and I
> knew he hadn't seen me accept any money. I walked up the
> block and there was his partner, writing a ticket to a parked
> car. I faded in the shadows and drank a soda until they left.
> Then I started in trying to make up for lost time. By 3:15
> I cashed in at the Chinese restaurant. The nice lady there
> let me get the buffet for 3 dollars. I was done for the day, [I

had made] around 46 dollars, and that was cool for a Tuesday. 46 dollars for about 3 hours is around 15 an hour . . . When I was walking back to the bridge, I saw 3 bike cops on the street. [They threatened me, but let me go on my way] Around 7pm I went back downtown for sunset and hustled up 20 more dollars. 660 pesos+ for the day, not bad. Too bad most of it goes up the needle. If I wasn't addicted I would have a lot more money in my pocket. I know I got to clean up and soon.

Yet during those times, cleaning up was a hollow promise that I could ill afford to make to myself. My life was all about keeping up with my habit and paying the rent. In between that, the basic necessities of eating and drinking, as well as keeping some clean clothes on my back, consumed my everyday existence. I tried to live in Felipe Angeles as much as possible. I regularly hung around the little neighborhood stores, such as Benny's and the Los Monchis burrito stand. Living there was less expensive, so a few pesos went further when it came to buying either meals on the street or snacks and sodas for the room.

The more I used heroin, the more my veins gave out. What was once an armful of veins had disappeared after years of repeated injections. I was shooting up in my feet, my legs, my stomach, and my underarms. The small moments of minor gains on the street did not outweigh the pain of overall failure and self-destruction. Although I often numbed myself to the world around me, by the summer of 2002, I was beginning to dread the realities of my lifestyle and to question my own existence. On May 9, 2002, I wrote:

> Being a dope addict is a pain . . . Its like tripping over your shoe laces over and over . . . I just did my morning 2 globos and am lying in bed watching TV . . . My stomach is growling as it always does when the body goes through the transition from halfway sick to the state of influence under heroin. Oh how it feels good to fade away this morning.

The daily routine of maintaining my habit and functioning on the street was a lot to handle. By that time I had a fan, a television, and a bag full of clean clothes to look forward to. But two days later, nothing much had changed:

Well another day is here [and] I hope today is as good as yesterday. I wish I wasn't hooked on heroin; it's getting to the point where I'm wearing myself down, and I dread shooting up when I can't even find a vein anymore. I just took a shot in my ankle and it really sucks. I'm waiting for the affect to wear in and I hope it's strong. Bumming money in the streets really sucks.

My nicotine habit was also getting out of control. I smoked so many cigarettes that I just threw the butts on the floor and swept them up when I had the time. This part of it all seemed like pure insanity. Sometimes when I looked around my room, hundreds of cigarette butts covered the floor. It was then that I would clean up the room, and then look at myself long enough to see that I needed a shave.

By this time, I was considering going through the pain of withdrawal again. Waking up sick everyday and shooting up just to feel normal and have enough strength to function was stressful enough, but my imagined projections of withdrawing on the street, or at Víctor's, made me realize that this lifestyle needed to stop. The main problem was that the part of me that wanted to stop was not powerful enough to overcome the part of me that wanted to stay within the false security that the availability of heroin seemed to offer. Seven weeks after the journal entry quoted above, here's what I had to say:

Well I just shot two globos and I feel it coming on. I didn't miss the shot and it feels good because I always miss a lot lately, since I have no veins left. Well I finished paying my rent . . . I like the calm of the morning. I hope everything goes good today; it is a Saturday and there should be a fair amount of money in the street today. Don't feel like writing much, it's very hot. Hope my sneakers dried last night. It never rains, but when it rains it pours. These streets were flooded big time. Well, time to get dressed and do it again.

The day before this entry, I had been out panhandling in El Paso until the early evening. It had rained so much that the streets were practically knee-deep with water. I had tied plastic bags over my feet to try to keep them dry, but it was no use. Much as I hated to spend the money, I broke down and bought an umbrella. Panhandling on El

Paso Street in the rain with an umbrella offered an easy way to blend into the crowds. Groups of people stood in doorways and alcoves, and I moved from group to group and ran my panhandling routine on them. Some gave, and the rain did not stop my routine or slow down the flow of money. Of course, walking over the muddy hillsides and pathways in Juárez made buying dope more a project than it normally was. But this did not seem to stop dealers and customers from their daily rounds. Bad weather offered protection and cover from the police. I often watched people run right across the border during rainy nights, and it seemed that many people in the underworld of the border relished bad weather for the protection that it offered.

ROUND TWO AT SOUTHWESTERN GENERAL

By the beginning of July, I was thinking about leaving Víctor's family's place. Víctor was locked up again, and his sister and her two kids had moved into his room. On July 4, 2002, I checked into detox at Southwestern General Hospital in El Paso. It was my second time there that year. I felt sincere as I went through intake that morning, but as the dope wore off and the cigarettes stopped tasting good, I had second thoughts. I began to feel real shitty, real fast. I don't remember how long I had been there, maybe a day or so, when I was in so much pain from withdrawal that I decided to take a hot shower at two in the morning. I remember taking lots of hot showers that day, and I usually put a metal folding chair in the shower and just sat there and let the hot water calm my aching nerve endings and stinging bones. This time, I stood up and let the hot water calm me down. For someone going through heroin withdrawal, hot baths or showers are the best short-term natural painkillers. Usually, I could sleep for a few minutes after a hot shower.

This time, however, I was not able to get out of the shower before I started blacking out. I remember trying to pick my foot up over the ledge of the shower floor, but my foot did not seem to make it. As I got out of the shower, I became really dizzy and fell on the floor. Everything around me looked like a cartoon, and I heard some crazy reverberating sounds. After I fell, the folding chair that was leaning up against the wall also fell and made a loud clanging noise. A nurse heard the noise as she was walking down the hallway and ran into my room.

When she saw me on the floor of the shower room, she called the night staff, and they helped me get up.

As they asked me all kinds of questions, it became apparent that I was medically unstable. They brought me downstairs to ICU (intensive care unit) and called the doctor. The doctor was on call, so it took him a few minutes to get there. They looked me over, and the doc told me that I was dehydrated. I was very skinny—skin and bones. The vomiting and diarrhea had depleted my body of what little water it had. Because I had been using so much heroin, my withdrawal this time was extremely painful, and I just could not hold down any food or liquid. They gave me some pills, but they were too weak to stabilize me.

The doctor wanted to put in an IV line and rehydrate me. This was a good idea, but there were no veins left on my arms. Most of the easy veins had been destroyed. It started to get painful as he poked my arms and tried to find a vein. I told him that he might have better luck with my legs. But after he and the nurse looked at the battleground that had become my legs, they decided that they would not attempt an IV insertion there. Finally, the doctor got serious and looked at my hands. Most of those veins were all dried up from continuous heroin injections, but the doctor found a small vein on the middle finger of my right hand. So there I was, going through heroin withdrawal in an ICU with an IV line pumping water into my middle finger. They kept me in ICU for twelve hours.

I began to feel a little bit better while I was there, and it was not long before they brought me back upstairs to the detox unit. I forced myself to eat some of the hospital food, but I still felt very weak. I did not sleep very well that night, but by the next morning, I had enough strength to shower and shave. While I shaved, I decided to leave the hospital and go back to Juárez. I do not remember exactly what happened, but my bag full of clothes seemed really heavy as I carried it on my back and walked out the front door.

LIKE A NIGHTMARE IMPOSSIBLE TO WAKE UP FROM

I carried my two bags down to the bus stop and waited. In the meantime, I asked anyone near me for some change. Between the money that I had on me and the change I bummed outside the hospital, I had enough to catch the bus downtown. I still felt weak and dizzy because of the withdrawal, but I knew that in a few hours, this feeling would be replaced by the rush and numbness of heroin. When I got downtown in my weakened state, I panhandled, but it was not easy. I think shaving that morning gave me an advantage; as I knew, people were more apt to give to a clean-shaven panhandler. Nevertheless, the routine was monotonous and painful. I carried those bags up and down Stanton Street and ran my lines on anyone who listened. After I had about twenty dollars in my pocket, I headed to Juárez.

I was not sure whether Víctor's family had cleaned out my room. After my dramatic experience at the hospital, I felt so removed from everything that I assumed that they had. As I imagined being home-less again, I dragged my ass back to Colonia Postal, the neighborhood of the casita, under the assumption that I could cop some dope from Marcos. When I got there, the sun was slowly setting beyond the hori-zon. Marcos was not home. I found someone on the street who remem-bered me, and I offered to turn him on to some dope if he knew where to connect. In a few minutes, I had five globos in my hand. The young guy on the street had an old needle that was so used that all the num-bers and lines had worn off it. I told him that if he didn't get some *clórax* (bleach) that I wasn't going to use it. He took me to his family's house and went in and got some liquid bleach and a cooker (a soda-can bot-tom). Inside an outdoor bathroom that had a little lightbulb hanging from the ceiling, I pasted two globos to the bottom of the can. Bad as I felt, my adrenaline increased. I was so close to instantly curing myself that the intensity of it all gave me enough energy to make it happen. Scraping the stuff into liquid form without any fire took longer than I would have liked, but I slowly scraped that shit very carefully, aware that one wrong move would ruin it all.

Once I had finished stirring it up, I took a piece of cotton from my sock, rolled it up into a little ball, and dropped in into the center of the small, quarter-size puddle of liquid heroin. Carefully, I stuck the tip of the needle on the cotton and drew the plunger back. As the needle filled up, I knew it was almost over. In a few more minutes, three days' worth of pain would all be a distant memory. An instant later, I stuck that dull needle into my armpit, pulled back the plunger, watched it fill up with blood, and emptied that shit into my body; the slow instant rush made everything painless once again.

I gave the guy a globo and headed back to Víctor's. There really wasn't anywhere else for me to go. I had some dope stashed away for in the morning and figured that even if I stayed on the street in Felipe

Angeles, I could still take a shower at my ex-girlfriend's house. When I got to Víctor's, I was happy to see that the lock was still on the door to my room; the keys were still in my pocket. Víctor's mom said hi to me, and I told her that I had been working in El Paso. I was really glad that I wasn't dope-sick when I went back there. As far as I was concerned, I had lucked out. My room was still there, just as I had left it. I had a whole bunch of used needles in the room, so I was all set to start running the next day.

The only thing Víctor's family seemed concerned about was the rent money, and a little bit more for the light bill. After a while, I regretted having left the hospital AMA (against medical advice), yet, as always, I soon forgot about all that. The hospital experience became embedded in my memory as a bad example of what would happen when I tried to stop using dope. It gave me more incentive to continue panhandling and surviving with my habit. One thing that I learned from it all was that I needed to eat and drink as much as possible. Yet the only way to do that was to keep myself medicated and stable. By this time of the summer, the days were very hot, and staying hydrated became almost as important as staying high.

In the middle of July occurred one of those days I'll never forget:

> Well here I am again. I still owe 50.00 pesos for the rent. Víctor got transferred from the County downtown to the Annex out on Montana . . . He's been clean for about two months . . . I probably shouldn't have left that detox AMA . . . Now I hardly got any veins left and it's crazy . . . I'm sweating already, it's been raining and the air is very humid here. Yesterday in the morning I was walking to Las Moras to go cop the D. I noticed a police truck and a forensics van. When I got closer [I noticed that] they were looking over a body in the street. It was a dead man. A corpse across the street from Felipe Angeles school, there it was covered up in a blanket, the feet sticking out the end, wearing work boots.

I had woken up early that morning to get my morning fix. As I walked down through Felipe Angeles toward Las Moras, down by the neighborhood school, I saw a guy lying on the sidewalk, feet facing the street. I passed by and did not pay him any mind. I thought that maybe the guy had been drinking and was out on the street sleeping it off. After I had copped and was returning to the room, the cops were there picking up the body. It was the first time that I had ever seen a dead person. I had not even stopped to think that the guy might be dead when I passed him. Although it lurked in the shadows of my lifestyle, death seemed distant to me.

However, death was never as distant as it seemed. Earlier that year, around January or February, when I was staying at Joe's, I had gone back to Altavista to get high at Pepe's place. Pepe's brother Víctor and one of the guys from the neighborhood told me that Pepe was dead. I don't know the exact details, but either an overdose or the lifestyle of using dope everyday wore him down enough to take his life. The last time I saw Pepe, he looked like a walking corpse. He was awfully skinny; his cheekbones were sucked in and made him look like a mummy or something. They told me that he just didn't wake up one morning. I went back there from time to time and got high with Pepe's brother Víctor. But I stopped going there altogether after he tried to pull a knife on me. When he pulled the knife, I just laughed at him and told him to go ahead and stab me. I had about seven dollars on me, and there was no way I was giving it up. He backed down, and we parted from each other's company. I never went back there after that unless I was just walking through the neighborhood.

Later that summer, someone else pulled a knife on me. It happened in Las Moras around six one afternoon, just after I had finished panhandling for the day. I was waiting in line to cop some dope when one of the junkies that always hung around the hilltop shooting gallery tried to test me. He pulled out a nasty-looking knife and told me to give him five pesos. I just laughed at him and asked him if he was going to kill me for five pesos (fifty cents). I knew he wasn't going to do it after he started to explain himself to me. As I approached the window of the house (there were so many customers waiting for them to start selling that they had us line up at a window and buy there), I told the dealers that there was a guy out here ready to kill me for five pesos. I joked about it and tried to minimize the whole situation—the last thing I wanted after copping was to have this guy following me with the knife and all. The people in the house knew me and knew I was a regular customer, so they told the guy with the knife to knock it off and get lost. I walked down the hill and never gave it a second thought. About a week or so later, I saw the same guy panhandling down at the Del Río store below Las Moras. I had just had a good day, so I gave him a cigarette and bought him a soda. We shook hands, and he never messed with me again.

A lot of the junkies in the neighborhood knew that I lived at Víctor's, and they gave me my space. Víctor's family was respected in that neighborhood; his brothers were known, and nobody ever came around there trying to steal anything, although someone once smashed the window of his brother's truck with a rock. My routine for the summer of 2002 was pretty much the same as ever. I was on the street every day, panhandling, dodging the cops, and maintaining my connections so that I wouldn't be sick. And my reflections on it all were pretty much the same as before: "Well I'm hot and sweaty and dirty and all messed up. I know I got to change this situation. I just wonder how and where. I just hope for a good long night's sleep. August 15th? Damn it's hot in here."

NEW DEALERS

That summer went by so fast that I can hardly remember anything at all about it. When I wasn't in El Paso panhandling, I was panhandling and hanging around Felipe Angeles. Sometime around the end of summer, Perico and the Las Moras dealers started selling less dope. New dealers were selling down by the river in Felipe Angeles. I went down there and copped some dope from them and got to know them pretty well. There were two brothers named René and Rocky. René was selling the stuff, and his younger brother, Rocky, was helping him out. As I noted sometime in 2002:

> René used to sell used cars in Juárez, his little brother Rocky is a junkie. I think that they had a lot of problems or something, so René decided to sell heroin. The house turned into a shooting gallery. Now René doesn't even use drugs, but Roc is a junkie so him and the boys start shooting dope outside and it turns into a fucked up situation: every other customer wants to shoot up on the premises. René is only making 30–40 dollars a day profit.

After a while, I knew the whole family, and if I showed up with some money to buy, they would invite me in and ask me whether I wanted something to eat. I became good friends with Rocky, and if he wasn't there, his mom would tell me to come in and sit down and wait for them.

They lived near the river, across from the Rescue Mission. There was the main house, where Rocky, his sister, and his mother lived. Then there was a small house behind the mother's place, where René lived with his wife and kids. The second house had been recently constructed and was surrounded by a wooden fence made of pallets. The dope they sold was good, and after a while, René started selling quarter grams of brown tar heroin for one hundred pesos each. He gave me six for the price of five. When I started buying from him, I was spending about five hundred pesos a day on heroin.

As my body deteriorated, I had a lot of trouble finding veins to shoot dope in. One day, I told Rocky that I was having trouble fixing because all my veins were gone. He was going through the same thing, so we started shooting each other in the neck. Shooting into a neck vein is hard to do alone; it usually requires an experienced shooter to help out. The first few times he shot dope into my neck, it was like a junkie's Christmas. But after a while, those veins became harder and harder to hit. This really became a problem when I had to sit there for what seemed like forever while Rocky moved the needle around, trying to hit a vein in my neck.

Pretty soon René and Rocky were the only dope dealers in Felipe Angeles. I was a regular customer, but so were all the junkies in the neighborhood. Every morning, the wooded area between their place and the river was occupied by all the neighborhood junkies, who used the woods as a shooting gallery. The cops didn't come around there often, but when they did, the place emptied out for the rest of the morning. If René didn't have any dope, he would say so. This usually meant a trip across town to another connection, such as Altavista, El Refugio, or maybe Marcos's place. If I showed up sick in the morning and they didn't have anything, Rocky often tried to help me by getting us a ride to go cop someplace else. I would get him high if he did that for me, but most times, I just caught the bus by myself.

I didn't like breaking my routine too much, so I often kept a morning fix under my pillow. I didn't like to go through all the drama of trying to find a wake-up fix while starting to withdraw. However, every once in a while, it happened. I think those experiences kept me vigilant and ahead of the game as much as possible. After all, fixing in a strange neighborhood in the morning was risky, and if it really went bad and you got picked up by the cops, things got real shitty, real fast. Aside from little run-ins with El Paso's bicycle cops, I didn't really have any problems with the police that summer.

After hanging around René and Rocky's for a while, I became familiar with the people who sold to them. It was an older couple, and they seemed all right to talk to. They did not matter that much to me, because I knew that without money for a fix, I would be just as sick as the next dope addict. Friendly as things seemed between Rocky, René, and me, I knew that I needed to keep panhandling every day. The only reason I got in with them the way that I did was because I was a steady customer. Unsurprisingly, if I didn't show up for a day, they wondered what had happened. René told me that he bought dope in small amounts that he knew could sell. If I didn't show up one day, it threw his routine off and left him holding dope that he was hoping to turn into cash. After a few raids by the police, he sold only to a few customers and was not so public about his dealing. This was because the cops wanted payoffs that cut too far into his profits. By selling only to a few select regulars, he turned over a fair amount of dope in private. Thus, these guys closed the public store and made the connection private.

Sometimes I showed up there and visited them for hours. I knew the whole family, and even got to know Rocky's ex-wife and daughter. When I showed up, they knew that I was picking up my daily supply, and it got to the point that I was using between six and eight quarter grams every twenty-four hours. As late as October 2002, I was still in some sense enjoying it: "No sé la fecha, y no creí que me tiré tan rápido y no me ponché. I didn't miss the shot and I'm happy to say that the blood flowed smoothly. Oh yea, I can feel it coming on . . . a numb sleepiness . . . another cigarette. I hope today is easy out there."

NO DRUG RUNNING FOR ME, THANKS

In Juárez, a lot of people propositioned me to run drugs across the border. Ever since my first year there, folks had offered me numerous chances to make some money by running drugs. But I made enough money as a panhandler. The people that René worked for also made me numerous offers. They were determined to talk me into running drugs for them. The old woman told me stories about how she had made more than $100,000 by running drugs. She told me about how she wanted to have something in her life, like a house or a car, insinuating that I too could have these kinds of things if I just took a chance and drove a few cars across the bridge. These people were dead serious about turning me loose with a carload of drugs. They said it was only marijuana and that it wasn't that much. The woman told me that she had eventually gotten busted, but she minimized the time she spent behind bars, saying that when she got out, she still had her money.

I thought this shit was totally insane, strung out as I was. A few years, five, ten, or twenty—these people were out of their mother-fuckin' minds. I did not even have a driver's license. One day, they even came looking for me at Víctor's place. Víctor's mother came downstairs, knocked on my door, and told me that someone was out there looking for me. She must have thought they were my friends or something. I went out to the end of the driveway, and it was the couple that René worked for. They tried to talk me into going, but in the end I just said no thanks.

The woman acted like a salesperson and tried to get me to act on her verbal suggestions. She offered me a thousand dollars to take a vehicle over the bridge. She said that they had it all set up: the customs officer was bought and paid for, so the only thing I needed to do was stay in the far left lane on the bridge. I thought about it. The thousand dollars sounded real good. It had been so long since I had a thousand dollars in my hand, and it would allow me to stop panhandling for a while. But I knew what would happen. I did not have a driver's license, and if customs asked me for my license on the bridge, it was going to be all over. I knew that if I told them yes, I would be putting myself in a situation that was much riskier than just panhandling on the street. This was another bottom that I did not want to reach. The stress and the worry were too much. They even offered to front me some dope so that I could be good and high when I made the trip.

The woman spoke good English and said that she was from New Mexico. She offered me various jobs at various rates. I could drive a car over the bridge and on to Albuquerque for five thousand dollars; I could drive one over the bridge to El Paso for $1,000. Didn't they realize that I was strung out? Did they think that I would make it all the way to Albuquerque without a fix? No way! There was no way that I was going to drive all the way up there and then take the bus home. Even under normal (legal) circumstances, I would not have left town. I knew that I would have been sick as hell by the time I got back.

As I leaned on the fence at the end of Víctor's driveway, the woman told me that all I had to do was deliver a car to the Wal-Mart parking lot in El Paso, catch a cab back to the bridge, walk across, and hand them the keys; they would give me a thousand dollars for doing that. I knew what the bridge was like. I had driven and walked across it countless times: the lines, the constant waiting, the people coming up to your car windows to sell you something or wash your windows, and then the questions at the port of entry. Where are you going? Whose vehicle is this? Yet the most dreaded would have been: let me see your driver's license. Imagine that! No, there was no way I wanted any part of it. I told Víctor's mother that the next time those people came looking for me, tell them that I was not there. The usual *no está* was good enough for them. I could tell Víctor's family the truth, and they would understand what had to be done. After that, Víctor's mom always told them that I was gone. Soon after, they stopped coming around to look for me.

Because Víctor's family already had one son (Víctor) locked up because of the insanity of drug running, they knew all too well what was at stake. Who knows? Maybe they did not want to lose the rent money I was paying them. I think Víctor's mom knew that I was strung out; she was just good-hearted and probably thought it best not to talk about that stuff. In any case, I never used out in the open and always hid my works. For the most part, I did this out of respect. Regardless, one good look at my physical appearance made it plain that I was a junkie and that I had been strung out for a very long time.

Speaking of Víctor, he was still in jail in El Paso. He had got caught while crossing the border down by the river one night, possibly running some marijuana. Later on, he told me that he had assaulted a Border Patrol officer. I don't know what happened, but Víctor thought that American jails were like hotels. He ate well and learned English while he was there.

Panhandling had been good to me. My Spanish was getting a little bit better, and a lot of the folks in the street knew me and always gave me a something when they could. Yet the thought of a thousand dollars stayed with me. With that kind of money I could take a few weeks off, eat some good meals, and get myself some new clothes. I could also have gotten some new eyeglasses. But the money would not have lasted that long. The more money I had, the more dope I used. The free time that the money would buy me would end up being used for shooting up and hanging out. Yes, it would break me from the daily routine of panhandling, but if I didn't panhandle, I wouldn't have a life. My panhandling network was my life. I was getting good at it, and it gave me

Endings and Beginnings   183

something to do. In a sense, panhandling kept me alive socially as well as physically. The thousand dollars wouldn't have lasted two weeks. When it was gone, I would have still been strung out (probably worse), and I would still have to keep panhandling. Thus, it seemed better to just keep panhandling and forget about everything else. In the end, there is no such thing as easy money.

THE SLOW SPIRAL TOWARD
ANOTHER DETOX

In the fall, I got on food stamps, and that helped out a little. Rocky and René did not hold it against me for not wanting to work for their connection. I still gave them steady business, and they were glad for it. Rocky and I were tight, so I suppose that this mutual arrangement benefited everyone. They were happy with things the way they were.

By early November I was becoming really tired of it all. I tried to get back into the El Paso County Detox at Southwestern General Hospital, but because I had walked out AMA last July, they would not take me back until November 11.

> Well you know it's time to quit shootin dope when you can't find a vein in 2 hours. Shit, I'm sooo fuckin mad. Wish that hospital would take me before the 11th. This shit is growing old. I bummed $50.00 in the streets today . . . only six more days to go.

I tried to use less, but this did not mean that I wanted to stop. As the weather grew colder, I thought about getting off the streets for the winter.

One thing about panhandling on the street was that the pennies did accumulate. As I noted on November 6:

> Well I'm broke again except for 200 pesos (approx 20 dollars) I have been saving since it's always good to keep something in your pocket. I only bummed thirty dollars today in the street, and the money went in one hand and out the other. So maybe it's better off that I'm broke that way I will not use as much. Less money, less drugs. I wonder if I

should sell my TV and cash in my pennies, or should I leave
them for Víctor's mom. It's about 30–35 dollars in pennies,
and I know I need the money more than them. As far as the
cigarette burns on the bed, well . . .

At Víctor's, I had about five coffee cans full of pennies and did not feel
like doing anything with them.

Much as I wanted to get off the streets, I knew that if I used my time
wisely, I could stay fixed and not be sick. I just did not want to get sick
from withdrawal before I had to.

During the last couple of months of 2002, I began writing more and
more in my journal. This entry, from November 7, was typical:

Well today I returned the library books after I bummed
50 dollars in the street. Damn this year sure went by fast.
I just realized it as I wrote the date down . . . I could have
made more money today if the people would just give a little bit more. Before I forget I'll write about the two pa-
chuco bike cops (Although I wish I would never remember them, I know I will forget them soon enough if I do
not write about them). I think they are related or something, maybe brother in laws, or cousins. Two Mexican-
American bike cops, they are the only ones that know me
by name. They are the only people downtown who know
my real whole name (unfortunately). It's from running all
those checks on me. I'll never forget the day I ran into the
ringleader and . . . the other rookies. It was Nov–Dec 1999.
I was out panhandling and the day was cold and windy.
I just got done hitting up some rich Mexicans when they
[the cops] saw them handing me the change. The older one
asked me for ID and when I went to reach in my coat for
my papers he went for his gun[—]like I was gonna be stupid enough to pull a gun on four cops. He didn't draw out
of his holster, but he was ready . . . When I pulled out the
papers he was at ease; he ran my ID and then I was on my
way. Although they hassled me a lot, they never stopped me
from getting 50–60 dollars a day . . . The younger one saw
me one day when I was jaywalking. The bastard had the
nerve to stop me for jaywalking one day when I was on my
way home from work. [It was] in the Spring of 2001 [after] I

had just loaded a shipment for a line driver. I had a hundred dollars on me and was in a good mood walking home from work when this idiot rides up on his bike and hassles me for crossing the street when the light says don't walk. I wonder if they really have any idea how much money I make each week from panhandling. I know they would have a fit and fall in it if they really knew—50 or 70 bucks a day isn't that much money, but multiply that by 7 days a week and that's [between] 400 and 500 dollars for my better weeks on the street. Well, I feel my shot kickin in, time to smoke a cigarette and dream a little bit.

I don't know why I started writing so much around this time. I never considered myself biblically religious, but after reading the Bible five times in a row—Old and New Testaments—I somehow thought I would try to record all this insanity so that someday, someone could make some sense out of it all. I remember that when I first arrived in the El Paso–Juárez area, I saw a saying painted on the side of the mountain in Juárez: *"Ciudad Juárez La Biblia es la Verdad Leela"* ("Juárez, the Bible is the truth. Read it.") For some reason, I decided to read it for myself and try to make some sense out of what was going on with me.

One thing I started to figure out real fast is that people are messed up, and it does not really matter where they were from or who they think they are. I think that I grew increasingly defensive as people became aware of me. The couple that supplied dope to Rocky and René started to look for me again; they kept trying to get me to drive for them. As I noted on November 8, they must have been

trying to play me for a sucker, offering me 2500.00 dollars to go to Albuquerque NM. I suppose the going rate is 5 grand . . . but when your ass gets caught at one of those checkpoints it's all over and you are through. I just can't stand the thought of spending one day in jail, much less 1–20 years. So I guess I will hit the streets again and try for 100 dollars at panhandling. It shouldn't be that bad, just 3 more days to go and the weekend is here, so the money should flow pretty good.

That morning went pretty well, and I made it back to the room for my midday fix around noon. Afterward, I started writing again:

I shot the quarter of dope into the little vein in my left middle finger and the blood registered on the first try, thank
god for small miracles. I just lit a smoke and in a few minutes the dope will be kickin in. I hope it holds me all day
so I can get the money I need for more. I bummed about
50 bucks yesterday in about 4 hours, so today should be a
lot better. Oh yea, it's kickin in good now. Another cigarette and I'm deciding whether or not to take my briefcase
with me. Last night I felt a pain in my heart and I wonder if
it wasn't a small heart attack or just some pain from smoking and or heartburn from junkfood. My diet hasn't been
the best lately; the best food I ate this week was the Chinese
buffet, which I should call the Korean buffet, since they are
all Korean and not one Chinese person works there. It's the
Mexican Korean buffet: vegetables with chile peppers and
Mexican hot sauce . . . I will walk after this cigarette.

Later on that day, I returned to the basement room at Víctor's family's place and began writing again.

Well its 6:00 [and] I just shot 1 quarter. [It's been] approx.
6 hours since my last shot. Damn, it's working already; must
be some new fresh dope [be]cause it hit me faster than the
stuff from in the morning. Burn in my fingers . . . It feels
fuckin good—need otro frajo y I hit the little blood vessel in my thumb in my left hand and it was a home run w/
very little pain . . . Anyway that quarter should hold me until 6:00am or so in the morning (damn that dope feels good
and I'm so glad I didn't miss that shot). I got three quarters for in the morning and 130 pesos (about 13 dollars) and
I guess it's all I need for now. I'm better off poor because if I
was rich I would shoot more dope and end up sicker sooner
or later. Yea, less money and less drugs, I guess I'm better off
that way for now, since I plan on detoxing starting Monday
and if all goes good Nov 11th will be the first day of the rest
of my life . . . I hope I don't get too sick this time. As long
as I taper down this weekend and shoot a little less I should
be O.K. Just need to go to bed earlier and enjoy my sleep
[be]cause it's gonna be awhile before I get another good
night's sleep once I start detoxing.

Well I got a box of snack cakes and some sodas . . . I hope
they show something good on TV tonight . . . I hope this
withdrawal goes quick and easy and that I don't experience
too much pain. If it all goes [well] by next Friday I will be
clean and the worst will be over. Hope I don't end up like
the last time in ICU with a bag of water going in my middle finger . . . Anyway another day is done and I hope tomorrow is better than today and that I get 80 or 100 bucks.

There just wasn't a lot to do when things went smooth. This gave
me a lot of time to reflect on what it was I was doing. It also gave me a
lot of time to write. The next evening I wrote some more:

Today I bummed 66.00 dollars; I was gonna go for 70.00
but I decided to stop after eating that plate of Chinese food.
I never knew regular pockets could hold so much change:
21.00 dollars in U.S.A. and 17 in Mexican—38 dollars in
change. I hope the people give more paper bills tomorrow . . . Countdown to detox on the 11th . . . I just shot
a quarter gram of heroin into my left hand between my
thumb and my pointer finger, into some hardass little vein
that hurt just a little bit when the needle went in, but the
blood registered and the needle filled with blood and the
dope went in with no bad feelings, even rather smoothly for
such a hard place to be shooting into, but I ain't got no veins
left anywhere, so I need to get it where I can. My lower legs
look like a battlefield with abscesses, bumps, and scars, and
my lower arms aren't much better. My upper arms and outer
chest is spent, the left side of my neck is all fucked up with
a big bump (abscess) that hurts when I sleep the wrong way
on it. The right side of my neck never had any blood to begin with [after a few shots]. I never had strong veins and
now they're all gone. Well, it's finally kickin in. At least a
peaceful moment; I'm glad today is over and I got the medicine I need for another morning. I can remember when I
had perfect blood veins, and I swore I would never shoot
dope with the needle. They told me eventually I would
quit sniffing and start shooting up, and yea, they were right.
Once I got hooked on shooting it was the beginning of
the end.

As I've noted, Saturday and Sunday were the best days to make money on the street. People had money and were on their own time. I think that people tend to be more benevolent when they are under less pressure and fewer time constraints. When people have time to spend, their humanity overrides worries about being on time. People do not tend to want to give anything when they are in a hurry.

The day before I planned to enter detox, my routine didn't really vary:

> Well I just shot my second quarter (sounds like a fuckin football game or something). Anyway, I shot it into the same place as last night—into the hand on the side of the pointer finger between the finger and the thumb. Now I'm waiting and writing: waiting for the effects to kick in. My stomach is starting to grumble and I am glad I didn't miss. To miss in the hand would really suck . . . it would hurt like hell and take forever to travel to the heart . . . Well, hopefully tomorrow is detox day and I hope I haven't waited this long in vain. Well, I feel it comin on (the high) and of course it feels good. Time for a cigarette and pretty soon time to hit the bricks for some more money.

That day, I had a difficult time making my usual quota. I knew it was my last day on the street, or at least I hoped it was. So that night, I poured out my frustrations in my journal:

> Yea, I made it through this fuckin day and I wish I was fuckin dead. Can't hardly find a fuckin blood vessel [with my] arms all fucked up. Blood veins in my neck all fucked up . . . I hope the detox lets me in tomorrow, all this goddamn waiting . . . I been wearing the same fucked up clothes for weeks and all my clothes are dirty, wish I had the . . . time to wash them, but it takes so fuckin long to panhandle [$]50.00. Joe was telling me that I should feel bad for lying for money and taking it from working people. Fuck that. Him and all those other so called businessmen lie for money everyday. Just [be]cause I use it for drugs and I am on the bottom of society it makes it wrong . . . Drugs should be legalized and you should be able to go to a drug store and pick your fuckin poison, just like in a liquor store.

Fuckin bastards drink until their faces are red and their families have fled the scene. At least marijuana should be legalized. It's natural much more than alcohol. As far as heroin goes, they already give out methadone for money, just like dope it's the same fuckin thing and the withdrawal is twice as bad . . . to make it so bad the clinic is only open when its daytime (worktime). So how [are] you gonna work and take meth at the same time. They should open at night and give out more take home bottles. I feel that heroin should be bagged and sold over the counter to confirmed addicts who need it and want it, instead of [them] withdrawing and being sick and buying it from illegal sources. Let the feds make the $ instead of organized crime. As far as cocaine, I feel it's the one thing we can all do without. It should be sold at the bars an[d] liquor stores with alcohol and if the people want to use it, it should be their own choice . . . At least if it was legal with a 21 year old age limit, it would help finance our government instead of the mafia drug lords. There would be less violence in the streets if drugs were legal. I hate cocaine, but if people want to do it that's their fuckin' problem. They [are] gonna do it anyway, one way or another, why not legalize it, sell it, document the users, and start more programs and rehab centers to help people stop and change? Like alcohol, there is casual use and then there is abuse. Less prisons and more rehab centers is what this country fuckin' needs. People ignore the issues. They see an addict on the street begging for money and they put em down, but they drink half their pay and use drugs themselves. I've seen it, I'm not blind. I've been robbed by the cops, bought my way out of jail time in Mexico, nobody knows nothing, nobody cares. Money, money, it's all about fuckin' dinero. If you got money you can't do nothing wrong. If you ain't got no money everything you do wrong is trying to get money. It's all about money . . . Drug addiction is a vicious circle and you're better off outside of that circle because once you're caught up in it, you're all fucked up. When you got no more material things to lose, you start losing personal thing, and then you lose an arm, or an eye, or your life or your soul. I've got to try to get out while I'm still able. Fuck what all the people think, what's done is done. It's time to move out and move through this. Tomorrow is the beginning.

That night was my last night at Víctor's place in Felipe Angeles. Víctor was still locked up, and my big day had finally arrived. The above statement, in retrospect, was a convergence of all my anger, fear, philosophy, uncertainty, and conditioned thinking that had built up within me over the last five years. At that time, I didn't have any idea what was going to happen next, but I knew that it was time to try something different. It felt funny to think that I was finally walking away from it all. I cleaned up the room and left everything there that I could not carry: "Well, at last it's finally here. Nov. 11th the day I have thought so much about and the day I have been waiting for all this time . . . Need to stay focused this time and not let stupid thoughts interfere with my recovery. Well I better clean up this room a little bit and take the clothes I'm gonna take . . . I hope I don't get too sick."

SOUTHWESTERN GENERAL, ROUND THREE

That morning, I shot up the last of the dope that I had saved and caught the bus downtown to the bridge. Walking across the bridge, it seemed just like another day. The only real difference was that my bags were full. Walking to the bus stop, it felt strange not to be asking anyone for any money. After a short wait, I caught the bus to Southwestern General Hospital. Walking into the hospital was like returning to last July. The intake was the same as before. In a while, I was up on the detox unit, walking around in green hospital pajamas.

If you were detoxing at Southwestern General, they expected you to participate in all of their workshops and presentations unless you were really sick. I don't remember exactly how long I was there before I fell into heavy withdrawal, but it wasn't long before I was throwing up and having diarrhea. They gave me something to stop the vomiting, but the pain of my aching bones and nerve endings was beyond comprehension. I took a bunch of hot showers and tried to pass the time by keeping as busy as possible. I could not eat for the first few days that I was there. Eventually, I forced myself to eat, no matter how painful it was.

Sitting in the workshops was interesting. Two counselors, Sam and Lou, gave presentations about all kinds of wild stuff, such as how brain chemistry changes when someone is under the influence of cocaine. Lou liked to show an old Frank Sinatra movie in which Sinatra plays a jazz drummer who is hooked on heroin and tries to kick his habit. Planned Parenthood gave classes on sexually transmitted diseases, and a couple of twelve-step recovery groups showed up and shared about how they helped people clean up.

It is impossible to describe the pain of withdrawal in words. Any physical recovery was slow and hard to detect. It was a major gain when I could walk from my room down to the cafeteria without feeling dizzy. Standing up and moving was painful, yet so was sitting down in one place for more than five minutes. During the workshops, I went from zoning out to crumpling up on a folding chair from just trying to bear it all. One night, someone from a twelve-step program spoke to the group. He said that if we really wanted to have a chance at changing our lives, we needed to get into a long-term recovery center after we finished our seven days at the detox unit. I knew he was right because in seven days I would still be feeling really bad. Going back out onto the street like that would surely have led me right back to where I had started from.

I was feeling sick, weak, and uncertain about everything: "Well it's Saturday [and] I've been here since Mon. Nov. 11th. I am still weak from the withdrawals. I am still shaking a little. I will stay here as long as I can to try to get my strength back." I began to worry; I sure didn't want to end up leaving the detox center for a homeless shelter. I knew that if it came to that, then I would just move back to Juárez, and probably to the room at Víctor's mother's place.

Weekends at the Southwestern General detox unit seemed pretty calm. Someone brought some movies in for Saturday night. The movies brought me out of myself long enough to allow me to forget what I was going through. I may have felt like a teenager as I watched them, but I sure did not look like one. The hospital windows offered a view of El Paso and Juárez, which were illuminated at night. As I sat there wondering what I was going to do next, I contemplated doing something new that would bring me more out of life than being a sick junkie on the streets of El Paso and Juárez. On Monday, I put it this way: "Well I'm still here and I'm still weak but the worst is over. I wonder what's next."

The hospital was on the verge of giving me a medical discharge. I had been there more than a week, which was considered sufficient for a detox. Just before the staff was going to discharge me, I told the program director, Sam, that I wanted to get into a long-term recovery center. He looked into it, and that afternoon someone from the Aliviane treatment center picked me up. This was probably the best thing that could have happened; if not for that place, I probably would have gone back to Juárez. In the condition that I was in, I would have been back out on the streets and using dope in no time.

ALIVIANE, ROUND TWO

I didn't really think much about it, but during the intake at Aliviane, I realized that I looked like a concentration camp survivor. I weighed about 159 pounds and was mostly skin and bones. I was still quite weak, and my head was spinning like crazy.

I think the worst thing about my first few weeks at Aliviane was that I could not sleep. But progress was steady, as I noted in a series of entries:

> I made it to the rehab center Aliviane. The fuckin' place is way out here in the middle of nowhere, but I guess it's alright. Whatever is gonna happen is gonna happen. I'm still weak and a little sick and dizzy. (November 22)

> Well I made it another day clean. It still fuckin' hurts but I'm feeling a little bit stronger. (November 23)

> Well I'm feeling a little better every day and it's time to start feeling a lot better. [I] did laundry today [and it's] still drying on the line. I wonder how long it will take to dry. I really enjoyed the enchilada lunch and all and I wish things were better for me. The counselor here showed me how to meditate; I just need to practice it. Anyway, I have 18 days clean. (November 29)

The Aliviane men's rehab center in Socorro, Texas, houses about forty clients at full capacity. There seemed to be about six counselors and a few more staff members running the place. The room that I slept in had three beds: a double bunk and a single on the floor. My first day there, I was assigned to the top bunk. Like many people who live in institutional settings, the only thing that I wanted was a small radio and a bottom bunk. Those first weeks were rough because I was still in the last phases of physical withdrawal. My bones hurt, I was still weak, and I could not sleep. In fact, for the first twenty-eight nights, I hardly slept at all. I just lay there, pretending to sleep. What made it worse was that I constantly had to get up in the middle of the night and go to the bathroom. My system was still weak, so climbing up and down on the bunk bed in a dark room was not easy or fun, especially when trying to be respectful of the person on the bottom bunk.

One of my roommates didn't like me too much. We just did not see eye to eye because he did not want to be there. The court system had forced him into the treatment center as a condition of his release from prison. He was some white dude from California or El Paso who had been conditioned by the prison system. I couldn't empathize with him; I was used to doing what I wanted to on the streets, and he was trapped in some petty prison mindset. I was too sick and tired to care. We almost got into a fight, but he stopped messing around with me after the conflict almost escalated into a situation that would have gotten him called out by his prison review board, or whatever they called the people who monitored his case.

Here is what happened. Everyone in the treatment center was assigned *talacha* (a house job). I never had any trouble with talacha and did whatever jobs they assigned me. I usually cleaned something like the floors or the bathrooms and did what I needed to do twice a day—once in the morning and once in the late afternoon. One day, my roommate wanted to do some extra cleaning. This was all right; he could do whatever he wanted. But when he tried to pull me away from my TV time when I was still feeling sick from withdrawal, I told him that it wasn't talacha time and that I didn't feel good (usually talacha is called by the group leaders). He mumbled some shit and went on cleaning with another patient who had just arrived that day; I think he was trying to teach the new guy how to do housecleaning. Whatever was going on, I just didn't want any part of it.

That night, during a group meeting, he called me a punk in front of the whole group. I had been there around a week and was still withdrawing and feeling real weak. I just looked at him and all those other people and told him to think whatever he wanted to; I was too weak to fight. By that time, the leaders of the group (the recovery center appointed two patients to group-leadership positions—usually people who were about to graduate from the program) had become aware of the situation and called him out on his behavior. Since he was my roommate, I talked with him afterward, and we got along well enough to live together. Many addicts are very strong-willed people who display self-centered characteristics.

My counselor at Aliviane was Jesse Martinez. He was an ex-junkie and Vietnam vet who had grown up in El Paso's Segundo Barrio. After he evaluated me, he told me that I was ready to change and that I would probably make it. Jesse took the time to talk to me, and we often talked for hours. He was a psychologist and knew a lot about staying clean. Aside from helping me through the toughest times in my recovery, Jesse became a good friend. I was lucky that he was my counselor; there is no telling how things would have turned out if someone else had been assigned to my case.

One of the first things that he taught me was to stay in the moment and not worry about the past or the future:

> Still in Aliviane but feeling better, the process of healing is working, but I still wonder what is gonna happen later. At least I got two new roommates, and they are cool. Not all stuck up like those others. OK anyway I'm still clean and glad everything is working out. Man I was really messed up; this time the withdrawal was long but not treacherous but too long. Still not sleeping. (December 6)

The day at Aliviane started at seven, when morning coffee was ready for those who wanted to get up and wait for it. After a while, I became used to waiting in line for things like coffee and breakfast. I think that for most of the guys there, morning coffee was one of the small pleasures that they looked forward to most. On weekdays between eight in the morning and eight at night, there were constant meetings and activities. On each end of the facility, there were a bunch of sectional sofas that would seat about twenty or so people. We sat on those sofas when counselors and speakers from recovery organizations spoke to us. I remember being so weak during my first month there that when one meeting was over, I just stayed in the seat and waited for the next one to start. I was practically too weak to get up. It seemed as if I were living in slow motion as everyone around me buzzed around in a great big hurry.

I think that a lot of the guys there had used drugs or alcohol just enough to get into trouble with the law or with their families, but had not reached the kind of bottom that enables one to reach a lifetime epiphany. Eventually, I began to sleep at night, and this caused me to begin to appreciate everything that I had just been through. I turned thirty-seven while I was there, and as my health improved, I became friends with most of the people there.

At Aliviane, half the meetings were in English and the other half were in Spanish. Since I spoke Spanish, somewhat, they let me participate in the Spanish meetings. This helped me a lot. I improved my Spanish and made friends with guys from Juárez who were there in the program. During my free time, I studied a Spanish-English dictionary that someone gave me, and my Spanish improved 100 percent while I was there. It was also good to give my mind something constructive to focus on.

As the holiday season approached, it became apparent that I was going to spend it there at the treatment center. This was all right with me; it was almost as if I did not want to leave. The food was good, and the showers had hot water. I had a small pocket radio and a bottom bunk. What more could someone want out of life? The holidays seemed to slow things down and reduce the tension at Aliviane. I spent a lot of my free time playing cards and trying to improve my Spanish. During the Christmas dinner there, I thanked the staff members for helping me regain the gift of health. By then, I was gaining weight and feeling a lot better. I almost didn't know what to do. It had been a long run during the spring, summer, and fall of 2002, and feeling healthy without drugs was like feeling brand-new again.

At Aliviane, I decided that I was going to try something besides heroin. Life seemed too full of other things to do to get caught up in that trap again. I knew that to go back would be to relive all the pain and misery I had just gone through. It seemed kind of funny, but after I gained weight and got a haircut, you couldn't tell that I had ever been a junkie. Many people looked at me in disbelief when told them how I had lived in active addiction. I think that my lifestyle was beyond the comprehension of most nonaddicted people.

My discharge date from the program was set for January 9, 2003. I had been clean since November 11, 2002. My bones still felt hot from time to time, but the more I stayed busy and kept my mind occupied, the less I felt the physical symptoms of withdrawal. The gains were incremental, so slight that you could not detect them from one day to the next. Physical recovery from heroin takes time, and in my case, it was a really long, drawn-out process. One of the biggest problems that I faced as my discharge approached was homelessness. The thought of going into a homeless shelter was disheartening. I tried to get into a halfway house, but they were all full. At Aliviane, I openly shared my dilemma at one of the Spanish-language recovery meetings. After the meeting, one of the guys told me that he would help me out. His name was Alfredo, and he even told the staff at Aliviane not to worry about me, saying that he would help me find a place to live. It was difficult for me to trust anyone at that point, but my counselor Jesse told me that Alfredo was from a wealthy family and that it might be a good opportunity to stay out of the shelter when I left the treatment center.

On my discharge day, Jesse congratulated me and signed my certificate of completion. I packed my bags and prepared to leave the Aliviane men's rehab facility for good. A part of me wanted to stay there. The treatment center was a safe place. There, I had food, clothing, and shelter. There, I had come out of heroin withdrawal and found myself, for practically the first time in my life. After I packed my bags, I called up Alfredo and told him that I was being discharged that day. He told me that he was on his way and that I was to wait for him. It felt really weird to sit in the lobby and wait for someone I didn't know to come pick me up and take me someplace to stay. I began thinking to myself that if worse came to worst, I could just go to the Rescue Mission and see what would happen.

LIFE IN JUÁREZ WITHOUT HEROIN

Alfredo showed up and took me across town to his family's house. He told me that this was just a quick stop before we went to the place that he had for me in Juárez. I was in no position to question anything. I thought that the least I could do was to see what this was all about before making a judgment. I was not too thrilled about moving back to Juárez, but Alfredo told me that it was in a different neighborhood from the ones that I had lived in before. At that point, I became optimistic about living in Juárez and decided to give it a chance.

That afternoon, we arrived in Colonia Partido Romero, where his family owned a set of large, fenced-in apartment buildings. We walked between the two buildings, and it became apparent that the apartments were all empty. Then he opened the door to one of the apartments. It was furnished with some very basic furniture and looked like no one had been living there for a while. Alfredo helped me turn on the gas and light the pilot lights on the stove, and pretty soon we had the hot-water boiler running. Alfredo told me that his family was letting me stay there for two months rent free, but after that, I would have to give them two hundred dollars a month to stay there.

I could not believe what I was hearing and seeing. Alfredo gave me twenty dollars and told me that he would stop by the next day. He showed up and took me to a supermarket. By the next evening, I had enough food to last a little while, cleaning supplies, and enough money to get me back and forth to El Paso without having to ask anyone for anything. I liked that little apartment on Calle Ignacio Zaragoza; it was quiet, secluded, and only a block away from several bus routes.

Not long after that, I began working part-time in El Paso, moving furniture. Every day, I woke up early and walked across the international bridge. I also began saving, for a change. Pretty soon, I had more than $1,000 cash in my pocket. I decided to put enough money aside that I would always be able to afford a place to live, no matter what happened. I was lucky to have met Alfredo. If not for him and his family, I would have left the rehab for a homeless shelter. Although it is difficult to guess the outcome of what might have been, I might have returned to my old lifestyle if things had worked out differently. In short, Alfredo and his family gave me something that numerous street junkies getting out of rehab did not have access to: stable and quality housing. For that, I will always be grateful to them.

On reflection, it seemed that I had survived by asking for some help in the same way that I had asked people for money every day on the street. This was one of the great things about living in Juárez and El Paso. I just couldn't imagine people extending that kind of benevolence to me anywhere else. Once again, I was fortunate to have met up with someone who cared enough about another human being to help him out a little. Who knows, maybe someday I will be able to help someone out in the same way—or maybe not. The main thing is that it happened because I shared my situation with someone who cared enough to listen. And after listening, he didn't just give me a song and a dance about what I should do. Instead, he took action and helped me. Even while I was maintaining my heroin addiction for numerous years on the street, some people there always tried to help me, as much as they could, by giving me a quarter or a dollar. It wasn't much, but it was a true, unconditional kind of support that allowed me to survive.

Although there have been significant changes in my life since early 2003, I will end the story there. I would also like to raise certain questions that pertain to recovery from drug addiction in general. Why, in a society that places so much emphasis on quality of life, are there are not enough halfway houses and reentry programs for people who have made it through the hardest part of recovery from drug addiction? When I was discharged from rehab, every halfway house I tried to get into was full. Where are recovering addicts supposed to go when there is no place for them? My experience has shown me that drug treatment centers are incapable of helping recovering addicts reenter society, other than by placing them in an already-overburdened system of homeless shelters. Why is that?

Is the cycle of drug addiction facilitated by the system instead of being disrupted by it? Is drug treatment a fallacy? Are places like Aliviane more about lip service than social service? Are they following through with what they have begun so that addicts can follow through with their recovery? Certainly, for the time I was there, my experience was very real. I physically recovered and was deemed to be well enough to leave the confines of an environment that was protected from drugs. But then what? What about social recovery? I once sat in a room with forty drug addicts and listened to a counselor tell us that it would be a miracle if one person in that whole room stayed clean. I thought to myself, I am that one. I am that miracle.

CONCLUSION

My intention in writing this book was to share my personal experience in the hope that someone would be able to develop a deeper understanding of what addictive patterns are all about. By no means do I want readers to develop any romanticized notions about life on the streets. The life of a street junkie is one of constant uncertainty; it is dirty, painful, and full of unfulfilled dreams. It is impossible to put into words the depth and breadth of my experience. What I have written about are my experiences as best I can recollect them. They are by no means representative of the experiences of people in Juárez or El Paso; they are personal experiences full of their own particulars, which are universal in theory but distinctly individual in reality.

On reflection, I was lucky to have lived long enough to experience recovery. The only reason recovery was possible for me was because of my personal surrender and spiritual awakening. Many people caught up in the cycle of addiction do not have the chance for that experience. Pepe from Altavista died in active addiction. Recently, I saw one of Marcos's relatives from Colonia Postal washing car windows near Puente Lerdo in downtown Juárez. One of his arms was missing. His sister-in-law, who panhandled in El Paso, looked alarmingly strung out and skinny when I saw her a few years later. She told me that she was too weak for withdrawal. She knew that she was going out, one way or another, but instead of surrendering, she was still in the midst of the struggle. These people looked like walking death the last time I saw them. Someone probably thought the same about me when they saw me at my worst moments in active addiction.

In 2008, my friend Víctor from Felipe Angeles died of a drug overdose down by the Rio Grande right below the University of Texas at El Paso. When I think of the multitude of addicts who do not slow down enough to find recovery, it becomes apparent that the reason they are unable to do so is because of their inability to stop the process of obsession and compulsion. Of course, there is more to this than just self-will run rampant. The social conditions and opportunities that exist in and around the lives of many addicts play significant roles in the outcomes of their lives. My friend Marcos from Colonia Postal lost a few of his kids due to diseases that resulted from poor living conditions and a lack of access to health care. His wife took the rest of the kids and disappeared, and the last time I saw him, he was strung out and alone, working a part-time job someplace in Juárez. I remember Víctor telling me that he knew that his chances of ever having anything in life were slim to none. This was one of the reasons why he chose to live the way he did.

As I revised this manuscript, my friend and mentor Jesse Martinez passed away. It was one of the first times that I had cried since I got clean. Jesse was my counselor at the Aliviane rehab center. He was someone who took the time and effort to listen to my stories and share some of his own. He was a major part of my life's new journey in recovery. I can't even begin to count all the times that he was there for me. When his daughter asked me to be the pallbearer at his funeral, I knew that if I refused, it would haunt me forever.

In 2003, when I left Aliviane, I would have never dreamed that I would find recovery in Juárez, but that is exactly what happened. As I stepped further into my own journey of change, I became aware of the deeper truths about life, which supersede its fallacies. As an addict, I idolized the chrome and the glory of economic conquest, consumption, and street-corner survival. In recovery, these things were revealed to be the trivial fallacies that they are. Yet if change is the main part of recovery—and it is—it came slowly for me. I began working in the moving-and-storage business again and walked across the bridge every day from Juárez to El Paso in order to go to work. The main thing that helped me make it through those early days was that I developed a network of friends who were just like me. If not for the help of others, I would have had a much more difficult time experiencing recovery.

Life was not easy during my early days in recovery. I lived hand to mouth and paycheck to paycheck. I walked and took the bus everywhere I went. Although this was a big improvement from panhandling, it was by no means a free ride. I woke up every day before sunrise and hit the streets, trying to find the ways and means to be self-sufficient through my own efforts. Yet the positives outweighed the negatives because heroin was no longer part of the equation. Living without using drugs in Juárez enabled me to enjoy various other aspects of life. My Spanish improved quite a bit, but more important was the increase in clarity that I experienced in regard to self and society. Later on, I learned that my experience on the border also involved a substantial amount of intercultural negotiation between and within the U.S. and Mexican social economies and cultures.

What I partly mean by this is that by living in Juárez and reentering the workforce in El Paso, I became part of a transnational economic system, one that has always existed on the U.S.-Mexico border. My job at Joe's moving company was both under and over the table, depending on when I worked there. Yet Joe was on his way out. His company was in Chapter 11 bankruptcy, and most of what I did there involved helping him sort out what he was going to take with him. Soon afterward, I worked at another moving company. Like many workers who crossed (and still cross) the border every day, I woke up at five and walked across the bridge from Juárez to El Paso. I did not really spend much of my personal time in El Paso. Living in Juárez became a new experience without the use of drugs, and I began to enjoy my new life there. Things were affordable.

As time went on, I moved into another apartment, one on Calle Damian Carmona in Colonia Partido Romero. The rent was $180, and with utilities, I could live on about $250 a month. My first few days there were interesting because I had no furniture, but with the money I had been saving, I bought a stove, a bed, and a refrigerator. One day on a moving job, a customer gave me a living room set, and before Joe left town, he gave me a desk with a chair. Also, a nurse named Angelica from the detox unit at Southwestern General Hospital gave me a kitchen table and chairs along with another twin bed. Before I knew it, my empty apartment was full of furniture. Of course, it would have been impossible to haul all of that stuff down to Juárez without the help of my friends in recovery.

Walking from my apartment in Juárez to the bridge and then to downtown El Paso every morning became a ritualistic time of spiritual meditation for me. As I walked past the panhandlers who sat on the corners by the bridge, some of them with scabs and track marks on their arms and legs, it reminded me how unforgiving street life could be. Entering the workforce as a daily border crosser associated me with the possibility of mendicancy all over again. Everywhere I went, I walked and took the bus. Eight-hour workdays turned into twelve-hour excursions, and twelve-hour workdays became sixteen-hour treks after which I slept about five or six hours a night. It still felt good to be out making money, and I began to appreciate what little free time I had. Every morning, the lines of pedestrians on the international bridges persisted. As I watched people much older than me walking, sometimes limping, across the bridge to work in manual-labor jobs such as construction, I developed a sense of self-gratitude. Between the economic reality of necessity and the new experience of recovery, there just wasn't any time to wallow in self-pity. I was having too much fun just enjoying the moment.

I thought to myself that a poor American could live well in Juárez. Things seemed to balance themselves out so that I was able to live within a mode of self-sufficiency that enabled me to experience some life-quality attributes that most Americans unknowingly take for granted. One of them was to have hot water. This was a big step up from living in places that didn't have it. Another was to have a kitchen. At the supermarket in Juárez, I could fill up a shopping cart with all kinds of groceries for around eighty dollars. The quantity of fruits and vegetables available made American grocery stores look depleted. Mangos, papayas, oranges, and all kinds of other stuff were sold at reasonable rates. One advantage that American consumers have over Mexicans is access to electronics such as televisions, stereos, and computers. For this reason, many residents of Ciudad Juárez buy these types of products in the States and bring them back to Mexico. One of the biggest tasks facing Mexican customs officials is regulating this importation of electronic goods.

I met my wife in 2003. She was an *estilista* (hair stylist) in a downtown Juárez *peluquería* (barbershop). I think we connected with each another because neither one of us had any family in Juárez. I once heard that the law of attraction says that like forces are drawn toward each other. This may have been one of the determining factors in our relationship. Today, we have a son, and I have an additional stepson. As we became familiar with our neighbors in the Juárez streets of Damian Carmona and Ignacio de la Peña, we developed a sense of community similar to that which I had experienced while living in Felipe Angeles and Las Canchas. The only difference was that this time the neighbors didn't associate me with mendicancy and drug addiction, not that they treated me any differently. No matter where I lived in Juárez, my neighbors always treated me respectfully. Aside from all that, I believe it's always good to get to know your neighbors and talk to them when you have the chance.

One of the major turning points for me occurred when I was injured on a moving job. I moved some cement lions to a customer's porch one day, and soon afterward, I began to feel a pain in my lower-right pelvis. I kept walking across the bridge, trying to ignore the pain, but when one of my testicles began swelling up, I knew that something was wrong. In the emergency room, the doctor told me that I had a hernia. My employer referred me to its insurance company. I collected worker's compensation insurance and spoke with a counselor from the Texas Rehabilitation Commission (TRC). The people at the TRC suggested that I train for another profession, so I told them that I wanted to become a substitute teacher. I really did not have any idea what teaching was all about, but I liked the idea of working with people in a classroom. The TRC sent me to El Paso Community College (EPCC). That was how I got into school. The injury turned out to be an infection that had been caused by excessive heavy lifting and strain. If not for that doctor's misdiagnosis of the hernia, I might not have had the break in my daily routine that allowed me to enter college.

THE MOVE TO ACADEMIA

I was surprised when I got straight As during my first semester. I had gone into it not really expecting anything more than to finish the work and pass the class. I suppose that the new self that emerges during recovery becomes manifested through new experiences, which are possible with a change in attitude and increased open-mindedness. In this sense, I was placed in an opportunity to manifest the construction of a new self by allowing myself to sit still, look, and listen to what was going on around me. I worked and went to school, and little by little, my world transformed itself. Needless to say, my worldview has changed significantly since 2002, when I made the decision to take a chance on a new way of life.

I grew a lot while at EPCC. After a while, I set standards and surprised myself by meeting them. As I developed academically, I realized the possibility for achieving things beyond my limited self-expectations. My recovery was a spiritual journey, and the college experience was the actualization of the change that journey offered.

Aside from negotiating the social terrain of living in Juárez and working and going to school in El Paso, I needed to find a balance between family, school, work, and recovery. The only way this balance became possible to maintain was by staying in the specific moment and trying not to presuppose future outcomes based on past experiences. Jesse Martinez had once told me that if I stayed clean, one day I would discover what it was like to find the calm in the middle of the storm. The keys to finding it are focus and balance. Finding focus and balance can be done only by staying in the moment and doing one thing at a time. It is that simple, yet so many people seem to have a hard time grasping the concept.

I graduated from EPCC in 2006 and graduated from UTEP in 2008 and again in 2010. I think the only reason that I worked so hard was the hope of realizing the emergence of the new self as a part of the change that I was experiencing in my recovery. I never lost sight of my foundation and remained vigilant of my own responsibility to self. This is important for anyone with any type of responsibility: if someone is untrue to the self, there is no way he or she will be able to be there for others. Another important reason why I took to education was because I liked, or learned to like, what I was doing, in the same way that I learned to like and accept myself for who I was.

Along with the opportunity for an education came the increased awareness of my own social position in relation to the dual worlds in which I lived. Mexico was nice, but I knew that there were few opportunities there for Americans in my situation. The survival of my family and myself was contingent upon my ability to cross the border and progress within the American economic structure. My son was born in 2005. I think it was from then on that I began to think further outside myself. My future seemed full of doubt and uncertainty until I realized that the solution was to let go of the need to control the outcome of the situation. Life became easier, and the calm in the middle of the storm seemed attainable. I think that the real secret to keeping my sanity amidst the struggles and poverty of everyday life on the border was to let go. For example, I cannot control someone else's feelings. Further, I cannot claim dominion over other people, places, and things. In this sense, responsibility does not equal total control. I think that as long as I stay true to myself, I will be able to be the best that I can possibly be for others.

I want to emphasize that this narrative celebrates change, balance, acceptance, and hope, but by no means does it ignore struggle and hardship. I deal with life on its own terms and do my best to accept reality as it unfolds before me. The uncertainty of the future and the experience of the past can be dealt with only by accepting the present.

When I got off the bus in El Paso during the summer of 1999, the changes that I subsequently experienced were inconceivable to me. Before then, in 1998, when I lived in Felipe Angeles, my identity was based on the fact that I was strung out on heroin. This was the common social denominator that transcended race, class, and gender. The people within my world at that time accepted me for who I was at face value and did their best to accommodate me within their own means. Surviving and maintaining our addictions meant so much to us that nationalistic constructs of identity hardly played into it all. I think that I experienced more racism within drug circles in the United States than I did in Mexico. Most of the people who raised questions about racial and ethnic identity were either Americans or people that had spent some time in the United States. That is not to say that people in Juárez did not have a social hierarchy, but I think it was more class based than race based. When I lived hand to mouth and day to day, I lived primarily in poor neighborhoods made up of people who were also struggling socially and economically. Their perceptions of life's ups and downs allowed them to be able to give to someone else who was also experiencing some sort of hardship. This is one of the main reasons why I was able to survive there.

Today, I do my best to avoid the fallacy of racial and nationalist paradigms; they all contain ulterior motives and hidden agendas for social positioning within a specific political economy. On the street, I learned to take people at face value and to realize that every person has distinct characteristics and personality traits, which supersede the stereotypical assumptions of universalized and prejudiced characteristics. This story is my story, and it is what it is. It is not an academic or expository work with a political agenda; it is the life experience of someone who wakes up every day and puts both feet on the ground. Today, I live in a transnational and multicultural household. In this vein, I have become part of the environment that I have adapted to. Maybe I have actualized a form of hybrid identification within my own consciousness. Just as I have learned that one cannot ever fully control other people, places, and things, I have also learned that my thoughts are my own, and they are not up for negotiation. It is in this that I believe that being framed within a certain social construct is unacceptable.

We moved out of Juárez in 2007. It was a big change for my wife, who grew up in Mexico. We often travel back to Juárez, and Mexico will always be part of who we are. Not long afterward, drug cartels began competing for control within the power vacuum of Juárez. Since 2008, thousands of lives have been lost in the struggle for economic control of the borderlands narcotics economy. When I think back to what the differences might have been for me if the same degree of bloodshed had occurred when I was there and using every day on the streets, I know that the outcome of my situation would likely have been quite different. Nevertheless, today's addicts use drugs and perpetuate the narcotics economy in the same way that we did then. And the systemic dynamics are very much the same. As a using addict, I developed relationships with various connections. Most of them knew me and appreciated my business. I can't see these dynamics of supply and demand changing just because of the current power struggles between competing interests.

I leave it to readers to draw their own inferences and conclusions from my experience in regard to the current tragedy facing the community of Juárez. In my own unobjective opinion, I feel that the violence in Juárez is the byproduct of poverty and the lack of state-sponsored compulsory education at the preparatory and university levels. Once the area's competing interests become stabilized and order is restored, business will continue as usual. It would be unrealistic not to believe this; the superstructure of both Mexican and American civil society is significantly ingrained with addictive behavioral patterns that will require a major structural change in order to actualize anything different. As I learned, insanity is doing the same thing over and over and expecting a different result. As mentioned above, change is the essence of recovery, and societal recovery is not exempt from this conclusion. Additionally, my recovery has shown me that change occurs incrementally and that no real change happens overnight. The changes that I experienced were painful, and the impetuses behind them moved slowly from fear, pain, and doubt to hope, gratitude, and love. I think that as a society, the borderlands community needs to move beyond the stages of the former so that it can benefit from the gifts of the latter.

The repetition and evolution of my experience between 1998 and 2002 exemplifies how addiction manifests itself in cycles. Self-destructive as they are, drugs are a social pacifier within impoverished communities in the same way that alcohol, the media, and sports are social pacifiers for rich and poor alike. They are a feel-good mechanism for people who have not yet found themselves. I suppose that aside from the easy availability of heroin, the main reason why I chose Juárez–El Paso as a destination was the possibility of change and cultural diversity that the border community offered. I had grown up with the idea of integration and cultural tolerance and then had traveled for the better part of my working adult life as a truck driver in the moving-and-storage business until my compulsive use of heroin almost led to my own self-destruction. I sensed something special about the border community of Juárez and El Paso, something new enough for me to be able to generate or actualize a life change that I was so desperately in search of. I remember hearing a counselor say once that when he entered into a relationship with other people, he looked them straight in the face and told them that he was "as is." Meaning that he was who he was and that was the way it was. This type of self-identification is premised upon the pillar of acceptance, the acceptance of self by self and self by others. When I arrived at the border, my own self-acceptance was numbed and filled by the use of heroin. As I lived here and slowly experienced my own life changes, I accepted myself for who I was, and others around me for who they were.

Change, for me, was not an abrupt shift. It was a combination of eclectic influences and experiences that occurred over a lifetime and came to a crescendo after my arrival in Juárez. I think that change within my own process of recovery involved the revision of spirit, mind, and body. Yet these three aspects of the self transitioned simultaneously, in no specific order. Of course, the spiritual awakening or awareness of the metaphysical self was for me, and is for the recovering addict, a necessary first step on the road to recovery.

Recently, Professor Campbell and I went to Juárez to talk to some people about drug addiction on the border. As we walked across the Santa Fe Street Bridge, it began raining. It was about six thirty in the evening, the same time that I used to call it quits after a day's panhandling. For a second, the rain and the ambiance of the bridge brought me back to the humility of living day to day and hand to mouth. Time and space became blurred as we crossed the international border, and the borders between my past and present became momentarily fused within my psyche. As we arrived in Mexico, there was a ruckus on the corner at Juárez Avenue near the bridge. A group being deported from the United States was vehemently protesting a check-cashing fee at one of the local establishments. A small squad of Mexican soldiers looked on with indifference. If I had been out panhandling, I probably would have asked them for some money, and they might have given me some. As we walked to the bus stop in Juárez, the rain continued. The streets swelled up with small lagoons of water that became transformed into instant cascades when vehicles raced by. I used to know where every puddle formed on my daily walk to the bridge. As I walked, there was a place where I did a balancing act on the edge of a sidewalk to avoid stepping in the water on both sides of it.

After we caught the bus, the rain fell like a monsoon. If we had been a minute later, we would have been caught in the storm. I wasn't used to seeing soldiers on the streets of Juárez. There was not as many of them around when I lived there. As we walked by a large building where they were stationed, I waved to the guards. After we had boarded the bus, another bus raced past and cut in front of us. Our driver, who had been accelerating, tried to avoid the crash by slamming on the brakes. Everything was wet, and the loud noise of the slippery screeching brake drums was followed by an abrupt collision. The driver got out to inspect the damage. I couldn't see too much, but I noticed that the lens cover to the brake light on the other bus was broken off. The lightbulb still worked. Both drivers seemed to shrug it off, and in another minute we were well on our way.

This was not my first bus accident in Juárez. One morning on my way to cop, the bus that I caught crashed into the side of a car and severely crushed it. It happened right in front of the police station. Another time, I watched a woman with a car full of kids pull out right in front of a bus that was going downhill on Avenida 16th de Septiembre in west Juárez. I was out there panhandling and practically held my breath as I watched the bus driver slam on the screeching brakes and narrowly avoid a fatal accident. Somehow, this near miss almost symbolizes my experience of navigating the risks of everyday life on the streets of Juárez and El Paso.

Although each person's story is unique, the dynamics of people's experiences contain common threads. In this sense, my story is not unique. There are others who have gone through similar, even if not identical, circumstances. Some people feel that the past is best left undisturbed and unspoken. I felt that way about my experiences in Juárez for a while. That changed when I realized that the past is gone forever, but the lessons we learn from it give us the awareness and reflective capacity to perceive and improve our present conditions. Our assessment of the past allows us to apply its significant conclusions to our journey into the future. If more can be deduced from this account than I anticipated, I am glad that I was able to contribute something that could help others on their own journeys.

EPILOGUE

In the now.

During the summer of 2008, I met Professor Howard
Campbell and shared some of my experience with him. At that time,
I had no idea that people would be interested in the everyday life of a
junkie on the U.S.-Mexico border. I had previously sent him an e-mail
regarding his research on drug trafficking in the borderlands, but I did
not expect anything more than a few passing words in response. For the
most part, people in my situation who find recovery and take another
shot at life find themselves in some sort of subaltern state when it comes
to their past and present life experiences. The last thing I expected was
to learn that someone might indeed be interested in these experiences
and that I would be writing this book, sharing some of the most dramatic details of my life with a variety of unknown readers.

Dr. Campbell was interested in what I had gone through, so I took
him on a tour of the neighborhoods that I had lived in between 1998
and 2002. At that time, those places seemed distant from the life I had
found in what I will call my post-Aliviane, or post-dope, experience.
Dr. Campbell mentioned that he remembered me from my graduation
from UTEP the previous spring. It felt odd to connect my present life in
academia with my past life on the streets of Juárez and El Paso. The two
seem so opposite and distant that it was almost as if I had been placed in
another life, one in which I was able to actualize who I was and who I
was becoming. Of course, this also involved a reflective return to who I
had been before I started using chemical substances in order to feel good
about myself. This dynamic change also involved a regression and a pro-
gression, senses of being and becoming that work simultaneously as the
new self emerges from the chaos of active addiction.

Recovery involves physical and metaphysical changes that must oc-

cur in order for it to be fully actualized in the life of an addict. I am using the term "metaphysical" to describe the internal dynamics of individual thought processes and experiences. Change is the true essence of
recovery. This is a commonsense notion predicated upon the idea that
insanity can be defined as repeating the same behavior over and over
and expecting a different result. As can be perceived from the trends
and patterns of my experience in Juárez and El Paso between 1998 and
2002, my actions and the results of those actions were repeated again
and again, thereby digging new, lower thresholds for what many recovering addicts describe as a bottom. Change is an age-old method for
turning a life around and is explicit in II Corinthians 5:17: "Therefore,
if anyone is in Christ, he is a new creation. The old has passed away;
behold, the new has come." I think that the first fundamental aspect of
change in recovery involves a metaphysical awareness of one's place beyond their physical positionality. Many describe this as a spiritual awakening: an epiphany in which the true meaning of self, society, and the
spiritual or metaphysical world becomes increasingly apparent. For an
addict in the early stages of recovery, this is a crucial part of the process,
and physical recovery cannot fully happen unless this metaphysical self-
awareness, or spiritual awakening, is experienced.

My spiritual awakening allowed me to perceive my relationship to
the universe around me. It enabled me to begin a journey of recovery
with an open-mindedness that allowed for various possibilities. More
than thirty years of living my way, artificially, had gotten me nowhere.
After hitting a social, spiritual, physical, and mental bottom, I knew
right away that the necessary changes involved accepting the idea of
trying something new. My recovery required me to embrace something
different from the behavioral patterns that had led me to administer my
own self-destruction from the tip of a needle. Spiritual awakenings are
not possible without personal surrender, that is, the surrender of self
in order to stay in the now and appreciate the moment. Too many addicts attempt recovery from the standpoint of wanting to re-create an
intense past experience or from wanting to help another—"I am doing
this for so-and-so." Although these kinds of reasons can provide ratio-
nalizations for entering recovery, by themselves they do not allow one
to fully experience the kind of spiritual awakening that is needed for an
honest recovery; they take the focus off the self and put it on an outside
particular. If this occurs, the cycle of addiction will continue until the
pain of staying the same becomes greater than the resistance to change.
In short, change and surrender are essential elements in recovery.

Too many addicts enter recovery with a focus on the past or the future and are unable to slow down enough to see what they have become. This is part of the metaphysical or psychological dynamic of the addict mind. Learning to stay in the moment cannot be overemphasized as a way to counter this type of thinking. Staying in the now allows one to experience an increased spiritual or metaphysical awareness that is necessary for the effacement of the insanity of active addiction. For me, arriving at a point where I was able to have this type of experience was a painful process. A lot happened before I was weak enough to give up and just let recovery from active addiction happen. Letting myself participate in life has allowed me to learn a few things about why I am the way I am as well as about why people who experience problems with drug and alcohol addiction are the way they are. Not surprisingly, the dynamic of active addiction can be found in natural human behavior to varying degrees.

In this sense, the physical and metaphysical are connected to one another throughout the dynamics of addiction and recovery. One of the most basic patterns of addiction, and the main reason why people use chemical substances (alcohol and drugs), is to feel good and fill an emptiness or void. After becoming conditioned to experiencing stimulation and pleasure by actively participating in addictive behavior, they develop a pattern of dependency that either levels off or increases, according to the desire of the individual. My own experience has shown me that time and exposure to drugs and alcohol play a significant role in the degree to which someone will become involved with these patterns. What fuels this dynamic is the natural process of obsession and compulsion.

Obsession is a thought process that begins easily enough by thinking about how good something will feel. It can be as innocent as thinking about a weekend football game and the six-pack of beer that goes along with it. It can be the thought of a sexual experience, or it can be the desire to do anything that will bring pleasure to the body and mind. In short, obsession is a thought. It manifests itself for the addict through personal gratification and becomes the driving force that targets the object of that obsession, whether it is a football game, beer, or anything else that gratifies someone's thoughts, obsessions, and desires. For someone who is physically addicted to a chemical substance such as heroin or alcohol, psychological obsession is compounded by physical addiction, which adds another dimension of pain to the mix. With or without physical cravings, obsession usually leads to action, which is the second part of the process of active addiction: compulsion.

Compulsion is the physical act that someone goes through to actualize an obsession. For a drug addict, it is the act of using drugs; it alleviates the obsession, putting it to rest temporarily. The insidious part of it all is that, for the addict, obsession returns and is followed by another act of compulsion. For someone who is mentally or physically addicted, this process becomes circular, like a tornado, and wreaks a whirlwind of self-destruction and harm on others. In sum: obsession is the thought, compulsion is the action, and addiction is the driving force that generates this circular process. By the time addicts find treatment, their thoughts are racing at light speed and the only way they can find recovery is to stop! Stop thinking for a while and slow down. For the addict who is going through pain, whether from withdrawal or personal loss, it is easier to slow down. Regardless of how someone comes to slow down, it is necessary to do so in order to attain some sort of metaphysical awareness.

When obsession and compulsion are left unattended in the life of an addict, the results are devastating. When using heroin or alcohol, an addict will always, sooner or later, require and desire more. This should not come as a surprise in a society where more is often deemed as better. Addicts use more, dealers sell more, and more money becomes available through the dynamics of obsession and compulsion. Compulsion pushed on by the obsession for more is what kills thousands of addicts every year. As you are reading this paragraph, someone is probably going to prison, rehab, or the graveyard because of his or her participation in this process. For an addict, obsession can become so strong that the only way to subdue it is through complete surrender. But for someone who is not ready or has not experienced enough pain, absolute surrender is beyond comprehension.

Anyone can fall into the trap of obsession and compulsion, and most people do. It is what drives consumers. People become obsessed with sex, gambling, drugs, alcohol, money, the Internet, video games, comic books, regular books, or whatever it is that takes them outside themselves or fills an inner void. In this sense, it is easier for most people to look outward than inward. The big difference between objects of obsession is that some of them offer social rewards, while others involve harmful and often life-altering side effects. In a general sense, the dynamics of addiction involve the use of people, places, and things to fill a void in one's inner self.